Life among the Texas Indians

◆ ◆ ◆ ◆

NUMBER 18
*Elma Dill Russell Spencer Foundation Series
in the West and Southwest*

D0813336

Life Among the

THE WPA NARRATIVES

Texas Indians

by David La Vere

TEXAS A&M UNIVERSITY PRESS
COLLEGE STATION

The paper used in this book meets the minimum requirements
of the American National Standard for Permanence
of paper for Printed Library Materials, Z39.48-1984.
Binding materials have been chosen for durability.

∞

Library of Congress Cataloging-in-Publication Data

La Vere, David.
    Life among the Texas Indians, the WPA narratives / David La
Vere. — 1st ed.
    p.   cm. — (Elma Dill Russell Spencer series in the West and
Southwest ; no. 18)
    Includes Bibliographical references and index.
    ISBN 0-89096-809-8 (cloth : alk. paper) —
    ISBN 1-58544-528-2 (pbk.)
    1. Indians of North America — Texas 2. Indians of North
    America — Indian Territory. 1. Title. II. Series.
E78. T4L3   1998
976.4'00497—dc21   97-32891
                                                        CIP

For my parents,
Dick and Ann La Vere

Contents

◆ ◆ ◆ ◆ ◆ ◆ ◆ ◆ ◆ ◆ ◆ ◆ ◆ ◆ ◆

◆ ◆ ◆ ◆ ◆ ◆ ◆ ◆ ◆ ◆ ◆ ◆ ◆ ◆ ◆

Illustrations

◆ ◆ ◆ ◆ ◆ ◆ ◆ ◆ ◆ ◆ ◆ ◆ ◆ ◆

between pages 108 *and* 119

Caddo Village
Home of Tawakone Jim, a Wichita Indian chief
Grass House interior
Red Horns' summer camp near Anadarko
Wichita sweat house on the Wichita dance grounds
Caddo Indians skinning beef, c. 1895
Tso-Tuddle and Red Bone, Kiowas, cutting meat
     after beef issue, May 1902
Kiowa Indians receiving rations at Anadarko
Comanches & Kiowas waiting for payment at
     Agency, January 28, 1901
At the Wichita payment, February 1899
Apache women with gifts for Comanche guests
Tonkawa Indians with their arbor at Anadarko
Kiowas at prayer, pre 1910
Wichita Indians playing monte
Two Presbyterian missionaries visiting an aged
     Apache woman, November 3, 1898
Comanche baby in coonskin-lined boys cradle,
     February 2, 1901
A class at Riverside Indian School
A council of Comanche, Kiowas, and Apache chiefs
Quanah Parker and his favorite wife
Quanah Parker on balcony of his home, c. 1904
Wichita Indian Stick Game

◆ ◆ ◆ ◆ ◆ ◆ ◆ ◆ ◆ ◆ ◆ ◆ ◆ ◆

Preface

◆ ◆ ◆ ◆ ◆ ◆ ◆ ◆ ◆ ◆ ◆ ◆ ◆ ◆

The stories and recollections in this book are by or about the Indians of Texas after they settled in Indian Territory. Some of these stories are sad, some are instructive, and some are funny. Some show a tremendous amount of sensitivity and enlightenment. Others reinforce longstanding prejudices. Some are filled with valuable details and some are vague, leaving the reader demanding more information. Nevertheless, this compilation of first-person accounts sheds light on how the Kiowas, Comanches, Caddos, Wichitas, Tonkawas, and Apaches remember their past. It shows the great earth-shaking cultural changes they faced during the last half of the nineteenth and first years of the twentieth centuries, and it shows how they adapted.

It was my hope to achieve a few things by presenting these recollections. First, I wanted to allow some measure of the Indian voice to be heard. Actual documented words of Indian peoples from the late nineteenth and early twentieth century are relatively rare, so in this book they get their chance to tell their stories. I originally hoped to use only stories told by the Texas Indians but quickly found that there were too few of them in the Indian-Pioneer Histories to make a book. There are many recollections by Cherokees, Chickasaws, Creeks, Choctaws, and Seminoles, but most of these have already been collected and published by Theda Perdue in *Nations Remembered: An Oral History of the Cherokees, Chickasaws, Choctaws, Creeks, and Seminoles in Oklahoma, 1865–1907.*

I can only attribute this lack of recollections by Texas Indians to the fact that they had received little, if any, emphasis on reading and writing English during the last decades of the nineteenth century. Unlike the Cherokees and Chickasaws, who had a hundred-year jump on white-oriented education, there were fewer Comanches, Kiowas, Caddos, Wichitas, Tonkawas or Lipan Apaches during the 1930s who were comfortable enough with English to provide an equal number of recollections. Also, some of these people, remembering their treatment at the hands of whites during the past decades, may have been hesitant to say anything at all in fear of reprisal. Despite this condition, I used almost every Texas Indian recollection I could find in the Indian-Pioneer Histories. However, in collecting the stories, it is possible that I accidently overlooked some about Texas. The only ones I intentionally omitted were those that told no story or provided little useful information. Fortunately, there were only a few of these. Still, I have included firsthand accounts on Indian warfare, hunting, farming, housing, dress, religious beliefs, ceremonies, and interactions with other peoples. I only wish there were more.

Despite this lack of Texas Indian recollections, I found that many whites, blacks, and other Indians had stories and recollections of their own about the Texas Indians. Soldiers, cowboys, ranchers, settlers, former slaves, preachers, teachers, Indian agents, government officials—as well as a host of Cherokees, Creeks, Chickasaws, Cheyennes, Delawares, and other Indian peoples —came into contact with the Texas Indians and often made keen observations about them. Their stories led to the second goal, which was to show first-hand the diverse attitudes and points of view, the cultural clashes, the sympathies and antipathies, and the confusion that resulted when all these different peoples came into close contact. Sometimes the stories are racist, with words and terminology unacceptable today. I believed it was important to include such comments because they show the opinions of the interviewees and reflect how people thought about Indians during the late 1930s.

I made no effort to censor or edit an informant's point of view, only correcting what seemed to me were obviously misspelled words and incorrect punctuation. Once again, I used almost every recollection given by these peoples concerning their relations with the Texas Indians. My only criteria were that the recollection be mainly a personal, first-hand account and that it provide some measure of informative or interesting information.

Keeping these two goals in mind, and because I was most interested in what Indians and non-Indians had to say about certain topics, I arranged the information according to subject matter. Long stories that covered a variety of topics were broken up and the relevant part placed under appropriate subject headings. As a result, individual Indians described their own people's dances, houses, games, clothing, methods of grieving, and their various experiences in warfare and on the reservation. Similarly, non-Indians, many of whom had very close relations with these Indian peoples, provided their own first-hand descriptions on many of these same topics. Each chapter deals with a specific subject or subjects. Within each chapter are subtopics. For example, chapter 1 deals with warfare, but there are subheads on raids into Texas, the Red River War of 1874–75, and such. Before each recollection, I provide the name or names of the Texas Indians the story describes. In many instances, the name of the Indian tribe does not always appear in the recollection, and the reader only knows which Indians are being talked about by the name at the beginning of the story. In this instance, I must beg that the reader trust me and rest assured that the story deals with the subject and the Indians mentioned. I was under the same limitations and sometimes knew only that the story was about a specific tribe, such as the Comanches, because the interviewer specifically identified the informant.

The question must be asked: do these stories and recollections provide any new information about these Indian peoples, or are they just interesting stories? It is my hope that they will both inform and entertain. Scholars already know a tremendous amount about the lives and experiences of these Indian peoples, and much of the information here will merely reinforce that knowledge. Still I believe there are some revealing sections, especially when Indian peoples describe aspects of their spiritual life and reservation experiences. I had long known that the government provided the reservation Indians with rations, but when I read a description of Ration Day by an Indian who participated in it, I obtained a much more vivid picture than what sometimes appears in government records. In other instances, the stories are merely interesting—a white doctor's account of smallpox ripping through a Wichita community; a white school teacher's story of trying to round up Caddo truants; a Texas businessman's explanation of entertaining Comanche chief Quanah Parker. All these provide a fascinating glimpse into life among the Indian peoples in southwest Oklahoma at the end of the nineteenth century.

Since all the recollections come from the Indian-Pioneer Histories collected in 1937–38, they open themselves to certain questions. Would an Indian tell a white interviewer the truth? Would a white person shade the truth? Were the interviewers themselves biased? What about Indians who could not speak English—were their interviews conducted through an interpreter? Did the interviewer interview them in their native language? Or were non-English-speaking respondents not interviewed? Unfortunately, with the Indian-

Pioneer Histories, it is impossible to tell as there is just not enough information provided. In some instances, interpreters usually were close English-speaking relatives. How often that was the case is not known. In most cases, the only background information provided is the name of the person being interviewed, their address, ethnicity, gender, date and place of birth, parents' name and place of birth, date of interview, and the interviewer's name. Sometimes the information is even less.

So can these recollections be trusted? My caveat would be that except in rare instances, one should not look to the Indian-Pioneer Histories for historical accuracy when it comes to names, dates, and places. Even William Hagan, an authority on the Comanches during the reservation period and author of *Quanah Parker, Comanche Chief*, warns that information from the Indian-Pioneer Histories must be used with care. Many of those interviewed were elderly at the time of the interview and sometimes confused things as they remembered events forty or fifty years earlier. On the other hand, descriptions of lifestyles, ceremonies, beliefs, and general events are reliable and can provide accurate information to historians, anthropologists, and general readers. Also, many of the events described are supported by other historical sources.

The only way ever to become truly proficient at distinguishing between myth and historical fact would be to become versed in the literature of the subject. Fortunately, there exist several excellent bodies of historical writing on the Indians of Texas. Probably the only complete overview of these Indians and their culture is W. W. Newcomb's *The Indians of Texas*. Howard Meredith's *Dancing on Common Ground* looks at the Southern Plains culture that developed among the Texas Indians. Elizabeth A. H. John's *Storms Brewed in Other Men's Worlds: The Confrontation of Indians, Spanish, and French in the Southwest, 1540–1795* provides the most complete examination of these Indians and their relations with the Spanish and French during the seventeenth and eighteenth centuries. There are many excellent monographs on individual Texas Indian peoples. On the Caddos, F. Todd Smith has written two histories: *The Caddo Indians: Tribes at the Convergence of Empires, 1542–1854* and *The Caddos, the Wichitas, and the United States, 1846–1901*, while Timothy Perttula's *The Caddo Nation* is more an anthropological and archaeological study. Vynola Newkumet and Howard Meredith's *The Hasinai* and Cecile Carter's *Caddo Indians: Where We Come From* are written by Caddo Indian people themselves. On the Lipan Apaches, there are Thomas F. Schilz's *Lipan Apaches in Texas* and John Upton

Terrell's *The Plains Apaches*. Unfortunately, except for the previously mentioned overviews and Susan Vehik's "Wichita Culture (A Study of the Tawakoni, Wichita, Iscani/Waco and Taovaya/Tawehash Social Groups)" in *Plains Anthropologist*, there is not much recently published on the Wichitas and even less on the Tonkawas.

Much more has been written about the Comanches and Kiowas. The old standard is Ernest Wallace and E. Adamson Hoebel's 1952 cultural history *The Comanches: Lords of the Southern Plains*. Two other fine studies are Morris W. Foster's *Being Comanche: A Social History of an American Indian Community* and Thomas Kavanagh's *Comanche Political History: An Ethnohistorical Perspective, 1708– 1875*. Stanley Noyes' *Los Comanches: The Horse People, 1751–1845* provides an early look at Comanche-Euroamerican relations, while William Hagan has written extensively on the Comanches during the last years of the nineteenth and early twentieth century in *United States-Comanche Relations: The Reservation Years* and *Quanah Parker, Comanche Chief*.

On the Kiowas, James Mooney's *Calendar History of the Kiowa Indians* and Mildred Mayhall's *The Kiowas* are considered the standards on Kiowa cultural history. Clyde Ellis has examined the Kiowa experience at the boarding schools in *To Change Them Forever: Indian Education at Rainy Mountain Boarding School, 1893– 1920*. The Kiowas have a reputation as being a very spiritual and artistic people. Kiowa oral tradition is examined in Maurice Boyd's *Kiowa Voices: Myths, Legends and Folktales*, while dances have been studied by Clyde Ellis in "'Truly Dancing Their Own Way': The Modern Revival and Diffusion of the Gourd Dance" in the *American Indian Quarterly* and by Ben Kracht in "The Kiowa Ghost Dance, 1894–1916: An Unheralded Revitalization Movement" published in *Ethnohistory*.

While much more needs to be written, it is my hope that the following stores and recollections will add a little to the understanding of these Indian peoples who once called Texas home.

◆ ◆ ◆

All the stories in this book arise from one source: the bound volumes of the Indian-Pioneer Histories housed in the Indian Archives of the Oklahoma Historical Society in Oklahoma City. During the Great Depression years of 1937–38, the Works Progress Administration (WPA), in conjunction with the University of Oklahoma and the Oklahoma Historical Society, decided to acquire firsthand recollections of people who lived in the Indian and

Oklahoma Territories during their early years. The project team, supervised by renown Oklahoma historian, Grant Foreman, mailed more than 25,000 questionnaires to people in Oklahoma. If a person responded positively, someone interviewed the respondent. More than eighty young historians, anthropologists, and ethnologists, including Lillian Gassaway, Thad Smith, Jr., Ophelia Vestal, Warren Morse, W. T. Holland, Rufus George, and Ethel Tackitt interviewed just about anybody—Indian, black, or white—who could provide an account about Oklahoma life in the nineteenth and early twentieth centuries. Most of these stories are not in question-and-answer form, but merely a recollection, a narrative, allowing the respondent to tell whatever story he or she wanted to tell. Only in a few instances did the written accounts appear as answers to questions. All these recollections and stories were typed and bound to form the Indian-Pioneer Histories.

One hundred twelve bound volumes and microfilm copies of these histories can be found at the Oklahoma Historical Society Indian Archives in Oklahoma City, Oklahoma. Because there is no volume forty-five, the last volume is numbered at one hundred thirteen. Microfiche editions can be found at the Western History Collection on the University of Oklahoma campus at Norman and at other universities around the country. Historians should be aware that the bound and microfilm editions are unlike the microfiche editions in that they are bound differently and therefore have a different type of index. For the purpose of this book, all recollections and all volume and page numbers come from the bound and microfilm editions found at the Oklahoma Historical Society Indian Archives in Oklahoma City.

◆ ◆ ◆

If imitation is the sincerest form of flattery, then I hope Theda Perdue of the University of Kentucky will feel flattered as her excellent book *Nations Remembered: An Oral History of the Cherokees, Chickasaws, Choctaws, Creeks, and Seminoles in Oklahoma, 1865–1907* served as a model for this work of mine. I was fortunate enough to attend a National Endowment for the Humanities summer seminar in 1994 on the ethnohistory of Southeastern Indians led by Theda and Mike Green. From this seminar, I became acquainted with their work and publications but also found that Theda and Mike tremendously influenced my thinking and writing about Indian peoples. I liked *Nations Remembered*, enjoyed the stories, felt it contributed greatly to the body of historical knowledge, and thought that I should do something similar one day. I then got involved in other projects and put the idea on the backburner.

Then in early 1996, an editor at Texas A&M University Press approached me with the idea of writing a book that used the Indian-Pioneer Histories to tell the stories of the traditional Indians of Texas now living in Oklahoma. With Theda's book serving as my model and the fact that I was already going to Oklahoma during the summer to research another project, I accepted Texas A&M's offer, and this is the product. Again, many thanks are due to Theda Perdue and the editors at Texas A&M University Press.

I owe a tremendous debt of gratitude to Bill Welge and Phyllis Adams and the whole staff at the Oklahoma Historical Society Indian Archives in Oklahoma City. The Indian Archives hold the bound volumes of the Indian-Pioneer Histories, where the staff made room for me and my computer and were most gracious in answering all my questions and putting up with my constant annoyances.

Other friends and colleagues also helped to make this book possible. For instance, thanks are due to the late John Impson at Blinn Junior College in Bryan, Texas; Clyde Ellis at Elon College in North Carolina; Brian Hosmer at the University of Wyoming at Laramie; and Bob Calvert at Texas A&M University. I also would like to thank my colleagues at the University of North Carolina at Wilmington; my special thanks go to the Department of History and to the Cahill Award Committee for providing financial assistance for this research. Additionally, I thank the Caddo Indian people near Binger, Oklahoma for their help, assistance, and acceptance. Again, many thanks go to my mother and sisters and to Cynthia Vail, Fitz Ebron, and Andrea Kalas— whose never-flagging support made the researching and writing of this book possible, easy, and enjoyable.

Life among the Texas Indians

◆ ◆ ◆ ◆

Introduction:
From Texas to Oklahoma

❖ ❖ ❖ ❖ ❖ ❖ ❖ ❖ ❖ ❖ ❖ ❖ ❖

About fifty miles west of Nacogdoches, Texas, a cluster of man-made hills goes by the name of Caddoan Mounds. The Caddo Indians lived here, built these temple and burial mounds around A.D. 900, but no Caddo people live here now. The city of Waco, Texas, was named for the village of Wacos, a sub-group of Wichita Indians; but no Wichita people live in the vicinity unless as individual residents of the city. Southwest of Fort Worth sits a tall hill named Comanche Peak. Now a nuclear reactor looks out over lands where Comanches once camped, but one would be hard-pressed to find a Comanche Indian living thereabouts. Similarly, there are no Apaches around the Apache Mountains in West Texas and no Kiowas along Kiowa Creek in the Panhandle. In fact, toward the end of the twentieth century, in a state where possibly millions of Indian peoples once lived, now only two recognized Indian reservations exist, and both of the peoples on those reservations are relative newcomers to Texas: the Alabama-Coushatta Reservation near Liberty houses Creek peoples who came to Texas in the early nineteenth century, and the Tigua Reservation near El Paso serves Pueblo peoples more connected to New Mexico than to Texas proper. Other than these, the people recognized as the "native" or traditional Indians of Texas have been killed off, have died off, or have been forcibly removed from the state.

Ironically, many of the state's symbols and legends are intimately linked with the Indians. The very name "Texas" stems from a Caddo word, *tesha*, meaning "friend." Spanish missionaries built the Alamo, the symbol of Texas independence, to save the souls of local Indians while enslaving their bodies.

The Texas Rangers, recognized as the law and order on the Texas frontier, drew as some of their earliest duties the role of protecting white settlers from the Indians. Warfare, in fact, the image most associated with the Indians of Texas, was brutal for both Indians and Euroamericans. This warfare, compounded with new and seemingly incurable diseases, plus the cultural disruptions brought about by war and disease, pushed many Indian peoples to extinction. By 1885, those of Texas who survived had been removed north of the Red River into Indian Territory.

Of the hundreds of different Indian nations or peoples who lived in Texas between 1492 and 1885, only half a dozen managed to establish themselves on reservations in Indian Territory, and it is these peoples whose memories make up most of this book. These traditionally Texas Indians—Indians living wholly or partially inside of the state before the Anglo-American settlers arrived—include the Caddos, Wichitas, Tonkawas, Lipan Apaches, Comanches, Kiowas, and Kiowa-Apaches. The stories and recollections in this book all either come from these six peoples or are recollections about them given by white and black Americans as well as other Indian peoples.

When did the first Indian people come to Texas? Ironically, most of these six Indian peoples do not see themselves originating within what is now Texas, but came here soon after their creation. The Wichitas believe that they were created in the Wichita Mountains of present-day Oklahoma and spread south of the Red River as far as the middle reaches of the Brazos River. The Caddos say they came from a cave at the confluence of the Mississippi and Red Rivers and traveled west to live in an area encompassing northeast Texas, southeast Oklahoma, southwest Arkansas, and northwest Louisiana. The Lipan Apaches, or Plains Apaches, were the easternmost group of the great Athapaskan migration south from Canada. They reached the southern plains of Texas and New Mexico in the late fifteenth and early sixteenth centuries. The Comanches, a Shoshonean people, originally came from the mountainous area of Wyoming and Montana and migrated onto the southern plains of Texas about 1700, claiming the lands as far south as Austin and the Pecos River. Similarly, the Kiowas, and the Kiowa-Apaches, who are Kiowa peoples mixed with Athapaskan peoples from Canada, came from underground, out of a hollow cottonwood log, around the headwaters of the Yellowstone and Missouri Rivers. They eventually migrated onto the Southern Plains in the Texas Panhandle about the mid-eighteenth century. Possibly the Tonkawas, who lived in Central Texas, on the Edwards Plateau, and near the Brazos

River are the only ones of the six who can be counted as originating in Texas proper, coming out of the ground after being uncovered by a great wolf.[1]

Thousands of years before these peoples came to the area and long before the Tonkawa culture emerged, big game hunters, called "Paleo-Indians" by archaeologists, lived in Texas. While all creation stories have them originating in this hemisphere, scientists believe that Paleo-Indians arrived in North America by crossing a Bering Strait land bridge, Berengia, between 30,000 and 18,000 years ago, during the last Ice Age. Paleo-Indians quickly migrated throughout the entire Western Hemisphere. By 12,000 years ago, using only spears, they hunted mammoths, elephants, giant bison, horses, and other large herd animals in Texas.[2]

Then, beginning around 8,000 B.C., the climate warmed, cloud cover disappeared, water holes evaporated as the plains dried, and the "great extinctions" began. As food and water sources declined, the great herd animals died off, with a little help from the Paleo-Indians, who staked out the few remaining water holes and killed those animals coming to drink or ran thousands over cliffs to get the meat of a few. By 5,000 B.C., the mammoth, horse, camel, giant armadillo, and other great herd animals had died or been killed off, leaving the buffalo and deer as the largest animals in North America. Then instead of following the herds, the early Indian peoples, living in family bands, cycled seasonally through a distinct territory, hunting smaller animals and gathering berries, seeds, and nuts. Anthropologists call it the "Archaic Period," and it was a good time for the Indian peoples. They suffered no epidemic-type diseases, as the bands were too small and too separated for disease to exist. There was plenty of leisure time since it did not take long for them to fulfill their needs through hunting and gathering. Contributing to this prosperity was the tremendous variety of tools they added to their inventory: flint darts, knives, and axes; snares and traps; stone pipes; woven baskets; and clay pottery.[3]

About 2,000 B.C., places in the eastern United States, the Southwest, and the Pacific Northwest moved into what anthropologists call the "Woodlands Period," characterized by the domestication of animals and plants and moderate-sized villages. The Indian peoples of Texas probably did not reach this period until after A.D. 500 when the cultures and peoples presently associated with the Indians of Texas began to form. Then, between A.D. 700 and 800, the corn-based Mississippian Cultural Tradition arose, stretching from the Carolinas to East Texas. During that time, a Caddo culture emerged in the area between the Arkansas River to the north and the middle reaches of the Neches, Angelina, Sabine, and Red Rivers at the south, forming the westernmost peoples of the Mississippian Cultural Tradition.

Several things mark the rise of the Caddo culture. Maize agriculture brought a population increase. With that came larger communities and villages with beehive-shaped grass houses. Since a community's survival and prosperity hinged on corn and corn depended on the earth, sun, and rain, a belief system emerged that was closely connected to those four things. Religious rituals, ceremonies, and activities surrounding the Earth Mother, the Corn Goddess, the Sun, and Sacred Fire arose which controlled the elements and ensured successful crops. Individuals who could "control" the elements eventually consolidated that power into a chiefdom political system and a ranked social order. This system or order included a high priest, the *Xinesí*, who governed several separate communities and handled the religious rituals; a *caddí* who governed single communities; and a whole class of nobles and commoners. Part of this Caddo belief system included building temple mounds and burying their chiefs and other high-ranking people with incredibly rich goods in burial mounds. The Caddos also developed a distinct stylized, engraved pottery and participated in long-distance trade relations with their neighbors to the East and West.[4]

The enormous earthen mounds and the richly carved pottery, shells, and sculpture showed the sophistication and brilliance of the Caddo culture. In the southern part of the Caddo area—along the Sabine, Angelina, and Neches Rivers of Texas—one of the earliest Caddo sites is the George Davis site between Alto and Nacogdoches, which began about A.D. 780. In an area commonly called the Caddoan Mounds, the Caddos built a village of round houses along with a ceremonial center complete with a conical burial mound and two platform temple mounds. Further north, during the same time— along the Arkansas River near Spiro, Oklahoma—the Caddos built huge temple and burial mounds and filled them with some of the most sumptuous burial goods found anywhere in North America: exquisitely engraved conch shells, engraved pottery, pipes, copper, ear spools, and other jewelry.[5]

Then around A.D. 1350, a climate change over the Great Plains brought drought conditions. The same drought displaced the Anasazis in New Mexico, and just as with the Anasazi culture, the Caddo society came under stress. Mound-building came to an end, and the great community at Spiro broke down. By A.D. 1450, with their economic support gone, the large chiefdoms at

Spiro collapsed. Most survivors migrated south to the Caddo villages along the Red River and East Texas, and some joined the early Wichita peoples living along the river valleys in the eastern Great Plains. The Caddos and their culture survived by breaking down into smaller, more family-oriented communities and bands. Though neither the Caddos, nor other peoples to the east, built any more mounds, the Caddos's chiefdom political system with its priest-chiefs, elaborate rituals, and ranked social system remained intact. By the time Europeans arrived in the area during the late seventeenth century, the Caddos lived in two distinct chiefdoms, the Hasinai chiefdom of East Texas and the Kadohadacho chiefdom at the Great Bend of the Red River near Texarkana. The Hasinai chiefdom consisted of ten, possibly more communities, including the Hainai, Nabedache, Nacogdoche, Lower Nasoni, Nadaco, Neches, Nacono, Nacachau, Nacao, and Nabiti. The Kadohadacho chiefdom included four communities: the Cadodacho, Upper Nasoni, Upper Natchitoches, and Nanatshoho. Other Caddo communities, not linked to any chiefdom, included the Ais of East Texas, the Petit Caddo, Yatasí, and Natchitoches along the Red River in Louisiana. From these communities, Caddo traders, renowned for their bois d'arc bows, ventured both east and west.[6]

While the Caddos were flourishing around the intersections of Texas, Oklahoma, Arkansas, and Louisiana, further west from the Salt Fork of the Red River in the south to the Smoky Hill River in Kansas to the north, the Wichitas lived in pit houses along the river valleys. Often referred to as Plains Caddoans, the early Wichitas were closely related to the Pawnees and Arikaras. All spoke a similar Caddoan dialect and to this day there are cordial relations between the Wichitas and Pawnees. From their homes along the river valleys of the prairies and plains, they hunted afoot for buffalo and other animals. The Wichitas used a less hierarchical social system than the Caddos, with chiefs wielding less power. Star worship, rather than sun worship, characterized Wichita cosmology. Still, the Wichita developed close trade relations with the Caddos to the east and the Pueblos to the west. Wichita encampments and villages also provided stop-over and rest-stops for Caddo and Pueblo traders as they moved across the Southern Plains. With the onset of the great drought beginning in 1350, the Wichitas moved east. While they probably absorbed some of Spiro's survivors, they also picked up corn horticulture and beehive-shaped houses from the Caddos. They also began migrating farther south, spurred on by the growing power of the Osages in Missouri and Arkansas. Spanish conquistador Francisco Coronado met Wichitas in

1542 in Kansas, and Bénard de la Harpe met them in central Oklahoma in 1719. By the mid-eighteenth century, the Wichitas lived between the Wichita Mountains in Oklahoma and the middle reaches of the Brazos and Trinity Rivers of East and Central Texas and consisted of five communities: the Taovaya, the Tawakoni, the Wichita, the Yscani, and the Kichai. The term Waco did not come into use until the early nineteenth century and was a name given to the Yscani community.[7]

Similar to the early Wichitas, but south of them and west of the Caddos, the Tonkawa peoples lived along the river valleys and streambeds of northeast to south-central Texas. They originally ranged all the way from the Red River southeast to the Colorado River. Prior to the great 1350 drought, they also lived in pit houses along the Central Texas waterways and then in brush shelters once the drought pushed them farther east and south. The Tonkawas lived an Archaic Period lifestyle up until the late seventeenth century, hunting and gathering to meet their daily needs while growing no crops. Even more egalitarian than the Wichitas and with a very loose political system, they ranged over a wide section of Central Texas, probably absorbing culturally a number of smaller bands of that area. By the mid-seventeenth century, the Tonkawas proper, Yojuanes, Mayeyes, and Yerbipiames composed the Tonkawa peoples.[8]

By the fifteenth century, these people of Texas had developed extensive long-distance trade relations. Caddo traders ventured all the way to the Pueblos of New Mexico, often stopping at Wichita and Tonkawa villages in between. Similarly, Pueblo traders made it as far east as the Caddo villages of East Texas. Early Wichita peoples exchanged buffalo meat and hides for corn and bread with both the Caddos and the Pueblos. This trade was seriously disrupted between A.D. 1450 and 1500 with the arrival of the Athapaskan peoples on the Southern Plains. These Athapaskan peoples had been migrating south out of Canada by following the expansion of the tall grasses in the Central Plains. The immigrant Athapaskans became the Apaches and Navajos of the Southwest, hardy fighters who learned how to thrive in both the desert mountains and the plains. Those who remained on the Southern Plains came to be called the Lipan Apaches. These hunter-gatherers, who chased down buffalo on foot and lived in skin-covered tepees, now formed new alliances with the Pueblo horticulturists and changed the overall Caddoan-Pueblo trade network. The Lipan Apaches, in reality not much different in lifestyle than the Tonkawas, began squeezing out the Wichitas as the main suppliers of bison meat and hides to the Pueblos and made it much more dangerous for Caddo traders to travel all the way to the Pueblos. By A.D 1500, the Lipan Apaches had taken over the Wichita-Pueblo meat-for-corn trade, while forcing Caddo traders to take routes farther south if they still wanted to get to the Pueblos. This trade rivalry led to conflict between the Caddos and Wichitas on one side and Lipan Apaches on the other, which remained sharp and bloody up through the late nineteenth century.[9]

So by the end of the fifteenth century, just as Spain began its voyages to the Western Hemisphere, the Indian peoples of Texas lived a fairly prosperous but complex life. The Caddo peoples, though not as grandiose as they had been two centuries earlier, remained a wealthy, powerful people of two or more chiefdoms governed by their separate Xinesis and participating in long-distance exchange networks. The Wichita people lived in communities from Kansas to the upper Red River area, growing small patches of corn and beans and hunting buffalo on foot. The Caddos and Wichitas traded with each other and developed close relations. Together they formed an antagonism against the Apaches, whose small, scattered communities vied for the same buffalo and trade relations with the Pueblos. Around the middle reaches of the Trinity, Brazos, and Colorado Rivers lived the Tonkawa Indians, probably the most typical of the early Texas Indians and similar to Attakapas and Karankawas, who hunted and gathered on the upper Texas Gulf Coast. Similarly, in far South Texas, a large number of small Coahuiltecan bands did the same. In southwest Texas, groups such as the Jumanos, hunted buffalo afoot and made trading expeditions to the Caddos, Wichitas, Tonkawas, Apaches, and Pueblos.[10]

While all these peoples participated in long-range hunts and long-distance trade, they also fought against each other. Violence between different peoples usually fell into three different categories: warfare, raids, and blood revenge. Offensive warfare was an attempt to take territory, conquer peoples to increase tribute, or deny other peoples the use of resources. Warfare could use hundreds or thousands of warriors, like the huge armies the Caddos could put into the field, or just a few men, typical of the Apaches or Tonkawas. Fights could involve long, drawn-out campaigns or quick, hit-and-run strikes. Raids were economic activities made by small parties of warriors to acquire resources such as horses, hides, captives, or food from the enemy and gain status and wealth for themselves. Blood revenge came about when a member of the clan or community was killed by someone from another people. When that happened, members of the deceased's clan or community were obligated to take revenge on the people who committed the murder. Most of the violence associated with the Indians of Texas was blood revenge.[11]

During the first half of the sixteenth century, contact with Europeans brought dramatic change to the world of the Indians of Texas. The change included more violence and more chances for wealth, status, and power. The first meeting came with Spaniards who had come from the South. The coastal Indians, such as the Karankawas and Coahuiltecans, made a few contacts with sailors and shipwreck victims, such as Álvar Núñez Cabeza de Vaca, who was stranded in South Texas during the late 1520s and early 1530s. Then in the 1540s, the Indians made contact with much larger Spanish expeditions coming from both the East and West. In 1541 the survivors of Hernando de Soto's expedition to the Southeast tried to escape back to Mexico by marching overland through East Texas. The Spanish, frustrated and tired of perpetual warfare with the Indians of the Southeast and constantly needing food, forage, and slave carriers, were in no mood to deal with the Caddo people. Caddo chieftains put up a spirited defense and sent thousands of warriors against the invaders, but Spanish troops prevailed, looting and burning scores of Caddo villages in Arkansas, Louisiana, and East Texas. Bringing even more terrible long-range effects, several sick Spaniards deserted and lived among the Caddo, thus spreading disease to a biologically unprepared people. The Spanish made it to Tonkawa territory on the Brazos River, where they realized the futility of marching across Texas. They turned back, burning and looting the rebuilt Caddo villages a second time, and made it back to Arkansas, where they built several small boats and sailed back to Mexico.[12]

About the same time, from the West, came Francisco Coronado. After devastating some of the Pueblo Indian communities, Coronado and his men, searching for cities of gold, marched into the southern plains of Texas. Astounded by the buffalo and the limitless horizon of the plains, Coronado, led by a Wichita Indian guide, made his way—as the story goes—to a grass-hutted Wichita village along the Arkansas River in central Kansas. Realizing he had been led astray and that the Wichitas possessed no gold, Coronado killed his guide and marched back to Mexico. He too left destruction, disease, and wary Indians in his wake.[13]

The de Soto and Coronado expeditions tremendously affected not only the Indian populations of North and Northeast Texas, but Indian peoples throughout the whole southern half of North America. The thousands of years in which the Indians had lived in small bands during the Paleo and Archaic Periods had filtered the Old World diseases from their blood. Soon after the incursions of de Soto and Moscoso, with no immunities, diseases began killing off the people of the Southeast in vast proportions. The population of the Caddos's area went from a possible 200,000 to 250,000 in the early 1500s to a population of somewhere between 8,000 to 40,000 in the late 1600s. Similar depopulations took place among the Wichitas, Apaches, Tonkawas, and others. Diseases brought both population and cultural loss. Among many of the Southeastern peoples, the epidemics decimated populations, often so fast that ancestral traditions were lost. In fact, because of the diseases that swept through the Southeastern Indians, archaeologists and historians now have only the smallest fragments of these Indian peoples' knowledge, philosophy, religions, and art symbolism that were in existence prior to the mid-1500s. Disease killed workers, leaders, specialists, and the people crucial to the continuation of the society—interpreters, craftspeople, healers, hunters, foragers, singers, dancers, and a host of others.[14]

Although Europeans essentially remained outside the modern borders of Texas for the next one hundred and fifty years, the Indian people still felt their presence. In 1598, the Spanish returned to New Mexico, and European metalware, cloth, and other manufactured goods began filtering throughout the extensive Southern Plains trade networks, eventually making their way to all Indian societies in Texas. While metal made better scrapers, hoes, and arrowheads, European-introduced horses brought the greatest changes. Some of these horses escaped from the Spanish in New Mexico; some were taken in raids by Apaches, Jumanos, and others. Thriving on the lush plains, horses quickly entered the trade networks and soon made their way to the Wichitas, the Caddos, even to the Illinois Indians and further East. The Pueblo Revolt of 1680 funneled even more horses into Indian hands, and by 1700 most Indian peoples anywhere near the Plains had access to horses.[15]

Horses were the perfect animal for the Indians of Texas. They could be eaten and so provided an additional food source if needed. They could be tamed to haul goods and carry riders. They extended the range of hunters so they could carry home more game, and they allowed a camp to move faster and farther. The use of horses changed the face of warfare as Apache, Wichita, Tonkawa, and Caddo warriors changed from foot soldiers to cavalrymen. The Indians could travel farther, strike quicker, and get away faster than ever before. Even a single man on a horse could wreak havoc on a village or change the course of a battle, and a member of a mounted party of thirty or forty could do even more. So horses also became a commodity, items to acquire and exchange. A man with plenty of horses possessed wealth, which brought status on its own and also aided him in acquiring military honors, from which came power within the community. A successful warrior who acquired many horses on his raids could easily gain the top reaches of power among the Apaches, Wichitas, and later the Comanches and Kiowas. Even the hierarchical Caddos made a place for a good warrior with horses.[16]

Horses soon ranged far beyond the boundaries of New Mexico and Texas. By the second half of the seventeenth century they had spread up the Plains as far as the Dakotas, Montana, even eastern Washington and Oregon. About this time, Indian peoples living in the woodlands and prairies on the verges of the Plains—such as the Shoshones, Lakotas, Cheyennes, Crows, and Arapahos—acquired horses. Some of these peoples had already been drawn to the Plains to hunt the immense herds of buffalo afoot, while others practiced horticulture at semipermanent villages. Now these peoples became horse-riding buffalo hunters following the herds. As all these different peoples flowed out to the great buffalo herds, they began to come into contact with each other, sometimes they made peace; sometimes they warred. As they crowded each other, some took the opportunity to move farther south. During the late 1600s, one of these Shoshone groups from Montana, Wyoming, and Colorado, the Comanches, now riding horses, began moving down the front range of the Rocky Mountains and into the Southern Plains of Texas, Oklahoma, Colorado, and Kansas. The Comanches migrated south not only to escape the warfare on the Northern Plains, but also to put themselves closer to the sources from which horses seemed to come.[17]

With horses already changing the lives of Texas Indians, the last years of the seventeenth century brought even more opportunities and changes. In 1685, the Frenchman Robert Cavelier, Sieur de La Salle, and a small band of colonists overshot the Mississippi River, landed on the Texas coast near Matagorda Bay, and built a small fort. A few years before, La Salle had sailed down the Mississippi River and claimed all the land drained by the river for France, naming it Louisiana. On Matagorda Bay, he realized he was somewhere west of the river. On several occasions he led exploring parties northeast into Caddo Hasinai territory, but he was finally killed by his own men, and only a few survivors made it back to French territory. Among the communities of the Hasinai chiefdom in East Texas, the French found horses, clothes, bells, and even papal bulls from the Spanish in New Mexico. They also found other Indian people visiting the Caddos to trade for bois d'arc bows. The Caddos greatly admired the Frenchmen's guns, needles, and metal goods and quickly exchanged horses and other goods for this metalware. They persuaded one Frenchman with his gun to make a raid with them against a Tonkawa village, where the firearm proved decisive and helped them take two women captives. They sent one of the women back to her tribe with a musket ball and orders to tell her people that the Caddos now had a new weapon and were prepared to use it again if necessary. Realizing the potential of the guns, the Caddos tried to get the Frenchmen to stay among them and marry Caddo women. Several did stay, but the rest eventually walked back to the Mississippi River.[18]

As word leaked out about the wealth of the Caddos and that Frenchmen were living among them, the Spanish sent several expeditions from Mexico to capture the French survivors. As the Spanish rounded up the French refugees, they saw the large Caddo villages and believed them ripe for a Christian conversion. So in 1690, the Spanish set up several missions in East Texas. These missions reaped no Caddo converts, and Spain abandoned them a few years later in 1693.[19]

Though the Spanish disappeared from Texas during the first years of the eighteenth century, the French established an outpost among the Natchitoches Caddos on the lower Red River in Louisiana. Then in 1720, they expanded their presence by establishing another outpost at the Caddo Cadodacho village near the Great Bend of the Red River. From these posts the French sent traders out to the Caddo and Wichita villages in Texas, exchanging firearms, ammunition, kettles, knives, axes, cloth and clothes, and a variety of other things for Caddo and Wichita horses and deer hides. The French also provided an annual distribution of goods to the Caddos and Wichitas to secure their alliance. The Spanish felt threatened by this French presence and to counter it, reestablished a series of missions and presidios among the Caddos in East Texas. They hoped the Caddo would give up their villages and live around the missions, become Catholic Christians, provide manual labor, and be allies of the Spanish in return for saving their souls and protecting them from other Indians.[20]

The Caddos and Wichitas eagerly played the two European powers against each other. The French wanted horses and hides, and the Caddos and Wichitas were more than happy to acquire these through capture or trade and exchange them for French firearms and manufactured goods. The prosperity of most individual Frenchmen in that area depended upon the Caddos' and Wichitas' providing them with horses and hides for shipment to France or her other colonies. The way to acquire these was to send a trader out to a Caddo or Wichita village and, through gift-exchange and trade, have him provide these Indians with the goods they wanted for the horses and hides. To ensure that the French kept a steady supply of these goods coming, the Caddos went to great lengths to pull these French traders into their kinship network, urging them to marry Caddo women or to be adopted into Caddo families. The Caddos believed that their new, and apparently wealthy, French kinsmen would thereafter always provide manufactured items and good deals to their Caddo families and kin.[21]

As for the Spanish missions in East Texas, the Caddos mostly ignored them, except to provide corn and meat to the missionaries and soldiers in exchange for some Spanish manufactured goods or to raid the corrals for horses and cattle. The Caddos did not give up their villages to live among the missions, as they did not need the protection the mission promised; after all, with the guns provided by the French, the Caddos were better armed than the local Spanish troops. Neither did the Caddos convert to Christianity, being fully satisfied with their own religion. By the 1740s, Spain again abandoned most all the missions in Caddo territory and gave up any pretense of missionization.[22]

In West Texas, the Lipan Apaches also acquired horses. This acquisition allowed them to expand their territory over much of the western Southern Plains and also become dangerous neighbors to the Pueblo Indians. Prior to the coming of the Spanish, the Apaches and Pueblos had an interdependent meat-for-corn relationship. Now, with their villages under Spanish control, the Pueblos and their Spanish conquerors raised large herds of horses, cattle, and sheep and so became targets of Apache raids. Spanish militia and their Pueblo auxiliaries often gave chase, sometimes as far as the Arkansas River valley, and occasionally recovered their possessions. But the action was like trying to swat mosquitos. There were too many Lipan Apache bands and too many young warriors hungry for the status that raids and spoils brought.[23]

For the Lipan Apaches, the turn of the eighteenth century saw them as masters of the western Southern Plains. Their situation changed as the Comanches made their way into the area and contested them for control. While Europeans, Americans, and later scholars have often disagreed over the number and names of Comanche bands, the advancing Comanches were divided basically into five major divisions and many minor ones. The Penetakas became the largest, southernmost, and the tribe most involved in Texas for the next one hundred and fifty years. They eventually established themselves among the headwaters of the rivers of central Texas, from the Cross Timbers to the Edwards Plateau. The Noconis ranged north of the Penetakas, centered about the Red River. North of the Red River and the Noconis roamed the Kotsotekas, and the Kwahadis lived west of them in the Texas Panhandle. The Yamparikas, the northernmost Comanche band, lived around the Cimarron River in southern Kansas. Mounted Comanche warriors, also wanting horses and the status that came with raiding, struck the Apaches, the Pueblos, and the Spanish. The Spanish in New Mexico, over the next few decades, alternated between punitive expeditions and attempts to make peace. The Apaches put up a spirited resistance, but gradually gave way before the Comanche onslaught and slowly withdrew off the plains and toward the desert south where they continued raiding the Spanish settlements in South Texas, New Mexico, and northern Mexico.[24]

Comanche and Apache warfare in West Texas had a tremendous impact in East Texas and shaped alliances that would last for the next one hundred and fifty years. As Apache and Comanche warfare intensified during the eighteenth century, both peoples constantly needed more weapons, firearms if possible, but mainly metal-edged weapons—with which most battles were fought—such as knives, axes, hatchets, or metal strips to make arrow and lance points. Because the Spanish hoped to stop Apache and Comanche raids on Spanish and Pueblo settlements by limiting the amount of manufactured goods they received, all now turned east toward the Indians who possessed trade relations with the French in Louisiana. Comanches developed a trade network that extended to the Wichitas and on to the Caddos. Manufactured goods flowed west from French Natchitoches to the Caddos to the Wichitas and eventually to the Comanches. Back came Apache horses, buffalo and deer hides, and slaves. Similarly, the Lipan Apaches developed their own trade network. It extended east to the Tonkawas, on to the Attakapas, then to the French outposts in southern Louisiana. By the mid-eighteenth century, two trade networks extended from French Louisiana across Texas: a Caddo-Wichita-Comanche network in the north and an Attakapan-Tonkawa-Apache network in the south. Members of these networks usually possessed peaceful relations with their trade network partners but often raided the peoples of other networks. It was this interdependency along one network and competition for the same resources with the other that brought such conflict between some of the Indians of Texas. It also explains why the Comanches, Wichitas, and Caddos hated the Apaches and Tonkawas and vice versa. This competition and enmity brought raids, counterraids, and revenge killings between these Indian peoples for decades to come.[25]

While the Indians of Texas had warred and raided each other since time immemorial, the entrance of the French and Spanish to Texas and the growth of Euroamerican trading and military outposts, missions, ranches, and villages fueled the frequency and intensity of the Indian wars. European manufactured goods, at first luxuries, soon became necessities. The need for these manufactured goods, Indian attempts to acquire them and control their distribution, and the status and power the acquisition of these goods brought to an individual made warfare in Texas a vicious circle. Indians raided other Indian peoples or Spanish outposts, usually for horses, hides, or slaves, and then exchanged them to their trading partners or French traders for firearms and ammunition, which helped them become better warriors. An individual gained status by displaying bravery on the raids and by acquiring wealth—such as additional horses, guns, and a variety of manufactured goods, which they gave away as gifts therefore showing their generosity. The Spanish hoped to stop the constant raids by limiting Indian access to firearms, but found that impossible as long as French traders from Louisiana supplied the Indians with what they wanted.[26]

Not only did the influx of European manufactured goods change the nature of Indian diplomacy and warfare, it also changed Indian culture and society. Horses, as already noted, changed Indian economics, warfare, their social status system, and the very life of the village and camp itself as people changed from walkers to riders. Next came the gun. Firearms, while important, played a much larger role among the Caddos, Wichitas, and Tonkawas than they initially did with the Apaches and Comanches. The Caddos, Wichitas, and Tonkawas found the gun ideal for deer hunting, which they did afoot. Production of deer hides increased, and those brought them greater shares of European merchandise. Conversely, it was almost futile to use a gun to hunt buffalo from horseback, so bows and arrows remained the primary weapon of the buffalo hunt, at least until bullets came along. For warfare, the mid-eighteenth century trade muskets were rather inaccurate, notorious for breaking, and just about impossible to reload while on horseback. In a horseback attack, the normal tactic used by the Indians was to fire an initial volley and then resort to bows and arrows, lances, or war clubs. In dismounted warfare, which sometimes occurred, the gun could be used to better advantage, but muskets were not known for their accuracy. Despite their deficiencies as weapons, the Indian peoples liked firearms because they gave them a psychological advantage over those without them. And if by chance the musketball did strike its human target, the ball came fast, was unseen, and usually left a horrible wound. So the Indians of Texas demanded even more weapons, musketballs, and gunpowder in their exchange relations with Europeans.[27]

Other European items created their own changes. Arrow points cut from metal, such as wagon wheel hoops or old kettles, replaced stone arrow points. Metal kettles and glass jars replaced homemade pottery. Hide clothing gave way to cotton, linen, and woolen cloth. Metal hoes supplanted stone blades or buffalo shoulder blade hoes, making the growing of crops easier and more productive. Shards of broken glass and mirrors became hide scrapers and increased hide production. Europeans did not have to force these goods on the Indians; rather, Indian men and women saw how these new items could save labor while increasing the production of a person, household, or village, and they liked what they saw. They demanded evermore quantities of these goods in their exchange relations.[28]

While Indian physical culture changed from their contact with Europeans, so did some of their basic social structures. French and Spanish traders wanted horses, buffalo and deer hides, and slaves from the Indians. This demand changed Indian warfare to long-range, lightening-quick raids. The treatment of captives changed. Prior to the coming of Europeans, most captives were by-products of warfare and were usually tortured to death as blood revenge for people killed in past battles. By the early eighteenth century, the Spanish in southern Texas, New Mexico, and Mexico; the French in Louisiana and the Caribbean; and the English from the Atlantic Coast demanded ever-increasing numbers of slaves. So when the Comanches or Wichitas captured Apaches, rather than putting them to death—especially if they were women and children—they exchanged them along the trade network to French Louisiana or to the Spanish in New Mexico. Apache slaves became so common around French Natchitoches that a large Apache community still exists in western Louisiana. Not all captives were traded away. Some, often women, children, and young boys, were adopted into the various Indian societies to make up for continued population losses.[29]

As buffalo and deer hides became valuable commodities and because the tanning of hides was considered woman's work, those Indian men with sure access to buffalo herds, such as the Comanches and Apaches, found that having more wives allowed them to acquire more goods and status. So polygamy became more common. A man's status also began to be determined not only by his generosity, his bravery, and how many horses he owned, but also by how many wives he could afford to keep. Such an opportunity for high status was open to any man, whether the son of a chief or a former slave boy adopted into the tribe.[30]

Among the Caddos, who placed a much greater importance on social ranking and inherited positions, hereditary chiefs still wielded tremendous power. But as disease continually depleted the ranks of the nobility, status and power often fell upon the person who controlled the distribution of European-manufactured goods and therefore acquired more hides, horses, and wives.

In fact, European diseases and the lack of Indian immunities to them dramatically changed Indian societies. Disease decreased the Caddos in the 1500s and terrible afflictions still cropped up periodically among the Indians of Texas. According to historian John Ewers, no less than thirty epidemics devastated the Indians of Texas prior to 1820. Smallpox was the most common scourge. It ravaged the Texas Indians at least once every generation. Measles, cholera, malaria, whooping cough, and influenza also contributed and all hit children and teenagers particularly hard. Those who survived gained some immunity to the next attack. According to Ewers, by 1890, the Tonkawas had been reduced by 97 percent, the Caddos by 94 percent, the Wichitas by 89 percent, the Lipan Apaches by 88 percent, the Comanches by 77 percent, and the Kiowas by 43 percent. The Indians adapted to these dramatic losses in population by coalescing with other similar bands, joining with wholly different peoples, or by adopting outsiders into their families and bands.[31]

These diseases brought about a tremendous population loss and cultural destruction. Still, despite the diseases and the changes brought by contact with the Europeans and their manufactured goods, much remained the same for the Indians of Texas. Buffalo were still hunted with the bow and arrow. The Apaches and Comanches still followed the buffalo up and down the plains within their own territories, while the Wichitas, Tonkawas, and Caddos made seasonal hunts to the plains in the fall and winter of the year. Women still tanned hides and did beadwork. In the Wichita and Caddo villages, the women continued to do all the farming and controlled the house and hearth. The Caddos, Wichitas, and Tonkawas all still lived in beehive-shaped grass houses, while the Comanches and Apaches lived in buffalo-hide tepees.

So, for most Texas Indians, excepting for the ravages of disease, most of the eighteenth century could be considered a time of plenty. Horses, firearms, and other useful European manufactured goods had appeared and made Indian life a little easier. As long as the Europeans continued bringing in a steady supply of needed manufactured goods, then all would be well. Though diseases might periodically ravage them, the Indians realized little could be done about it. While war and raids could be devastating, they remained a poor man's way to acquire status and power and continued as an important aspect of life for all the Indians of Texas.

The wild cards in all this were the French and Spanish. The French fit in best with the Indians' way of life. Not interested in farming Indian land nor in Christianizing them, their demand for horses, hides, and slaves fit in just fine with the Indians' lifestyle. By the 1740s, at least one French trader, who usually doubled as a gunsmith, lived in or regularly visited every Caddo and Wichita community. There they often married Indian women, sired mixed-blood children, and tried to uphold their kinship obligations with the Indians. Frenchmen in Natchitoches developed close relationships with the Caddo and Wichita communities and depended upon their military assistance. In return, French firearms, ammunition, and manufactured goods spread throughout these Indian societies of North and West Texas.[32]

The Spanish baffled the Indians. Spaniards of every class arrogantly believed everything about the Indians was inferior and therefore felt compelled to change it. Spanish missionaries told the Indians their religious beliefs were sinful, their way of life savage, and their tendency to use warfare to gain status and wealth wrong. Instead, the missionaries proposed they give up these characteristics, settle at a mission, and work at manual labor for the padres. If they were good and obedient, they would receive metal goods, be protected from their enemies, and go to heaven when they died. None of the Apaches, Comanches, Wichitas, Tonkawas, or Caddos accepted the Spanish offer as they preferred their traditional lifestyle over what the missions offered. They already possessed a conduit to manufactured goods through the French in Louisiana and were not sure what the Spanish could protect them from. The successful Spanish missions were located in South Texas, deep in Spanish territory, among the more settled, agricultural Coahuiltecan peoples. In contrast, the Spanish missions in Central and East Texas became way stations and supply depots for the Indians. When times were hard, the Indians might briefly live at a mission. When times were good, they would raid the horse herd or store house for supplies.[33]

If these North Texas Indians, *Norteños*, as the Spanish termed the Comanches, Wichitas, Caddos, and Tonkawas, did not desire Spanish religion, neither did they fear the Spanish military. Spanish presidios were few and the regular army minuscule, with most of the troops made up of colonists and Indian allies. The soldiers' pay was meager, supplies inadequate, morale low, and conversely, the thought of battle with the Apaches or Comanches struck terror in the hearts of the troops. The only thing that kept the Apaches and *Norteños* from all out war against the Spanish was that the Indians understood the role Spain played in their own economics. While the Indians depended upon French goods from Louisiana, they always needed more, and the Spanish were a major supplier of these valued manufactured goods. Spanish goods made their way to the Apaches and *Norteños* through gifts, trade, and raids on the missions, presidios, and villages of the settled Indians of South Texas, New Mexico, and Mexico.

Despite their weak presence in Central, North, and East Texas, the Spanish still believed they controlled the Indians. Blindly ignoring their own weaknesses, the Spanish often blundered when it came to Indian diplomacy. In 1758, the *Norteños* decided to show the Spanish just how weak they actually were. In Central Texas, the Spanish had built Mission San Sabá where they hoped the Apaches would congregate, give up their buffalo hunting, and halt their raids on Spanish settlements in South Texas and northern Mexico. The Apaches refused to settle at San Sabá and in March 1758, an Apache party stopping at the mission appeared particularly jittery and left after a short stay. Soon after, a large war party of Comanches, Wichitas, and Caddos attacked and destroyed the mission, killing two priests, eight residents of the mission, and two soldiers who tried to come to the rescue of the mission. Spain vowed revenge against the *Norteños*. The next year, Colonel Diego Ortiz Parilla led a force of more than 600 soldiers and Indian auxiliaries, which included thirty-four Apaches, toward the Red River, defeating a Tonkawa village en route. At the Red River, they found the Indians holed up in the fortified, palisaded Taovaya Wichita village. Indian fire was so hot from the village that Parilla could not besiege it. Suddenly a large party of warriors sallied out of the fortification, soundly defeated Parilla, captured two of his cannons, and sent him and his allies scurrying back toward San Antonio after suffering more than fifty casualties. In later years, the Comanches and Wichitas explained that when they saw the Spanish becoming so friendly with their Apache enemies by building a mission for them, they believed that the Spanish had now sided with the Apaches and were now their enemies. So they attacked first.[34]

Even as the Comanches, Wichitas, and Caddos were defeating Parilla on the Red River, events taking place on the Atlantic seaboard and in Europe were shaping up to affect dramatically the lives of the Indians of Texas. Between 1754 and 1763, the British and French fought the French and Indian War and in 1762, rather than lose it to the English, France gave Louisiana to Spain. For the *Norteños*, this change from a French to a Spanish Louisiana had the potential to be disastrous. There had always been a constant need for guns and ammunition for hunting and raiding purposes, but now this need had grown greater. Beginning in the 1760s, the Osages from Arkansas and Missouri began making their own raids against the Caddos, Wichitas, and Comanches. The Osage raids soaked up firearms and ammunition, not only on defense and counterraids, but also in the additional hunting the Indians did to make up for hides taken by the Osages. With the Spanish now controlling New Mexico, Texas, and Louisiana, theoretically they could cut off the supply of firearms, ammunition, and manufactured goods, which would force the Indians to make peace, possibly even settle in missions.[35]

Fortunately, the Indians of North Texas had nothing to worry about. In 1770, Spain threatened the *Norteños* with cutting off their supply of manufactured goods, but Spain's weakness made their threat hollow. In Louisiana, Spain acquired a tremendous stretch of territory, but could not afford to replace all the French officials with Spaniards. Therefore, French officials, such as the Natchitoches fort commandants and official traders to the Caddos and Wichitas, remained at their posts, only swearing allegiance to Spain. Suspicion between Texas and Louisiana remained. Exacerbating this situation was the fact that Louisiana came under the administration of Havana, while Texas came under the Viceroyalty of New Spain in Mexico City, making close coordination extremely difficult. At the same time, while Spain hoped to stop the Indian's raids on Texas settlements by controlling the trade to them, their fear of an Anglo-American grab for Louisiana and Texas caused Spanish officials to see the Indians as armed barriers against any American expansion.[36]

To institute this Indian barrier against the Anglo-Americans and to stop raids in Texas, the Spanish initiated peace talks with most of the Indians of North Texas. Still, they faced a dilemma. Remembering the fate of San Sabá and realizing they could not make peace with both the Apaches and Comanches without angering one or the other, the Spanish decided the Comanches were the lesser of the two evils, or rather were the more to be feared. The Indians of Texas saw no reason not to make peace with the Spanish, as this would only keep more manufactured goods coming in to their villages. By 1771, the Caddos, Tonkawas, and Wichitas had signed a peace treaty with Spain, and by 1787, the southernmost Comanche bands had made peace with Spanish authorities in both Texas and New Mexico. Driving the Indians' willingness to make peace was their need for more goods in the face of increased Osage and, by now also, Choctaw raids. Spain, hoping to solve two problems at once, offered gifts and merchandise in return for peace and redirected Comanche and Wichita raids away from Spanish settlements and against the Lipan Apaches.[37]

Still, peace was a nebulous thing. Just because one band made peace did not mean another band of the same people did so. Also, young men wanting status often disregarded the words of the chiefs and made horse raids on their own. If by chance an Indian was killed by the Spanish on these raids, then the obligations of blood revenge demanded that clan or band members must retaliate. This situation, compounded by another Spanish attempt to make peace with the Apaches, meant that by the early 1790s, Comanche and Wichita raiding parties again struck deep into the Spanish settlements of South Texas.[38]

Although the Penataka Comanches, Wichitas, Tonkawas, and Caddos made peace with the Spanish, the Spanish still feared these Indians might be swayed to an alliance with England. To prevent this possibility, Spain authorized only licensed traders to visit the Indian villages and trade with them. Merchandise shortages brought about by the American Revolution meant Spain could not provide enough trade goods or gifts to meet the Indians' needs, so, much to the anger and fear of the Spanish, the Indians welcomed both licensed and unlicensed traders to their village. These unlicensed traders, many of them French creoles from Spanish Louisiana, undercut the prices of official Spanish traders and undermined Spain's ability to regulate the goods going to the Indians. The Indians often dictated prices, the amount of annual gifts they were to receive, and usually ignored Spanish orders to trade only with Spanish-licensed traders.[39]

Increasing attacks by the Osages and westward-moving bands of Choctaws drove the need for evermore weapons and merchandise for the Indians of East Texas. To replace ammunition as well as stolen horses, some of these Texas Indians again raided Spanish outposts. Even worse for Spain was that in the late 1780s and early 1790s, much more fierce and warlike peoples began streaming into Texas from the North. Northern bands of the Comanches, as well as the Kiowas, began appearing in Texas and raided Spanish outposts and ranches. The Kiowas were a Plains hunting-gathering people speaking a distinct language who considered themselves originally from the northern-most reaches of the United States around the headwaters of the Yellowstone and Missouri Rivers. They were friends and allies with the Crows, Arikaras, and the Canadian Athapaskan peoples—the same peoples who had earlier moved south and became the Apache peoples of Texas, New Mexico, and Arizona. In fact, one group of these northern Apaches—though speaking a different language than the Kiowas—attached themselves to the Kiowas and became a distinct part of the Kiowa people, thus forming the Kiowa-Apaches. Six divisions comprised the Kiowas: Katas or Biters and Arikaras; Kogui or Elks; Kaigwu or Kiowas proper; Kingep or Big Shield; Semat or Kiowa-Apaches and Kongtalyui or Black Boys. In 1775, the Dakota peoples drove the Kiowas and Comanches further south into the Southern Plains of Texas, Oklahoma, New Mexico, Colorado, and southern Kansas. In 1790, the Comanches and Kiowas made a peace and became strong allies. This peace has lasted up to this very day, and the two peoples remain closely associated with each other.[40]

In 1789, tired of Osage raids, seven hundred Penataka Comanche and Wichita warriors attacked Osage villages in northern Arkansas. This attack dealt such a serious blow that it can be considered a turning point in that it prevented the Osages from expanding onto the Southern Plains. Still, while Osage raiders may now have been hesitant to advance too far into Texas, they kept up their raids on the Caddo and Wichita villages along the upper Red River. Because of these raids by the Osages and the ever-advancing Choctaws, continual epidemics of disease, and the need by the Caddos and Wichitas to acquire hides and horses to feed themselves and purchase weapons, a tremendous fission and fusing gripped the Indians of Northeast Texas. Some Caddo and Wichita villages along the upper Red River moved further south to escape Osage raids by 1800. Small villages often combined with larger ones for protection or broke apart with its members scattering in search of safety. Many communities ceased to exist as their members died off and the survivors joined other communities. For example, of the ten communities that composed the Caddo Hasinai chiefdom in East Texas, by 1800 only four communities remained: the Hainai, often called the Tejas; the Nadaco, which came to be called the Anadarko; the Nacogdoche, and the Nabedache. Similarly, of the great Kadohadacho chiefdom at the Great Bend of the Red River, only the Cadodacho remained and it was this community that eventually gave the name "Caddo" to all these peoples. Likewise, some Wichita and Tonkawa communities also disappeared—such as the Wichita Yscani—which became the Waco and eventually melded into the "Wichitas." The Mayeyes and other Tonkawa bands eventually all came to be called "Tonkawa."[41]

Then, in the first decade of the nineteenth century, several events took place that brought dire consequences to the Indians of Texas. In 1803, the United States purchased Louisiana. Instead of having a weak Spanish government to the east, the Indians of Texas now had powerful Americans to contend with. While the Spanish wanted the Indians as allies and trade partners, American settlers who streamed into the area wanted Indian land for farming. Many Indian peoples of the eastern United States, having their fill of the aggressive Americans, streamed into Texas to get away from the Americans. As early as 1790, the Spanish had invited several bands of Choctaws to settle in Louisiana and by 1796, some of these Choctaw bands had petitioned the Spanish government for permission to settle in Texas, something the Caddos vehemently opposed. This movement of eastern Indian peoples into Texas increased after the purchase of Louisiana by the United States government.[42]

In 1810, the Mexican War for Independence began and lasted for more than a decade. The war brought turmoil to Texas. Spain virtually abandoned the colony when it began losing the war. Most of the Euroamerican population of Texas deserted it for the safety of Mexico or Louisiana. As a result, the Indian peoples of Texas had the area almost to themselves. The Comanches, Kiowas, and Lipan Apaches continued their buffalo hunts unmolested. On Texas's eastern border, the Caddos, Wichitas, and Tonkawas continued planting corn, beans, and squash; hunting deer for hides; making winter buffalo hunts to the plains; but still they tried to stem the tide of Osage, Choctaw, and other eastern invaders.[43]

Once Mexico gained its independence in 1821, it tried to firm up its control of Texas. Seeing the lack of colonists in Texas and fearing both the power of the Plains Indians and the aggressiveness of the United States to the east, Mexico instituted a policy of inviting both "peaceful" eastern Indians and Anglo-Americans to settle in Texas. In some ways this action was merely accepting reality since some eastern Indians—such as the Cherokees under the leadership of Chief Duwali—had already established themselves in Texas during the winter of 1819–20. Soon, even more eastern Indians, such as bands of Shawnees, Delawares, Kickapoos, Choctaws, Creeks, and more Cherokees migrated into Texas and settled on lands traditionally claimed by the Caddos, Wichitas and Tonkawas. About the same time came the first true American settlers into Texas, led by Stephen F. Austin. Granted land by the Mexicans, they were the first of an enormous wave of Americans that would come to Texas during the next few decades.[44]

The coming of Americans to Texas posed serious problems for all the Indian peoples living in Texas. Prior to the 1820s, most Anglo-Americans in Texas—such as Philip Nolan and Anthony Glass, like the French traders before them—wanted the Indians as business partners and so developed a good relationship of providing firearms and other European goods in exchange for hides and horses. The new Americans coming into Texas fell into two categories.

First came a new breed of entrepreneurs: the Santa Fe Trail traders. Beginning in 1821 and taking advantage of the more open trading policies of the Mexican government, American traders hauled huge wagons filled with cloth and metalware from points in Missouri and Arkansas to Santa Fe, New Mexico. At Santa Fe they exchanged the goods for silver and gold. The Santa Fe Trail cut directly across West Texas and through lands claimed by the Comanches and Kiowas.[45]

The Comanches had long had contact with Euroamerican traders and were not awed by these peoples. For the first seven years of the Trail's existence, peaceful relations reigned between the Comanches and the traders. Still, the Santa Fe Trail traders had never before met Indians like the Comanches and Kiowas, and eventually a clash of cultures took place. As these traders crossed West Texas, the Comanches and Kiowas often approached them. As their culture required, they asked the traders for gifts. Gift exchange was a cornerstone not only in Comanche and Kiowa culture, but to all American Indians. Gift giving made strangers into family and potential enemies into friends. No meeting, council, or transaction could begin without an exchange of gifts. The giving of a gift created a special bond—a kinship of sorts—between the participants which brought with it a host of obligations; the same obligations any kinspeople would have toward each other. From gift giving and kinship, a person might receive such items as food, clothing, shelter, protection, advice, assistance, or even a spouse. When a man wanted a wife, he gave her and her parents gifts. Euroamericans often mistakenly saw this as "buying" a wife. Between the Indians and the Anglos, each gave what they had. An Anglo among the Indians might receive food, shelter, horses, and protection while the Indians expected their rich Anglo brothers to provide them with guns, manufactured goods, tobacco, and such.[46]

For many Anglo-American Santa Fe Trail traders—possessing a shopkeeper's mind toward profit and loss—the demand by the Comanches and Kiowas for a gift reeked of bribery and extortion, and so they often refused. For the Comanches, a refusal represented a terrible insult indicating that a person or group willingly chose to be their enemies. With the refusal to give a gift, violence usually erupted. Comanches and Kiowas might then target the offending group of traders and steal their stock, raid the wagons, or even try to kill them. Naturally, the traders responded with violence. When a Comanche was killed, the obligations of blood revenge meant that the death must be avenged with the killing of a Anglo-American. Just as Anglo-Americans made little distinction between Indian groups, neither did the Comanches and Kiowas, so one group of traders might pay for the actions of another group. By 1828, violence between the Comanches and Kiowas and the Santa Fe Trail traders became so pronounced that the traders demanded protection by the army. Over the years, the government attempted to make peace treaties with the Comanches and Kiowas and stationed troops along the Arkansas River in order to provide some protection for the traders before they entered Mexican Territory.[47]

The second group of Americans that troubled the Indians of Texas were ranchers, planters, and farmers. Many of these settlers came from the states of the lower South and brought with them old prejudices against Indians. Also, cotton was booming throughout the nation. The cotton gin, high demand by the textiles mills of New England and Europe, and high prices being offered made cotton the poor man's way to get rich. All that was needed was good land, and so Mexican Texas beckoned.

Even the rules and barriers set up by Mexico, such as conversion to Catholicism and the Mexican government's official disapproval of slavery, posed no problem as the Mexican government strictly enforced neither. During the late 1820s and early 1830s, the many Indians living in Texas presented the only true barrier to American settlement. And these Indians, immigrant Anglo-Americans reasoned, could be pushed from their lands, just as Andrew Jackson forced the Creeks to cede millions of acres of land after the Creek Civil War of 1813–1814.

By the early 1830s, the Caddos, Wichitas, and Tonkawas living in East Texas, as well as other Indian peoples living in this region, found themselves either surrounded or hard pressed both by immigrant eastern Indians and Anglo-Americans. The Indians of Texas and the eastern immigrant Indians

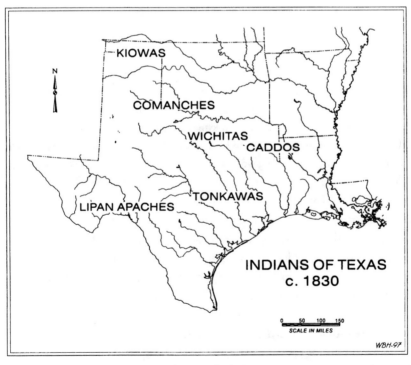

Map by W. Burlleigh Harris.

competed for the same resources, and violence often erupted in East Texas. Even worse was the conflict with white newcomers. Though the Mexican government tried to recognize Indian rights, Anglo-American settlers who received large land grants from Mexico often claimed lands on which Indians already lived. Problems developed over horses and cattle as Indians did not share the same beliefs in private property and ownership as the Anglo-Americans did. Without fences, Anglo-Americans often let their livestock wander in the woods or prairie with merely a brand to identify them. To many Indians, a wandering horse, cow, or pig was fair game so they caught and kept the animal, a practice that led to accusations of theft by whites. Similarly, Indians usually let their own unbranded livestock wander. But white settlers, considering them mavericks, often claimed them for their own.[48]

For protection, the Caddos in East Texas relied upon the power of their Great Chief, Dehahuit, who lived on the border between Texas and Louisiana and stymied all efforts by the United States to take Caddo land in Louisiana. Dehahuit died in 1833, and in 1835 the United States forced the Caddos in Louisiana to cede their land and move west. The Louisiana Caddos split, with most moving to Texas to join their Hasinai Caddo kin; some Caddo bands briefly moved to Mexico, and some moved to Indian Territory that the United States Congress had created north of the Red River in 1825. Other Indians, such as the Tonkawas and some Wichita communities, tried to move west. The Tonkawas—characterized as thieves and beggars by the Texans who misread Tonkawa culture of asking for gifts and the status a man gained from stealing from non-kin—were despised by the Texans, and also by the Wichitas because of Tonkawa friendship with the Lipan Apaches. As the Wichitas prepared to invade Tonkawa territory in 1824, the Texans, fearful of such a large Indian war party, prepared to expel the Tonkawas, but the Lipans agreed to take charge of them and moved many Tonkawas west to settlements along the Llano and San Sabá Rivers in central Texas. Unfortunately, East Texas Indians wanting to move farther west found their paths blocked by the Comanches, who attacked the Tonkawas and other immigrant Indians, such as the Cherokees. The Comanches also attacked American settlers who got too close to their traditional lands. [49]

As tensions increased between the Anglo-Americans and the Mexican government during the early 1830s, the Texans saw the Indians as both potential enemies and allies. Hoping to persuade them to side with the Texans in the event of war with Mexico and hearing that Mexico had already made overtures to the Indians, the Texans sent Sam Houston to meet with the Indians in East Texas. On February 23, 1836, the Caddos—as well as many immigrant Indians, such as the Cherokees, Biloxis, Choctaws, Alabamas, and others—signed an agreement in which they promised to remain neutral and reside on a small reservation in East Texas, giving up all claims to any land outside the proposed reservation. Out west, the Lipan Apaches were split, with one group friendly to the Texans and another siding with Mexico. Despite this division, most Indians lived up to their neutrality during the Texas War of Independence. Still, the next year, 1837, the Texas Senate rejected Houston's treaty.[50]

Even the Comanches, Kiowas, and Apaches did not cause many problems for the Texans during the revolution. While the robbing of non-kin was accepted, even encouraged, and though raids and the acquisition of horses added to a man's status and wealth, the Comanches, Apaches and Kiowas were not at war with the Texans. To imply that "the Comanches" might declare war on the Texans overlooks the tremendous number of factions dividing the Comanche peoples and most Indian societies. None of these Indians of Texas identified themselves as belonging to a "tribe," but rather as members of a family, maybe at most a clan. They were "Comanches" or "Caddos" or "Tonkawas" because they spoke that language and were connected to other Comanches, Caddos, or Tonkawas respectively, by being members of the same clans, possessing corresponding religious beliefs and similar cultures. Therefore, the name "Comanche" is a name given to a people, not a single political entity, such as the "Republic of Texas" or the "United States of America." No one chief governed the "Comanches," or "Kiowas," or "Apaches." Many different "divisions" or "communities," such as the Penatakas, Kwahadis, Yamparikas, and Noconis, comprised the Comanche people. An ever-changing number of bands, each led by its own chief, made up each of these divisions. Some of these bands from the same division—or even bands from other divisions—might join together at certain times of the year, but rarely, if ever, did they act in concert.[51]

Besides, a Plains Indian chief's power was extremely limited. While certain families may have been looked upon as chiefly families, in reality a Plains chief gained power not from heredity, but through practicing four cardinal virtues: bravery, fortitude, generosity, and wisdom. If a man eventually displayed all these virtues, the people of the band bestowed power upon him, and he governed through a moral authority. His power increased as word of his virtues grew; as his success in raids, hunting, and diplomacy continued; and as he became recognized as a man who provided for his people. By these actions, more and more people would be attracted to his band, and it became easier for him to sway the opinion of other bands and chiefs. Because a chief's power was conferred upon him by his people and was maintained by his success, it could be withdrawn by continued lack of success. This meant that a chief's power was severely limited. He could rarely order his people to do or not do something; he could only advise. This was one reason chiefs had trouble controlling the younger warriors who saw raids as a way to increase their own status and show their own virtues. Because the chief could only coerce his followers in certain times, such as when actually on a raid or hunt, any person or group who disagreed with the chief's policies could withdraw to another band, or even form their own band and strike out on their own. Because of this tendency, there were scores of Comanche, Kiowa, and Lipan Apache chiefs.[52]

This pattern baffled most Texans and Americans, who expected leaders to exert control over their followers. Most Texans and Americans believed that if they signed a peace treaty with one Comanche chief, then they had signed a peace treaty with the entire Comanche people and expected the chief to make all the Comanches uphold the agreement. In reality, a peace treaty with one chief was just that, an agreement with that chief. As long as his people accorded him power and listened to him, then he might persuade them to uphold the peace. Other band chiefs from his own and other divisions did not have to abide by this treaty. In fact, people of his own band— if they disagreed—could often ignore the peace agreement, as many young men looking for status did. Most Indians of Texas used a similar political system. It was the misunderstanding of this system that led many Texans and Americans to describe the Comanches, Kiowas, Apaches, and other Indians as "treacherous" and as "renegades."[53]

Ironically, at this time during the first half of the nineteenth century, Texans and Americans held the Plains Indians to a standard that they themselves refused to accept. Texans and Americans ignored the sovereignty claimed by each Comanche division and refused to accept that warriors would not listen to their chiefs, but they championed the rights of the state to ignore laws made by the United States and Mexican federal governments. At the same time, Americans often disregarded laws of their own state if they happened to disagree with them. This confused the Indians. If the government promised one thing, such as a guarantee of land, then why did whites violate this promise and settle on lands promised to the Indians? How could white juries continually leave white men unpunished for crimes against Indians? Why was one Indian group often punished, even mistakenly, for the alleged crimes of another Indian group? Why did the promises made by the Texas and United States governments change with each new President? Whites made similar complaints. Why could a chief not control his people? Why did the rules of blood revenge mean that Plains Indians often killed an innocent white person for the killing of an Indian by a different white person? Why could Indians not recognize personal property rights?

These differences guaranteed violence throughout Texas. Few Plains Indian bands fought against the Texans during their war for independence, but as Texas filled up with settlers after independence, these two peoples came into much closer contact. Many white Texans viewed the Indians as a way to get rich; after all, the Indians had long traded with Euroamericans and were a source of valuable horses and hides. While some Texans traded with Indians in a fair and equitable manner, some whites mistakenly viewed the Indians as childlike and believed they could cheat the Indians with impunity. The Indians knew when they were being cheated, and because kin did not cheat kin, therefore someone who cheated them was non-kin and subject to raids and violence. One of the most famous raids in Texas history resulted. In 1836, John Parker, who had built Parker's Fort near Groesbeck in Limestone County, allegedly had gone on a horse-stealing raid with some Comanches and Kiowas and then cheated the Indians out of their share of the spoils. Angry at his behavior, in May 1836, a band of Noconi Comanches and Kiowas attacked the fort, killed most of the inhabitants, and took five captives. The most famous were Mrs. Rachel Plummer, who later published an account of her captivity, and nine-year-old Cynthia Ann Parker, who eventually married a Comanche chief and gave birth to one of the great chiefs of the Comanches: Quanah Parker.[54]

Discounting any idea that the Indians may have had some justification for their attacks, these kinds of raids angered and terrified Texas settlers. Texans responded in kind, raiding Indian villages, and often killing women and children. Unfortunately, these were not always the same Indians who had committed the raids. Because of this behavior, many Indians, even Plains Indians, hoped for a peace with the Texans and the establishment of a boundary line between them and the Texas settlements. Fortunately, with the election of Sam Houston as the first president of the Republic of Texas, it appeared that Indian relations in Texas would take a turn for the better. Houston, who had been adopted by the Cherokees and even briefly married a Cherokee woman, possessed an enlightened view of Indian relations for that time. Unlike many of his fellow Anglo-Texans, Houston believed that Indians possessed a right to their lands. As president of Texas, Houston tried to establish cordial relations with all the Indians in Texas. The Indians, as did Houston, realized that most violence erupted when whites settled on lands claimed by the Indians.[55]

By mid-1838, Houston had reached some agreement with the Comanches, Kiowas, Lipan Apaches, Caddos, Wichitas, and most of the Indians of Texas, even guaranteeing Indian lands in West Texas. For the farming Indians living in East Texas, Houston tried to place them on reservations that were also closed to white settlement. Despite the guarantees, Houston found he could not control his own people who believed the Indians had no right to the land and saw them as "savages" who stood in the way of their own economic prosperity. These Texans continually, often at their own risk, settled on lands claimed by the Indians. Then, when Comanche or Kiowa bands attacked, they bitterly complained to the Texas government and demanded that the Indians be punished. According to one observer, Houston commented: "If I could build a wall from the Red River to the Rio Grande, so high that no Indian could scale it, the white people would go crazy trying to devise means to get beyond it."[56]

While Houston was making peace with the Indians, the United States had been attempting to do the same with the Plains Indians north of the Red River. As early as 1825, Congress had considered making the area north of Texas a place to put Indians removed from the east. President Andrew Jackson explained in his 1830 message on Indian Removal that he believed these eastern Indians would emigrate to this area, which would be guaranteed them, where they would be outside the limits of any state or territory and be "subject to no other control from the United States than such as may be necessary to preserve peace on the frontier and between the several tribes."[57] So throughout the 1830s, the United States government extinguished Indian land claims east of the Mississippi River, then forced these Indian nations— such as the Cherokees, Choctaws, Chickasaws, Creeks, and Seminoles—to move to Indian Territory, now the state of Oklahoma. The Indians called this forced removal the "Trail of Tears."[58]

As the government negotiated those removal treaties, the eastern Indians constantly voiced their worries about moving to the vicinity of the Comanches, Kiowas, and Wichitas, whom they called "wild Indians." The United States government promised to protect the eastern Indians in their new homes, and to fulfill this promise sent a commission headed by former North Carolina governor Montford Stokes to make peace with the Southern Plains Indians. In 1834, the Stokes Commission, accompanied by five hundred Dragoons and painter George Catlin, traveled out to the lands between the Red and Canadian Rivers in search of the Comanches, Wichitas, and Kiowas. The ill-fated expedition, where one hundred and fifty Dragoons in wool uniforms died from summer heat and cholera, met only a few Indians. Still, this was the first meeting between representatives of the United States government and some of the Comanche, Kiowa, and Wichita bands. The meeting led to the 1835 Treaty of Camp Holmes which established a peace between some of the Comanches and Wichitas and the United States and the eastern Indians moving into Indian Territory. While the Kiowas avoided the Camp Holmes treaty negotiations, some Kiowa bands did sign a similar treaty in 1837.[59]

It was one thing for representatives of the United States or Texas to sign a treaty with the Plains Indians, but it was another for the representatives to eliminate the root causes that spawned the violence. Rarely, if ever, did the treaties provide for arbitration in the event one side felt the treaty had been violated by the other. Even if arbitration had been prescribed, most whites of that day, who took for granted white racial superiority and appropriated for themselves privileges not granted to other peoples, would not have abided by arbitration anyway. During the mid-1830s, most southern states adopted harsh laws against the Indians, including prohibiting Indians from testifying against whites in courts. Whites demanded that if an Indian broke a white law, that Indian should be tried in a white court, but steadfastly refused that any white be subject to Indian law. Since, in the minds of most whites, Indians were "savages" without any property rights or claim to the lands—which whites saw as reserved for them only—the chance of peace in Texas would be slim indeed.[60]

Ignoring Houston's guarantee of Indian lands, white residents settled on Indian lands and the Indians—especially the powerful Comanches—fought back. While whites were outraged at Indian attacks, the Texans made little effort to distinguish between peaceful Indians and those Indians who actually attacked Texas settlements. In late 1838, blaming the Caddos for attacks on Texas residents, Texas General Thomas Rusk crossed into Louisiana and disarmed a large band of Caddos near Shreveport whom he blamed for raids into Texas. Playing upon this warfare, Mirabeau Lamar, campaigning against Houston for the Texas presidency, believed that Houston's policy of reserving lands for the Indians limited white settlement and therefore white economic prosperity. Knowing his constituents' beliefs that whites were racially superior to Indians, and claiming that the Indians were agents and allies of Mexico, Lamar promised to exterminate them. This promise helped secure his election. Once inaugurated as Texas's second president, he instituted his policy. All Indians suffered, but instead of putting an end to the Indian "problem," it only increased the problem as Indians fought back.[61]

Indians did not limit their attacks only to Texans, but remembering old animosities, still raided and attacked their old Indian enemies. Comanche and Kiowa bands continued attacking the Lipan Apaches. This warfare became so pronounced that by the early 1840s, most Lipan Apaches retreated into Mexico or began living with their Apache kin in New Mexico. Wichitas, Comanches, and Caddos continued attacking the Tonkawas. In 1833, the "year of the falling stars," a band of Osages attacked a Kiowa camp near present-day Lawton, Oklahoma, when most of the Kiowa men were away hunting or visiting. The Osages captured the Kiowa's Tai-me Medicine Bag, one of their most sacred religious icons, killed most of the women and children, and then cut off the heads of the dead and placed them in metal pots for the Kiowa men to find. This place has ever since been called "Cut Throat Gap" and "Cut Throat Mountain." Comanches and Kiowas sometimes raided the immigrant eastern Indians. Chickasaw, Choctaw, and Creek families in Indian Territory often lost horses and cattle to Comanche raiding parties, while Shawnee, Kickapoo, Pottawatomi, and Delaware parties hunting buffalo on the plains sometimes came under attack. Eventually, the Shawnees, Kickapoos, and especially the Delawares became close trading partners with the Southern Plains Indians.[62]

This conflict between Indian bands played into the hands of Texans and Americans and made warfare against the Indians even more vicious. Recalling old animosities and responding to the obligations of blood revenge, parties of Lipan Apaches and Tonkawas sometimes rode with the Texas Rangers when attacking Comanche villages. Caddo, Tonkawa, Wichita, even Penataka Comanche scouts and auxiliaries tracked down Comanche and Kiowa bands for the Texans and the United States Army. Without the help of these Indian auxiliaries, the Americans would never have been able to have located the villages. Despite this assistance, Texans and Americans quickly forgot this invaluable service and turned on their allies whenever circumstance dictated.[63]

During Texas President Lamar's administration, raids and warfare see-sawed back and forth as Comanche, Kiowa, and Wichita bands and Texans attacked and counterattacked. Eventually, war weariness gripped both sides. As early as 1838, some Comanche chiefs requested a peace council with the Texans in hopes of agreeing to a boundary line separating Comanche territory from the ever-westward moving settlers. Nothing came of this attempt as Texas officials refused to be limited by any boundary line.[64]

In 1840, some Penataka Comanches again requested a peace council and were invited to San Antonio. In the spring of that year, about twelve Penataka Comanche chiefs along with fifty-three Comanche men, women, and children—bringing with them a couple of Texan and Mexican captives—arrived at San Antonio. The council turned bad from the beginning as the Texans were outraged at the sorry physical condition of Matilda Lockhart, the white captive the Penatakas brought in. The Texans demanded the chiefs turn over all the white captives of the Comanches. The Penatakas explained that this was the only captive they had, which was probably true, while other Comanche bands possessed other white captives. This band could only speak for itself, and it would take a lot of trade goods to ransom those captives from the other bands. Angered at what they saw as a blunt refusal, the citizens brought in an armed band of Texas Rangers to intimidate the Penatakas. When the Texans then tried to take the Comanche chiefs hostage to force a return of captives, fighting broke out, which spilled outside. In the melee, thirty Comanche men—almost all of the chiefs—three women, and two children were killed, while the Texans suffered seven killed and eight wounded. The Council House Fight was a severe blunder by the Texans. Indians throughout the Southern Plains saw this event as evidence of Texas treachery and as good as a declaration of war. The Council House Fight can be considered the spark that caused the Southern Plains Indians wars which lasted until 1875. From this point on, the Comanches and Kiowas became implacable foes of the Texans and distinguished between Americans, whom they liked, and Texans, whom they hated.[65]

To take blood revenge for the Council House Fight, large raiding parties struck deep into the Texas settlements. Penataka chief Potsanaquahip, or Buffalo Hump, and his Comanche and Kiowa warriors seized the town of

Victoria in August 1840 and a few days later sacked Linnville on Lavaca Bay. As Buffalo Hump headed north, the Texas Rangers—along with Tonkawa scouts—caught up with his party, attacked, and forced the Comanches to abandon the goods taken from Linnville. Other Comanche bands also suffered at the hands of attacking Texas Rangers, but by 1841, most settlers were tired of Lamar's policy and the endless warfare it caused, as well as its tremendous expense calculated at more than $2.5 million. In late 1841, Texas voters re-elected Sam Houston as president of the republic in hopes of bringing peace.[66]

Now with Houston back as president, he tried to remedy the situation. In September 1843, at Bird's Fort on the Trinity River, the Caddos, Delawares, Shawnees, and some Wichita bands signed a peace treaty with Texas. Next, Houston hoped to create a permanent peace with the Comanches, Kiowas, and Apaches by establishing a boundary line between them and the Texans. Though Houston created an imaginary boundary and charged the Texas Rangers with stopping whites from crossing into Comanche and Kiowa territory, the line was never accepted by either the Texans or the Comanches, so nothing came of it. With the Comanches already wary of white promises, with whites continuing to invade Indian lands, and with the Texas Rangers tending to ignore white encroachment but shooting any Indian found near white settlements, Houston's peace policy came to nothing. So Comanche and Kiowa raids continued while the Texas Rangers and armed bands of settlers counterattacked.[67]

Also, while Texas attacks could be devastating, particularly when they killed women and children and burned villages, Comanche and Kiowa raids began becoming economically profitable for the Indians, especially the taking of captives. Captives had always been an outcome of Indian warfare. In earlier days, captives may have been killed as part of blood revenge and in some instances still were. On the other hand, captives added to an Indian household's production capabilities. For farming Indians, a captive, essentially a slave, could help in the fields or tan hides. For Plains Indians, young male captives became horse herders. By the late eighteenth and early nineteenth century, as increased warfare and disease took their toll, captives were adopted into the band in order to shore up a dwindling population. Many of these captives became assimilated and accepted into Indian society, such as His-oo-san-ches, a mixed-blood Mexican boy named Jesus Sanches who had risen to become a highly esteemed Comanche warrior and who had his portrait painted by George Catlin in 1834.[68]

By the 1840s, the Texan and American dread of having non-Indians held by "uncivilized" Indians played into Indian hands. Anglo-Americans offered huge ransoms for non-Indians captured by the Plains Indians. Realizing that money and manufactured goods could be "purchased" with captives, Comanches and Kiowas stepped up their raids in order to take them. While some of these captives were adopted into the band, most were taken to be ransomed. Comanche and Kiowa warriors raided the Texas and northern Mexico settlements, but also kidnapped African-American slaves held by the Chickasaws, Choctaws, and Creeks living in Indian Territory. Then parties of Delawares, Shawnees, and Kickapoos living along the Canadian River in the central part of Indian Territory would venture out to the Comanche and Kiowa villages where they would exchange goods for these captives. These immigrant Indians brought the captives back to places such as Fort Gibson in eastern Indian Territory and collected the ransom offered by the United States government, the family of the captives, or the owners of the slaves. This custom became a great scheme practiced by Indians throughout Indian Territory and continued until the 1870s.[69]

Indian-white relations became even more confused when the United States annexed Texas in 1845. The Wichitas, Comanches, and Kiowas possessed friendly relations with the United States and distinguished between Americans and Texans. Suddenly Texans became Americans and United States officials had a difficult time explaining this change to the Indians and why they should not raid Texas settlements any more. Texans now demanded that the United States do something about the Indians, urging use of the army to protect them from Indian attacks. Representatives of the United States government met with bands of Penataka Comanches, Wichitas, Tonkawas, and Caddos at Council Springs in 1846 and signed a peace treaty in which the Indian bands would recognize the authority of the United States in Texas and in turn the United States would provide them with traders and merchandise. Despite this treaty, by insisting on a strict allegiance to states' rights and standing on the annexation clause which gave Texas ownership of all its public lands, the State of Texas refused to allow the United States government to make reservations for the Texas Indians. This refusal conflicted with the United States policy which recognized Indian land claims by right of occupancy and believed these could only be extinguished by treaties. According to the State of Texas, the Indians had no rights to any land in Texas no matter what the federal government said.[70]

For the next few years, the federal government and the Texas state government wrangled over jurisdiction. The Penataka Comanches, by this time not near the military force they once had been, decided to make a treaty in December 1850 in which they promised not to venture south of the Llano River without the permission of an army officer. Several bands of Caddos, Wichitas, and Lipans also signed this treaty at Spring Creek near San Sabá. Still, other northern Comanche and Kiowa bands, frustrated at the ineffectualness of the federal government in preventing Texas settlers from claiming land in their areas, stepped up their raids on white settlements. The Texans usually took out their aggressions on the peaceful, settled, agricultural peoples, such as the Caddos and some of the Wichita bands. In 1854, with no cessation in hostilities in sight, the Texas legislature gave in to federal government demands and allowed two reservations to be set up in Central Texas along the Brazos River. One, at the mouth of the Clear Fork, would be for the Penataka Comanches; the other, on the main fork of the Brazos, would be for the remnants of the Caddos, Tonkawas, Delawares, Shawnees, and such Wichita peoples as the Wacos and Tawakonis. Some Tonkawas decided to move south to Mexico and join with the Lipan Apaches living there. These reservations were placed under the supervision of Indian Agent Robert S. Neighbors. Still, thousands of Kwahadis, Noconis, Yamparikas, and other Comanche divisions, the Kiowas, as well as some Wichitas, and a few Lipan Apache and Tonkawa bands roamed at large in and out of Texas.[71]

The agricultural Indians on the Brazos Reserve lived a life similar to what they always had. They resided in family-oriented villages; built cabins and used wagons; wore clothing similar to the Texans of that day; planted crops of corn, beans, and squash; raised herds of horses and cattle; and sometimes went hunting for buffalo or deer on the plains. Adjusting to reservation life proved a little more difficult for the Penataka Comanches on the Clear Fork Reserve. The Penatakas had never lived in permanent villages like the agricultural Indians did, but migrated when they needed food and fresh grass for their many horses. Unused to the more restricted life, many Penatakas continued hunting buffalo off the reservation, while some of the young men, desiring the status of warriors, left the reservation to live with the other Comanche divisions for awhile and then return home to Clear Fork. The government, under the supervision of Agent Neighbors, provided blacksmiths, doctors, and model farmers in hopes of making these Indians into Christian small farmers. In all, most Indian people on both the Brazos and Clear Fork

Reserves proved to be peaceful, prosperous residents, always ready to provide contingents of warriors to serve with the Rangers or the army as scouts against the other Comanche, Wichita, and Kiowa bands.[72]

Just about all Indian peoples—even peoples such as the Kiowas who possessed warrior societies—wanted a peaceful existence. Most hated to be on the run, sleeping fitfully, and always looking over their shoulder for the next attack. Most wanted to be left in peace to pursue their own existence, see their children grow up happy and healthy, and live to an old age to play with their grandchildren. These Indians of Texas now hoped that with the reservations, secure in their lands, and by abiding by all the rules laid down by the government, they could now live this peaceful life. It was not to be, however, as the nearby Texans would not allow it. Most Texans viewed the two reservations as a waste of good land, which by all rights should go to white people. Settlers soon pressed the edges of the reservations. Some actually tried to set up farms and ranches inside the reservation boundaries but were run off by Agent Neighbors and troops from nearby forts. The settlers also had grave suspicions about having hundreds of Indians living in their midst, no matter that Agent Neighbors swore they were peaceful. Eventually the reservation Indians became scapegoats. When non-reservation Comanches, Wichitas, Kiowas, and Kickapoos made raids into Texas, the settlers, frustrated at their inability to capture the fast-moving raiding parties, blamed the reservation Indians. Some Comanches from the Clear Fork Reserve may have made a few raids against whites; these were few and there is no proof that any of the Brazos Reserve Indians ever committed any attack or crime against the white settlers. In fact, the Indians of both the Brazos and Clear Fork Reserve often themselves became targets of raids by non-reservation Comanches, Kiowas, and Kickapoos. Still, the Texans blamed them for any raid, kidnapping, killing, or horse theft committed in the vicinity. White mobs patrolled the edges of the reservation, stole Indian stock, and killed Caddos, Wichitas, and other Indians caught alone. Texas citizens constantly agitated for removal of these Indians.[73]

By 1859, the situation had become intolerable. In early May, mobs raided the Brazos Reservations and killed several Caddos, demanding the right to exterminate the reservation Indians. Then, on May 23, 1859, a white mob of more than 250 men, led by John R. Baylor, who had at one time been a special agent to the Texas Indians, invaded the Brazos Reservation and killed several Caddos. They were finally driven off by agency personnel and troops guarding the reservation. Although the mob had been repelled, extermination talk among the settlers continued. Agent Neighbors realized that as long as these Indians lived in Texas, they would never live in peace, and would, in all probability, soon be massacred by the Texans. So in the summer of 1859, Neighbors, fearing for the safety of the Indians, packed them up and led them north across the Red River into Indian Territory. Here the Caddo, Wichita, Tonkawas, and Penataka Comanches, all Indians who called Texas home, experienced their own Trail of Tears. Abandoning their houses, crops, and most of their herds of cattle and horses, they took only what they could carry in a few wagons, leaving behind the land where their ancestors' bones were buried. For the Shawnees and Delawares, it was a second exodus. In Indian Territory, the government leased land from the Choctaws and Chickasaws and created the Wichita and Affiliated Tribes Reservation headquartered at Fort Cobb in the western part of Indian Territory. Members of the white mob, incensed that Neighbors had not allowed them to kill the Indians, murdered him when he returned to Texas.[74]

The Texas Indians had barely settled in Indian Territory when the Civil War began. Representatives from the Confederacy approached the expelled Indians with hopes of making them allies in the event of a Union invasion. Though they signed peace treaties, most Texas Indians wanted nothing to do with the conflict. Some Caddo and Wichita bands moved to Union-held Kansas—some of the Indians moved further west to get away from the war— but most stayed put and either paid lip-service to the Confederacy or remained neutral. The biggest event of the Civil War for the Texas Indians was the Tonkawa Massacre on October 23, 1862, when parties of Shawnees, Delawares, Wichitas, and Penataka Comanches attacked and just about wiped out the Tonkawa Indians. Who instigated it remains unclear. The Wichitas and Comanches blame the Shawnees. Equally unclear was the reason. Some claimed that it happened because the Tonkawas were cannibals and ate some Shawnees; other say that it was blood revenge because the Tonkawas had killed some Wichitas. Some say that the reason for the killings was because the Tonkawas sided with the Union rather than the Confederacy. Others say it was merely an attack by the Union-allied Shawnees and Delawares on the Confederate-held Wichita Agency who took the opportunity to get rid of the Tonkawa. In reality, the Tonkawas were always the odd ones out among the Indians of the Brazos and Clear Fork Reserves. The Caddos, Wichitas, and Comanches had been links in a trade network for more than one hundred and fifty years

THE MAJOR RESERVATIONS

c. 1885

0 _____ 100
SCALE IN MILES

and therefore were friends and allies. The Tonkawas had been part of the Lipan Apache trade network and therefore allied with enemies of the Comanches, Wichitas, and Caddos. The Shawnees and Delawares, since coming to the Southern Plains, had become trade partners with the Comanches, Kiowas, Wichitas, and Caddos. Probably old animosities came to the surface, and the Tonkawas paid for their ancient alliance. A few Tonkawas escaped back into Texas.[75]

The Civil War also brought increased Indian-white violence to western and central Texas. With the federal army gone and most white men serving in the Confederate army, the westernmost white settlements were left with little defense. At the same time, with most guns, ammunition, and manufactured goods being funneled into the war, the Comanches and Kiowas had a difficult time acquiring the goods they needed. To overcome this shortage, they stepped up their raids inside of Texas. In the summer of 1864, Comanche and Kiowa raids threatened the Santa Fe Trail, the supply route to Union-held New Mexico. To protect the Trail, Union Colonel Kit Carson and his New Mexico Volunteers attacked Kiowa warriors at Adobe Walls in the Texas Panhandle on November 25, 1864. Both sides suffered losses in the fierce fight, with Carson and his men barely escaping defeat. Though the battle secured the Trail, it did not deter Comanche and Kiowa raids on Texas farms and ranches.[76]

When the Civil War ended, the federal government determined to bring about peace with the Plains Indians. The 1864 Sand Creek Massacre—when the Colorado Militia attacked Black Kettle's peaceful Cheyenne village and killed and scalped men, women, and children—shocked the Eastern establishment and Washington politicians. It spurred a peace movement. In October 1865, government representatives negotiated the Little Arkansas Treaty with the Comanches, Kiowas, Kiowa-Apaches, Southern Cheyennes, and Southern Arapahos—pledging them reservations in the Texas Panhandle—but Senate revisions and opposition from Texas and Kansas virtually annulled the treaty, and no reservations came out of it. For the other traditional Texas Indians, the government reestablished the agency at Anadarko, Oklahoma, for the Wichita and Affiliated Tribes Reservation, which included the Wichitas, Kichais, Caddos, as well as some bands of Delawares, Shawnees, and Penataka Comanches. As for the Tonkawas, the government moved them and a few remaining Lipan Apaches to the old Nez Percé reservation in northern Indian Territory in 1885, near the present-day town of Pawnee, Oklahoma.[77]

While the Wichitas and Caddos were reestablishing their reservations on Indian Territory, the Kiowas, after the failure of the Little Arkansas Treaty, continued their raids. Dealing with similar problems with the Southern Cheyennes and Southern Arapahos, the federal government now determined to make a lasting peace with the Southern Plains Indians. In October 1867, the government negotiated the Treaty of Medicine Lodge Creek with the Comanches, Kiowas, Kiowa-Apaches, Southern Cheyennes, and Southern Arapahos. The treaty authorized the creation of two reservations in western Indian Territory from lands taken from the Cherokees, Chickasaws, Choctaws, Creeks, and Seminoles as an indemnity for some of them fighting for the Confederacy. The Cheyennes and Arapahos got three million acres between the 37th parallel and the Cimarron and Arkansas Rivers. Immediately south of this location, the Comanches, Kiowas, and Kiowa-Apaches received a reservation located between the Washita and Red Rivers. In return for ceding all the other lands they claimed and for ceasing their raids in Texas, Kansas, Colorado, and eastern Indian Territory, the government promised to provide them with food, clothing, blankets, firearms for hunting, as well as seeds, plows, and other farming implements. The government would also send people to teach them to farm and missionaries to instruct them in Christianity. Most Comanche and Kiowa chiefs, resigned to their fate, signed the treaty, but Satanta, an influential Kiowa chief who felt he would be hemmed in, refused to sign and led his people down into Texas.[78]

On the reservations, the Texas Indians experienced differing situations. The agricultural Caddos and Wichitas, no longer threatened by white mobs, reestablished their traditional lifestyle of growing corn and other crops while supplementing it with periodic hunts of buffalo and deer. This situation was complemented by periodic distributions of government supplies, such as flour, beef, and cloth. For the Comanches and Kiowas, the reservation experience proved much harsher. Under the terms of the Medicine Lodge Treaty, because the Comanches and Kiowas would eventually no longer be able to roam the Southern Plains and supply their needs through buffalo hunting, the government guaranteed to compensate them with food, clothing, and blankets. Government indifference, bureaucratic foul-ups, corrupt contractors, and primitive transportation facilities meant that supplies often came very late and usually short. At first, the allotment delays caused few problems because stipulations in the Medicine Lodge Treaty allowed the Comanches and Kiowas to hunt buffalo south of the Arkansas River in the Texas Panhandle as long as buffalo roamed in that area.[79]

Still, problems resulted from the restrictions the reservation placed on the young men, for whom status and power came through raids and warfare. As the young men chafed at the restriction, anti-treaty chiefs—such as the Kiowa chiefs Satanta, Big Tree, and Satank—gained even more influence. Soon raiding parties of Kiowa and Comanche warriors struck deep into Texas, New Mexico, and eastern Indian Territory only to return to the reservation to receive their share of allotment goods and boast of their exploits. In 1871, General William T. Sherman, commander of the Division of the Missouri, under whose jurisdiction came the reservation, arrested Satank, Satanta, and Big Tree. Satank was killed while trying to escape, and Satanta and Big Tree were imprisoned at the Texas State Penitentiary at Huntsville with the hopes that this would stop the raids. It did not and in 1873, under pressure from humanitarian groups and the Indian councils in eastern Indian

Territory, the state released the two Indian prisoners. Kiowa and Comanche raids continued.[80]

If the late allotments and the imprisonment of their chiefs did not cause enough anger, adding to the discontent of the Comanches and Kiowas were American horse thieves from Kansas who stole Indian ponies. Whiskey peddlers created problems by selling cheap whiskey to the Indians on credit, getting the Indians so deeply in debt that they had to forfeit what little cash they received from their allotment. American buffalo hunters proved to be the worst problem. In the late 1860s, American buffalo hunters, armed with high-powered rifles, began invading the plains. By 1870, they had wiped out the buffalo on the Central Plains, taking only the skin and leaving the rest of the carcass to rot. Now they cast greedy eyes on the remaining buffalo on Comanche and Kiowa hunting grounds south of the Arkansas River. In that same year, the government gave them permission to begin hunting on the Southern Plains. Soon buffalo became harder to find by Comanche and Kiowa hunters, and with the always too little and always too late government food allotments, the Comanches and Kiowas began to starve. Ignoring the Indians' complaints about buffalo hunters, the government did nothing. In some instances, army officers encouraged the hunters, realizing that killing off the buffalo, the Plains Indians' food source, was the best way to permanently subjugate these Indians. With this action, buffalo hunters became even more aggressive and banded together into large groups for protection and ventured into the heart of Comanche and Kiowa hunting grounds in the Texas Panhandle and the Llano Estacado.[81]

Comanche, Kiowa, and Southern Cheyenne anger boiled over in the summer of 1874. On June 27, about three hundred Comanche and Cheyenne warriors attacked a group of buffalo hunters at Adobe Walls—the same place the Kiowas and Kit Carson fought it out in 1864—and so began the Red River War. The hunters, with their high-powered rifles, held off the Indians but quickly left the area once the Indians retired. The Indians, realizing there was no turning back, began attacking settlers, travelers, and even army detachments in Texas, New Mexico, Colorado, and Kansas. By early September, thousands of Comanche, Kiowa, and Cheyenne men, women, and children, possibly totaling twelve hundred warriors, had left the reservation and made their main camps on Texas's Llano Estacado. As the cold days of winter approached, the United States Army responded, putting more than five thousand troops into the field. Utilizing the concept of "total war," the army destroyed Indian villages, food supplies, and horses in order to let starvation take its toll. Cold weather, hunger, and relentless pursuit by young army officers, such as Colonel Ranald McKenzie who defeated the Comanches and Kiowas at the Battle of Palo Duro Canyon in September 1874, finally wore down the Indians. By the summer of 1875, the Red River War was over and the Comanches, Kiowas, and Cheyennes were back on the reservation. This episode ended Indian warfare on the Southern Plains. Satanta was sent back to the Texas State Penitentiary at Huntsville where he committed suicide in March 1878. Seventy-four other warriors, some of them not involved in the war at all, were imprisoned for three years at Fort Marion, Florida.[82]

Defeated and now thoroughly dependent upon the United States government, the Comanches and Kiowas tried to emulate their Caddo and Wichita neighbors by planting crops and herding cattle. In September 1878, the Comanche-Kiowa agency was relocated to Anadarko and consolidated with the Wichita Agency. There, all four Indian nations relied upon the government allotments of cattle, flour, and clothing. Still, the Indians learned how to make do. Living on lush grasslands, the Indians, especially the Comanches under the leadership of Quanah Parker, the mixed-blood son of the captive Cynthia Ann Parker, often leased their lands to Texas cattlemen and received cash payments, called "grass money." Reservation resources sometimes became targets of unscrupulous whites; for example, white settlers often slipped onto reservation lands and stole timber to be used for fence posts, housing, and firewood. Indian Police Forces had to be created to keep white thieves out of the reservations.[83]

During the next twenty-five years of reservation experience, the Comanches, Kiowas, Caddos, and Wichitas underwent tremendous cultural change. Not only did the Comanches and Kiowas have to adjust to farming and ranching, all four nations now came under the influence of Christian missionaries and teachers. By the late 1870s, Catholic, Presbyterian, Methodist, and Baptist missions had opened in Anadarko and around Fort Sill, Oklahoma, near where many of the Comanches and Kiowas resided. They experienced varying degrees of success in converting the Indians to Christianity. Although many Indians might attend church on Sunday, most still attended their traditional ceremonies and dances. Quanah Parker—one of the younger Comanche chiefs during the Red River War and who later became the main spokesman for the Comanche people—along with some of the Caddo chiefs, founded the Native American Church, which blended traditional Indian beliefs, peyote use, and Christianity. In the early 1890s, the Ghost Dance, a revitalization movement which promised the disappearance of the whites and the return of traditional Indian ways, spread throughout all Indian peoples of the Plains. While particularly strong among the Lakota Sioux in South Dakota, it had some adherents among the Southern Plains Indians, but a few, such as the Kiowa chief, Apiatan, rejected it outright.[84]

The United States government also forced an American-style education system upon the Indians. Day schools, such as the Riverside Indian School at Anadarko, opened and taught Indian girls and boys domestic and mechanical arts, respectively. Besides English, basic reading, writing, and arithmetic, the girls were taught how to sew, cook, and clean. The boys were taught how to farm or be carpenters. Many children were also sent far away from their families to boarding schools, such as Rainy Mountain Boarding School near Gotebo, Oklahoma; Chilocco Indian School in northern Oklahoma; Haskell Institute in Lawrence, Kansas; or Carlisle Indian School in Carlisle, Pennsylvania. At these schools, their hair was cut and they were prohibited from speaking their Indian languages.[85]

The biggest threat to traditional Texas Indian culture came from the ever-increasing number of whites living on and around the reservations. White storekeepers, preachers, teachers, government officials, and ranch hands lived on the reservations, while white settlers and ranchers claimed lands around their edges. Many of these white men married Indian women and produced mixed-blood children. As Indian women came into contact with white women, dress styles and cooking methods began to change. Often the government itself tried to force culture change, as government officials tried to outlaw traditional dances and ceremonies.

Still, for many government officials and philanthropists, the Indians did not give up their old ways fast enough. By the mid-1880s, many "friends-of-the-Indians," dismayed at reservation poverty, felt the biggest detriment to Indian progress toward "civilization" was the reservation land held in common by the Indians. Washington officials believed the best thing for "civilizing" the Indians would be to break up the reservations, give each Indian family its own plot of land, and make them into small farmers. This approach ignored the notion that peoples like the Caddos and Wichitas had been farming successfully for hundreds of years, and that the Comanches and Kiowas, who as horse people possessed no tradition of agriculture, were doing well as ranchers with tremendous herds of horses and cattle. Despite the almost unanimous protests by the Indians, the United States government passed the Dawes Severalty Act of 1887. The Severalty Act would give one hundred and sixty acres of land to each head of an Indian family and lesser amounts to unmarried or orphan Indians. All excess land would be auctioned off by the government with the money from the sales going into Indian accounts to pay for education, the purchase of stock and farming implements, and such. Most whites, especially ranchers, railroad companies, and oil companies strongly supported the act.[86]

The Dawes Act finally caught up with the Comanches, Kiowas, Wichitas, and Caddos in the 1890s as the Jerome Commission began negotiating the allotment process. Congress finally allotted the Wichita and Affiliated Tribe's reservation in 1895 and the Kiowa-Comanche Reservation in 1900 by breaking up the reservations and allotting plots of lands to individual Indians and families. Most of the Texas Indians protested the break up. Lone Wolf, a prominent Kiowa leader, took the case all the way to the Supreme Court. In 1901, despite the Indian protests, the government opened the remaining lands in both reservations to white settlement. The Supreme Court supported the break up in *Lone Wolf v. Hitchcock*, which more or less said that Congress had the power to disregard any Indian treaty and make laws for the Indians. Many of the traditional Texas Indians, who had prospered as ranchers with their ability to use the common land, now found themselves much poorer with their allotment too small for ranching and the land too poor for farming on such a small scale. Within just a few years, many Comanches, Caddos, Kiowas, and Wichitas had lost their land to whites. With this loss, many of the traditional Texas Indians sank even deeper into poverty that has characterized their lives up to rather recent times.[87]

Although these Indians of Texas all suffered similar experiences at the hands of the whites—defeat, confinement, subjugation, and attempts at destroying their culture—they remained wholly different peoples with completely separate identities. Separate peoples lived in their own area of the reservations and often, despite pressure from the government and the melding influences of farming, religion, and education, managed to continue their ancient ceremonies. The Caddos continued performing their Turkey Dance, which recounted the history of their people; while the Kiowas, under pressure from the government, abandoned the Sun Dance, but took up the Gourd Dance. All groups, in their own ways, felt themselves superior to the other peoples around them and in many ways kept themselves separate from the others. Some Comanche and Kiowa parents hesitated to send their children to the same schools. There was an even greater gulf between the more agriculturally oriented Indians, such as the Caddo and Wichita, and the former buffalo-hunting Comanches and Kiowas. This separateness exists even to this day.[88]

By the late 1930s, when the Works Progress Administration (WPA) historians conducted the interviews that make up these Indian-Pioneer Histories, it had been eighty years since they had been driven out of Texas; sixty years since their defeat in the Red River War; and thirty-five years since their reservations had been broken up. It is the years between the end of the Red River War and the 1930s that comprise most of the recollections recorded in the Indian-Pioneer histories. In reading these histories, one is struck not only by the great cultural changes that the traditional Indians of Texas underwent, but also by their dramatic ability to retain so much of what was culturally valuable to them. While much changed, so much also remained the same.

Chapter One

◆ ◆ ◆ ◆ ◆ ◆ ◆ ◆ ◆ ◆ ◆ ◆ ◆

Raids and Warfare

◆ ◆ ◆ ◆ ◆ ◆ ◆ ◆ ◆ ◆ ◆ ◆ ◆

Warfare was an integral part of the traditional Indians of Texas, but especially for the Comanches, Kiowas, and Lipan Apaches. By displaying bravery in battle and by acquiring the spoils of war, a young man gained status and wealth through warfare. The Kiowas also had warrior societies, which were groups of men who pledged themselves to protect the band or village and attack their enemies. One of the warrior societies of the Kiowas was the Tonkonga, or "Black Legs." Over the centuries, Kiowa and Comanche warriors fought many groups, including the Apaches, Tonkawas, Pueblos, Spanish, Mexicans, Texans, Americans, sometimes their Caddo and Wichita allies, and sometimes even other bands of Comanches and Kiowas. The last war fought by the Comanches and Kiowas collectively was against the United States in the Red River War of 1874–75. They were defeated and placed on a reservation in southwestern Oklahoma. Still, individual warriors from these traditional Texas Indians have served bravely in United States armies in World War I, World War II, the Korean Conflict, Vietnam, and the Gulf War.

KIOWAS

Every child, both male and female, is born a Pho-li-yo-ye, or Rabbit. An old man is put in charge and as soon as a child can totter he is taught to dance in the circle of the Rabbits. When a big feast and dance is to be held the old man goes throughout the camps calling out: "Rabbits, Rabbits get ready; paint your faces; be prompt; come to the dances; plenty to eat; grand time."

The children come from all directions, all ages from the youngest to those just entering manhood and womanhood. They dance, jumping around the circle, mimicking the motion of a rabbit and keeping time with the two forefingers of each hand lifted like a rabbit's feet running. At the same time they make a little noise like the rabbit. The tom-tom is the only accompaniment to the performance.

In this way the young people are trained for war, for every boy must be a warrior and every girl a warrior's wife.

There are five orders of soldiers, the Ti-e-pa-ko, the Tsai-e-ton-mo, the Ton-kon-ko, the Ah-tle-to-yo-ye, and the Ko-e-Tsain-ko. The five orders make up the whole army of "Dog Soldiers." The Ko-e-Tsain-ko is made up exclusively of those who have distinguished themselves in war.

Any member of the other orders may become a Ko-e-Tsain-ko, who has achieved some notable deed. They are distinguished by a red sash made of painted skins, and use only rattles made of deer hoofs, instead of the usual rattle gourd. The different orders are always watching the Rabbits and as the boys grow old enough for the army it is a race to see which order will catch them. In this way the ranks of the "Dog Soldiers" are kept filled by the captures from the Rabbits.

When a Rabbit is captured by an order he is sent to capture another Rabbit for his file man and close companion in the army. Then the choice is made and the pledge is made and sealed by the smoking of the pipe, which make them boon companions ready to die for each other. They are no longer Rabbits, but of a higher order of the Kiowa soldiery.

J. J. Methvin, White Missionary to the Kiowas and Comanches
Vol. 36, pp. 110–11

COMANCHES, KIOWAS, AND APACHES

I have had several fights with the Indians and had to kill to save my own life. The only trouble we ever had with the Indians was with those from the reservation and [Comanche, Kiowa, and Apache] tribes. . . . They fought with bows and arrows in a particular fight I was in on the banks of Red River. They used flint-pointed arrows and later the spike point. Their arrows were a foot and a half long usually made from good hickory wood. The point was placed in the slit end of the stick and a strip of animal hide wrapped around this to hold it in place. This would be dried till very hard. When it went into the flesh it was very hard to be removed as the point softened and many times had to be left in the flesh until it could be cut out. One man I recall was shot and I rushed to him and jerked the arrow from his leg which had gone from one side of his leg to the other and in jerking the arrow out it left the point in his leg.

Mitchell Arendell, White Resident of Chickasaw Territory
Vol. 72, pp. 74–77

COMANCHES

The Indians fought the white people [around Fort Cobb]. The Indians crowded the whites until they had to run their cannons into the Washita River.[1] The cannon sank in the sand. A bunch of us tried to raise one of the cannons. We tried diving but could do nothing. There seemed to be a ringing noise when the ring hit the top of the cannon as if there was a knot on a spring near the end of the barrel. I came near drowning in this channel at the bluff. Arrow heads were found here. One man plowed up an old gun on a hillside near this place. I am sure there is a cannon at the bottom of this river channel here because we could hear a metallic ring when we made a strike.

Emory King, Comanche
Vol. 86, pp. 446

COMANCHES AND KIOWAS

One morning in 1868 this wagon train left Fort Richardson, [Texas] commanded by [the boss] Warren, and it was loaded with sacks of shelled corn on its way to Fort Griffith [Fort Griffin, Texas]. Before the wagon train pulled out it was short one driver and Mr. Warren asked me if I wanted to make the trip. How I got out of making this trip I don't recall, but another man was hired to make the trip and, after seeing what happened, I was glad I did not go. This wagon train had made one day's drive and camped and early the next morning before it pulled out for another day's drive they were attacked by the Comanche Indians and only five escaped alive and three of the five were wounded. The boss of the train was killed and one of the men was wounded so badly that he could not get away. The Indians tied his feet to one wagon and his hands to another wagon and while he was swinging this way they built a fire under him and burned him in two; after this the Indians took the sacked corn out of the wagons and must have laid the sacks in front of them on their ponies and cut a hole in the sacks and rode in a large circle, and the corn was scattered all over the prairie around where this massacre took place. There were over four hundred Indians in that raid; it was later learned that Chief Big Tree was one of the chiefs on this raid and according to what he told at his trial, the white man that was burned after being wounded to where he could not get away, had lain on the ground, and with his two six-shooters, had killed several of the Indians and that was why they had burned him.[2]

J. R. Massagee, White Freight Driver in Western Oklahoma
Vol. 108, pp. 113–19

COMANCHES

It was understood that the Comanche Indians had a belief that their medicine men could go to a certain place and go through certain ceremonies, after which they could instruct the warriors as to what they should do. There was such a ceremonial place on Pease River, called Medicine Mound, to which the Comanches were accustomed to go.[3]

Seventeen Comanche Indians, with their medicine man, were making this pilgrimage when they were discovered by some buffalo hunters, led by a man named Vaughan, who had a buffalo camp near. These buffalo hunters began shooting at the band of Indians with their long-range buffalo needle guns, whereupon the Indians made for the Medicine Mound, thinking that they would be safe when over the mountain, but these buffalo hunters had a way of elevating their guns and dropping the bullets where they desired over the rise of the mountain. In this way all but three of the Indians were killed and among the three was a medicine man whom the Indians put to death for instructing them incorrectly.

James Cosner, White Cowboy in Comanche Country
Vol. 100, pp. 278–87

Raids into Texas

COMANCHE AND KIOWAS

I was about eight years old when there was an uproar with the Indians, the Comanches and Kiowas. The white people had gotten word that the Indians were on the war path and coming and murdering the people and burning the houses as they came. The people were gathering at my younger brother's house for safety and my older brother, Arther Hartkil, had lent his gun out to a neighbor whose name was Mr. Tom Fitspatrick. My brother went to get the gun and he, Mr. Fitspatrick, his wife and two daughters were on the way back when the Indians overtook them and murdered my brother and Mr. Fitspatrick and scalped Mrs. Fitspatrick and kidnapped the two girls. They shot Mr. Fitspatrick and killed him but literally shot my brother all to pieces; it was because my brother made a fight that the Indians butchered him up.

When they scalped Mrs. Fitspatrick she tied her apron over her head and ran from my brother's house and had gotten almost to the gate when she fell on her face, dead.

Mary E. Rayfield, White Resident of Montague County, Texas
Vol. 70, pp. 434–38

COMANCHES AND APACHES

When I was fourteen years old my parents moved to Denton, Wise County, Texas; this was in 1876. While you may not be interested in what happened in Texas, still this concerns Oklahoma as Oklahoma Indians were connected with it. Some of the Indians of southern Oklahoma were raiders, and most anything bad you wanted to call them. I am an Indian myself, but we were civilized, or so called, and didn't participate in raids and killings and robbery. The early settlers were exposed too, and suffered greatly from these Indians raids. The Apaches and Comanches were the worst and in every "light moon" or when the moon was about full, was when these raids would take place. The band of Indians, sometimes fifty or more, would make their raids and steal horses principally; they didn't bother cattle. They would kill the settlers and capture the girls and young women and take them away with them. I helped fight off just such a raid when I was fourteen years old, in Wise County, Texas, down near Decatur, Texas. They raided a school, burned the building and killed some of the children and kidnapped two girls. I had the satisfaction later, from 1876 to 1880, of chasing these raiding Indians and giving them some of the same treatment they had given the white settlers. I was a Texas Ranger during those four years. We guarded wagon trains across the country but our main territory was on the Mexican border, from Brownsville to El Paso, on the New Mexico line.

George L. Poston, Cherokee-White Resident of Texas
Vol. 40, pp. 284–89

Just a few years before we moved to Jimtown, the Comanches made their last raid into that part of the country. I think it was in February 1872 that nearly two hundred of them came down Mud Creek in what is now Stephens and Jefferson county and crossed the Red River into Texas, swinging down toward Denton. They were on a horse-stealing expedition and were gathering up horses as they went. The white people had sighted them coming and had sent riders on ahead to warn the settlements. At one place a man heard the news and had sent his two boys out to bring in his horses. The boys had found the herd and were riding on the old "bell" mare, followed by the rest of the herd, when eight or nine Comanches tried to stop them. They kept right on running and the Indians fired on them with arrows. One arrow struck the boy riding behind, in the back and killed him. His brother held him on the horse until they reached home. When the Indians saw that they had killed the boy, they gave up the chase. That boy was the only person killed during the whole raid.

As the Comanches progressed south and east they found things were getting hotter for them and they turned north and recrossed the Red River at Gains Crossing and headed up Walnut Bayou (now called Walnut Creek) until they reached a placed called Battle Spring Prairie. (Battle Spring Prairie is between Oswalt and Cheek in Love County.) At this point they evidently thought they were far enough away to be safe and stopped and went into camp.

An Indian by the name of Col. Gaines, a full–blood Chickasaw, for whom Gainesville, Texas was named, had a big farm on the north side of the Red River and was working about fifty Negroes. Gaines and these Negroes set out in pursuit of the Comanches and found them encamped at Battle Springs Prairie. The loose horses were grazing on the prairie and the Indians had camped back in the timber. Gaines and his men slipped around and rode in between the loose horses and the Indian camp and began to shoot and holler. The Indians, frightened by the unexpected attack, retreated off to the northwest and Gaines and his men drove the horses home.

Will Brown, White Resident of Chickasaw Territory
Vol. 1, pp. 380–86

Raids Against the Chickasaws, Choctaws, and Seminoles

Grandmother told me of an exciting adventure she had with the Comanche Indians near the Arbuckle Mountains when she was a girl. She and a neighbor girl decided to ride to another neighbor's house, about five miles away, one day to do some sewing. There were very few sewing machines in those days and when a woman was fortunate enough to own one, the neighbors for miles around would use it.

It was a beautiful clear fall day, and as the two girls rode along they saw a herd of horses being driven by one man, who they thought was the slave of the people to whose house they were going. The girl suggested that they race with this man as he drove the horses. No sooner was this suggestion made, than they were off at full speed. To their horror they soon discovered they were not racing with a slave, but with a Comanche Indian. They turned their horses around in an effort to retreat. The Indian gave a yell and a host of Indians appeared. The girls looked back and to their amazement they were being followed by this band of Comanches.

Grandmother wanted to jump from her horse and hide in the underbrush near the trail, but the other girl wanted to go on and try to outrun them to the house. Finally Grandmother felt that the best thing to do was to get off the horse. This she did. The horse continued to run, and Grandmother crouched in the underbrush near the trail. The Indians rushed madly past her. The material which she was carrying fell to the ground as she jumped and the other girl dropped hers at about the same place. As the Indians raced by they stooped from their saddles and picked up the cloth. Grandmother was so frightened that she hardly dared to breathe. The Comanches continued their chase after her girl friend and as she entered her home they shot and killed her. Grandmother was indeed glad that she had left her horse. They took both the horses as they left.

Grandmother said that many a night she has heard noises near her home which she thought were made by the Comanche Indians. She would awaken all her children and they would flee to the woods for protection. The Comanche raiders were much dreaded by the Chickasaws. When the Choctaws and Chickasaws separated, after coming to the Territory, the Choctaws gave the western part of the land allotted them to the Chickasaws, because they were afraid of the Comanches who were their neighbors on the West.[4] The

Chickasaws received better land, but the Choctaws didn't have to fear the Comanches. They were too far away to be bothered by them.

Ida Cunnetubby, Chickasaw
Vol. 21, pp. 348–52

COMANCHES

The Comanche Indians were of a hostile tribe and many times they would come over into the Chickasaw country and steal horses and cattle, which seemed to be their greatest desire. Sometimes they would get away with the stock then again the Chickasaws and Choctaws would run them down and fight it out with them and at such times nearly always regained possession of the stolen stock. The Comanches generally came in small bands and for this reason could usually be beaten down or driven back to their country if over-taken before reaching the boundary line of the Chickasaw and Comanche countries but the Chickasaws would nearly always give up the chase when reaching the Comanche line.

Janie Elizabeth Ray, White Resident of Chickasaw Territory
Vol. 113, pp. 250–53

COMANCHES AND KIOWAS

The Plains Indians would raid my grandpa's farm and steal horses, cattle and grain about once or twice a year. Grandpa killed three Indians on one of these raids. He was given a contract from the Government to furnish beef to soldiers at Fort Cobb and Fort Arbuckle. He had a large herd of cattle.

One time Grandfather was sent on a scouting expedition with Captain Marcy[5] to Salt Lake but at Santa Fe, New Mexico, he became too ill to go on and lay for weeks with fever.

At another time he was taken with soldiers to a Wichita Indian village, east of Rush Springs, on Rush Creek because he knew so many of the Indian languages at the village and could talk the language. An Indian from the village had killed a soldier at Fort Arbuckle and an uprising was feared be-cause friends of the soldier were on the way to the village to kill the Indians. Excitement was running high, and soldiers were sent to keep down trouble, but reached the village in time to see the head of the Indian, who had killed the soldier, brought in to white friends. Further trouble was avoided by the presence of several weeks of the soldiers at the village.

Walter L. Moncrief, Choctaw Resident of Wichita Territory

Vol. 108, pp. 356–61

COMANCHES

I recall several raids made by the Comanche Indians. The Comanches would come from the west in bands or in small gangs and would steal the cattle and horses of the Chickasaws and would run them back west on their own range. The only way that the Chickasaws could get their cattle and horses back was just to trail the Comanches up and whip them out and get their stock. I recall once when my father and I lived south of the Arbuckle Mountains near the frontier, that the Comanches raided one night and the next night following. Father and I tied our horses in the yard around the house and father and I stationed ourselves back of the house to guard.

Well, about eleven o'clock that night two of those Comanches crawled over the yard fence and were trying to steal our horses and father shot one of them. He fell in the yard and the other ran and just as he jumped the fence, father let him have it and he fell just over the fence.

Joe Colbert, Chickasaw

Vol. 20, pp. 177–80

KIOWAS AND COMANCHES

The Comanche and Kiowa Indians used to make raids on us. They would steal from us the same as from white people. I remember, when a small child prowling through the woods and finding ashes of camp fires where they had camped, one day I found an arrow point. It was made of hard steel. We didn't dare leave a crosscut saw outside. They liked to get hold of them for arrow points. They weren't inclined to fight with us, unless we tried to catch them if they had stolen something. They would kill and scalp us.

Dinah Lewis Frazier, Chickasaw

Vol. 3, 582–85

We had lots of trouble with the Comanches. The people in the neighborhood had a lot of horses, and the Comanches liked to steal horses. I remember one night when the Comanches were on a raid, my father rounded up all of our horses and put them in the lot, to keep the Comanches from stealing them. The next morning they had driven off all of the horses except one small colt, which was not big enough to jump the fence. They made another raid one night when there was a big snow on the ground. All of the settlers for miles around gathered at the Edmond Pickens home. After the raid the men (eighteen in number) started out after the Comanches. There was also one Negro in the crowd. There were somewhere between two and three hundred Comanches in the raid.

The Chickasaws caught up with the Comanches at about where McMillan is now located. They were so badly out-numbered it was impossible to get the horses back. Part of the Comanches would go ahead with the horses while the others stopped to fight. The Negro, William Henry, was riding a mule. He had on a large overcoat and he pulled it over his head and started running. The Comanches got both his gun and coat. One of the men let the Negro ride back with him to the Pickens home.

One of the Comanches got after Dave Pickens. Pickens shot him, but the other Comanches carried him away. After the battle, it was discovered that Dave Pickens had an arrow sticking in the back of his saddle, through into his overcoat. Every one started to help remove the arrow, since it would have been impossible for him to have gotten out of the saddle with out being hurt by the arrow. They all got too excited or something, anyway the arrow cut Pickens in the side; just a small place. The arrow was poisoned and Pickens lived only a few days. He died just as soon as the poison went through his system.

On another raid the Comanches entered a home and were about to cut a woman's finger off to get her ring. She offered a jug of molasses if they would give her time to remove the ring herself. One of the Indians knocked her down with the jug, and took his hatchet and cut her finger off.

They also made a raid near Baum. On this raid they ran into two girls on horseback. One girl jumped from her horse and yelled at her sister to do the same, but the girl was so badly frightened that she stayed with her horse. The Comanches ran her into her own yard, killed her, and took the horse.

A year or two after these raids the United States government gave the

Chickasaws permission to go into Comanche country and look for their horses. They went and found horses in large numbers, but none of their own. A few years later I went on a visit to Lawton and met a real old Comanche. I asked him why it was that we never found any of our horses. I said, "Remember anything about Comanche used to steal horse?" He said, "No, me from Texas, steal horse in Texas, bring over here. Steal horse over here, take him to Texas." That was the whole story. The horses that were stolen from the Chickasaws were carried to Texas, and the horses that were stolen in Texas were carried to Lawton.

Overton Lavers, Chickasaw
Vol. 6, pp. 316–21

COMANCHES

My father had a big herd of ponies on the range and if he wanted to trade off some of them, he would go see the Indian Agent at Anadarko. There were three agencies in the Territory, one at Anadarko, one at Fort Sill[6], and one at Fort Reno.[7]

One time a bunch of Comanche Indians stole some of our ponies and started toward Fort Sill with them. We got on their trail and kept following them. After three or four days we came upon them on Big Beaver Creek, near where Lawton is now. They had the ponies staked along the bank of the creek and were swimming in the creek. When they saw us they began to scram and opened fire. We returned fire. We killed four of them and the rest of them got away. None of our men were hurt. We got our ponies and returned home.

All the Indians were pretty friendly except the Comanches and Kiowas. We had to watch them pretty closely.

Henry Belton Perry, Choctaw-Black
Vol. 70, pp. 173–78

APACHES

The Apaches gave the Seminoles trouble when in the midst of their wanderings after they had been forced to leave their old homes. They were never satisfied in the new country and they took up to wandering around in different parts of the country under their new leader, Wild Cat, while A-ha-lak

E-math-la was serving as medicine man all this time. The Apaches plundered and stole from the Seminoles anything they could get. When this trouble arose, the Seminoles were trying to make settlements but the Apaches were daring enough to steal some horses from them. The Seminoles could not do without their stock. A-ha-lak E-math-la took up the trail of the Apaches and followed the trail that led to a stream of clear running water. The stock had been driven across the stream at one place but instead of crossing at the same place, my great grandfather went or followed the course of the stream for a short time when he finally fell on his stomach to take a drink from the stream. Before he stood up or before he ever hardly realized what was happening, an arrow had been shot from the opposite bank of the stream and found a mark on my great grandfather's left cheek. Glancing across the stream, he saw an Indian woman where she had lain in wait for such prowlers as he.

It is told that he didn't think much or was much concerned about the arrow, but he just pulled it away from its place in his cheek but he leisurely began to doctor himself. Probably there is no one now that can do what he did—he forced his tongue to the wound on his cheek and began to lick the place. There was no bleeding of the wound, and, in all, the incident did not seem to bother him. The woman on the opposite bank witnessed all this incident, and when she saw what the medicine man was doing to heal his wound, quickly disappeared into the thickets.

Tanyan Wesley, Seminole
Vol. 46, pp. 198–202

Indian Warfare on the Plains

KIOWAS

Cut Throat Gap was named because, according to Indian history, passed on by word of mouth from generation to another, it was here that the Osages cut the throats of old men, women and children while the Kiowa warriors were off scouting.

The heads were put in copper kettles and left in the canyon. When the warriors returned they found what had happened. One old woman had escaped by crawling into the cliffs and hiding there. She lived to tell what happened.

Col. Schyler, of Frederick, Oklahoma told me he found or saw a copper kettle in a farm house yard all bent and mashed. He learned later that the kettle had been picked up at this gap and was used as a water bucket for horses.

Guy Quoetone, Kiowa
Vol. 8, p. 305

WICHITAS

[According to Osage beliefs, when an Osage person dies, they must go out and kill an enemy and bring back the head to appease the evil spirit who had allowed their kinsman to die. This story tells of such an incident in the late 1880s or early 1890s and was probably the last time this ritual killing took place.]

The last [Osage] party of this kind was led by Bill Conner and Three Striker. I had this story from Bill's own lips. They proceeded to the plains of Western Kansas. The first person appearing to their view was a lone horseman, a white man, riding on the barren plains. The Indians, immediately upon spying him, proceeded at great speed, as they always rode their best horses on these occasions. They soon overtook and surrounded the rider. Conner's horse had fallen into a dry hole in the prairie and dismounted him, but he was soon astride a splendid horse again and joined the Indians who had the man surrounded. The white man, seeing that Conner had some white blood, fell on his neck and begged piteously for mercy. Bill's statement was to the effect that he counseled the Osage full-bloods to release this man, as the government was watching very closely acts of this kind, and if they took the life of this man, his head would probably be required for the crime. He finally prevailed upon the Indians to take his council.

The next man they met was a Wichita Indian chief. One of two of the party, either Conner or Three Striker, severed the head of the Wichita Indian and brought it back to camp, showing that they had complied with the order of the mourners. This act proved to be quite serious for the Osages, as the Wichitas assembled their warriors and came to Pawhuska to demand a settlement. They first asked for the head of Conner. Conner, of course, had made himself conspicuous by his absence at this particular time. A war council was called, and a settlement was agreed upon, whereby the Osages were to give the Wichitas three hundred ponies, a considerable sum of money and many blankets. This, as far as the writer knows, was the last war party that went out to carry out the custom that had hitherto been practiced.

W. E. McGuire, White Resident of Osage Territory

Vol. 35, pp. 177–88

COMANCHES AND TONKAWAS

This is a real story as it comes to my mind that took place in 1866, although I was just six years old. Trouble between the Tonkawa and Comanche Indians. A Tonkawa Indian killed a deer one evening and hung it in a tree. The Comanches waited until the Tonkawa came back after it then they attacked him. In the fight they killed him, but he also killed one of the Comanches.

The Tonkawa Indians got the Comanche Indian and took him to a little village, Fort Griffin [Texas]; there they scalped him and cut his hands off. They built a bonfire of logs, put him on it, then took his scalp and hands and tied them on a pole and held them in the air while they put on a war dance. They buried the Comanche, and burned everything he had with him and killed his horse and put it on his grave. His mother wept and wailed and took a knife and slashed her breast all to pieces.

Along about the same time the Comanches scalped my brother. The scalp all grew back but right in the crown, but he died about a year later from the effects of it.

The Comanches also stole a little white boy, six years old by the name of Ledbetter. A Negro man whom they called Negro Britt was trading with the Indians, and he got the boy back about ten years later. The boy then was sixteen years old, but he was never satisfied with his folks anymore.

Negro Britt ran a train from Jacksboro to Ft. Griffin. This train was made up of five or six wagons and teams. The Indians surrounded them and killed all of the drivers but Negro Britt. My father said they went out to investigate the fight, and there was a bucketful of Winchester shells after the fight. . . .

My father and one of my brothers had a fight with six Comanche Indians, and they shot my brother through the head. The arrow went through one side right under the ear and it came out on the side right under the ear. My father cut the spike out, and killed one or two Comanches. Another time the old settlers got in a fight with the Comanches and they wounded one of Rawhide's boys, and they killed one of the Sutherland boys, too.

Daniel J. Jackson, White Resident of Texas and Oklahoma

Vol. 30, pp. 478–80

The Tonkawa Massacre

The Indians were quieted down by this time [1901] and were removed to their reservations, but located one mile and a half to the south of my place is ground [near Anadarko] where the Tonkawas were massacred. I have seen their skeletons in the early days. The skeletons were scattered over the hillside just as the Tonkawas were killed.

I shall not mention the tribes who did the killing because they are now educated and somewhat respectable Indians. These Indians killed women and children the same as men and left the bodies where they had killed them. Their claim for killing the Tonkawas is that they were digging up their dead after they were buried and eating them. They once had some captives of the tribes who later killed the Tonkawas, and they told these captives they were being fed some of their brothers.

John Clark, White Resident of Comanche Territory

Vol. 65, pp. 132–34

TONKAWAS

The forefathers of the Tonkawas had hunted and camped over most of Oklahoma and Texas, but the first any of the little band now located at the Oakland Agency can remember, was their being located in the Wichita Mountains. They went from there to San Antonio and Houston, Texas, where they lived in tents at the time; no houses were built at that time and white people also lived in tents. They next moved to Austin, Texas, where they picked cotton for a living; at this time they were a large and powerful tribe. It is not known how long they stayed there but high water caused the death of a large number of them and they were separated, some coming north and some going other ways.

Near the Red River they killed a great number of buffalo, the Indians' favorite meat. The meat was diseased; they ate of it and lots of them died. They were without money and nothing to eat; when an Indian has to do without meat very long he soon gets sick. The only living they had was roots, herbs, prairie turtles, and a few wild turkeys.

All the different tribes came together for a council at Waco, Texas. Some of the men came from Washington D.C., to council with them as to what they wanted to do. Four of the older men of the tribe now, were only small boys then; their names are Buck Bill, John Williams, Standing Buffalo, and Corporal Jesse. The Tonkawas had not been receiving any rations from the government until this time; so these government officials decided to issue them beef, sugar and coffee and told all the chiefs of the different tribes to come to Washington for a council. They started, some on foot, but later took the train. When they arrived at Washington, the council lasted for four days. Sam Houston was head of the Indian Affairs and he told Lasalo, the chief of their tribe, to go home and he would appoint Major Davis as their Agent (whom they greatly loved) and they were to have the land in the Red River Valley.[8]

When the Civil War broke out, the South asked the Tonkawas to help them but the chief said, "no." They were friendly to all white people. After the war, a number of the men were enlisted as United States Scouts. The Pawnees were having trouble at this time, so the Scouts were sent up there to make peace with them.

The commanding officer promised them they could have what they captured, and if that was not enough, they would be paid for their services. While they were away, the other tribes decided they must kill off the Tonkawas, as they were too friendly with the whites, so they had a regular massacre. The Comanches, Caddos, Wichitas, Delawares, Shawnees, and Kickapoos swooped down on the Tonkawas one morning before daylight, burning the agency building. The Agent, Colonel Leeper,[9] who made his escape, went to Wichita Falls, Texas. Over 2,000 of the tribe were killed at this time; about 700 were captured. Only one can now be found out of that number, a son of Lilly Wolf; he was captured by the Comanches and afterwards married. Only 400 were left after the fight. They were in such a confusion and afraid, that a good many scattered and were captured by other tribes. . . . The tribe was so badly scattered that the remaining ones had a council and were given a reservation in the Washita Valley with Major Davis as their agent, but he was killed and the papers lost. The other tribes were so hostile to them that the Government decided to give them the old Nez Percé Reservation, known now as the Tonkawa Reservation. They came as far as the Sac & Fox Agency and stayed there one winter (1885). Most of their ponies died and in the spring of 1886, they came afoot to this reservation, arriving here with only a few ponies in May 1886. They were poor but a happy people. About a year after this the Government began issuing them rations. Every Saturday every family was issued, per head, 5 pounds of beef, one-half pound of coffee, 1 pound of sugar and 3 pounds of flour.

Bertha Brewer Plummer, White Daughter of Agent to Tonkawas
Vol. 93, pp. 353–62

Captives

COMANCHES

Herman Lehmann was captured by the Comanches when he was nine years old and was raised by them; he lived with Father a long time and thought a great deal of him, he treated him as a father. The Comanches would tie Herman on a pony and turn the pony loose and watch it buck with the white captive tied to its back. They would also tie Herman with a ten foot rope to a tall sapling, bend it over as far as they could and let it flip back, thereby throwing Lehmann up in the air while attached to the rope. Father would laugh and joke [with] Herman after he became more civilized.

Herman Asanap, Comanche
Vol. 99, pp. 233–37

KIOWAS

I was born on the Washita River north of the present town of Carnegie. At that time there was no town or settlement of white people in the country and my people who were full blood Indians of the Kiowa Tribe did not count time like we do now; therefore I do not know in what day or month I was born but from the count of time which others of my people give me I am sure that I am seventy years old.

My father's name was Wolf's Breast or Wolf's Stomach and I cannot give any interpretation of the name into English for the reason that I never heard any.

When I was very little, so I was told by my people, my father was captured by soldiers and taken to Fort Sill and put in prison because he was a very great warrior and went on many fights against the white people; he with many other young Kiowas would not be civilized. They wanted to live like their people had always lived.

He was kept in prison for a long time and then my people said that the soldiers sent him to a prison that was on an island, somewhere in the East, I never knew where but awhile [later] they said that he had died in the prison.[10]

My mother's name was Went After Wood and as she was just a woman, there is nothing to tell about her, except that she helped make the home and get the food and looked after me.

Stephen Kotay, Kiowa
Vol. 32, pp. 435–37

COMANCHES

Nathan J. McElroy, who tells this story, was eleven years old when he was captured.

On Sunday afternoon of June 7th, 1869, I, with a group of other children, went down to the creek [near present-day Paris, Texas] to hunt berries and toward evening we started to return home. I told them that I would go over toward a little mountain and drive the horses home, as that was my task. My cousin, Robert Lackey, age nineteen, walked on with my sister, Ellen, age thirteen, my brother William Dorie, age seven, and the other children.

When I came near the horses at the foot of the little mountain, my dog began to bark and I soon discovered a number of Indians were there and they had the horses tied. I ran back as fast as I could go and the Indians were after me. My cousin saw what was happening and he grabbed my little brother, Dorie, or "Skinnie" as we called him and all started running for the house. They simply ran us down and overtook us. They killed my cousin Robert. Then they tied me on a horse and taking my sister, Ellen, and little brother, "Skinnie," each on a horse with an Indian, they set out, we were to learn, for the Indian Territory.

They were a band of Comanches on a horse stealing raid and we traveled two days and nights without stopping, only for a short time. At last after this long journey, we crossed the North Fork of Red River and came to the mouth of a great canyon which is now called Devil's Canyon in Kiowa County, Oklahoma. Here a great band of Comanche Indians were camped and in the valley to the north of the mountains, which are the Wichitas. The Wichitas and Caddos had a great encampment. There were more than a thousand I am sure. They were grouped a little to the east. The Kiowa Indians lived northwest, which is now in the vicinity of Lake Altus and Lakeside Park. These were all great bands of Indians.

At the big Comanche camp we rested two days and nights then the whole band moved about thirty-five miles northwest to what is now called Spring Creek; here the band again made a village and after a few days a band of thirty-six young warriors prepared for a horse stealing trip or raid and I was taken along with them. My sister, Ellen, and brother, Dorie, were left at the camp with the women and children.

This band of young warriors took me through what is now the Panhandle of Texas, New Mexico, Utah, Idaho, Montana, Colorado, Nebraska, and Kansas. I remember seeing the towns of Fort Sumner, New Mexico and Ogolalah [Ogallala] Nebr. The band of warriors gathered about two hundred horses. When we came back the tribe was at Fort Cobb, Oklahoma, then Indian Territory. My brother and sister were all right and I was glad to see them, but I had enjoyed my trip as the Indians were good to me. It is true we had nothing to eat but meat and some wild fruits which we found on the way, but the Indians killed plenty of deer, antelope and buffalo. They cooked the meat over a fire sometimes on a green stick sharpened into a fork and sometimes when we camped long enough they would dig a hole in the ground and pack it hard, then they would build a fire in it and make it hot burning coals and hot ashes. This they would drag out of the hole and place the fresh meat in it and cover the meat with leaves or straw and place the hot dirt over it and cover it all with the fire and leave it until it was thoroughly cooked.

I was owned by an Indian named Pascidia. He was about forty years old and as I had been raised to ride a horse and live much in the open, the Indian life was not hard for me and I was like all boys, so I soon learned to talk to them and enjoyed their rambling. They seemed to like me.

Indian bucks never work, so Pascidia had his own daughter, Vemne, (which means Clear Water in Comanche) and the daughter of Black Horse to wait upon me. I can't remember Black Horse's girl's name. I liked both of the girls and knew them for many years. Black Horse's girl died about two years ago.

My brother and sister were not so happy. They lived in the Indian camp with the squaws and papooses and helped them get wood and water as well as assist with the other camp duties. The squaws and children waited upon the bucks, who only killed the meat, while the squaws skinned the animal, cut it up and carried it into camp. This was hard work for my sister and little brother and of course they grieved for home.

All this time my parents and their friends were making every effort in their power to locate our whereabouts and finally a white man called Dutch

Bill, whose wife was a Cheyenne Indian and who traded with the Indians as they had a store near Fort Cobb, told my father that he thought we were among the Comanches. Father had also found in the Indian Territory a man who was his friend during the Civil War. He was called Pottawatomie Joe and these men agreed to help father by buying us, through the Cheyenne Indians from the Comanches.

Father sold his farm and stock in Texas and brought $1950.00 to the Indian Territory and through Dutch Bill and his wife and Pottawatomie Joe we were bought from the Comanches by the Cheyennes and returned to our parents in November of 1869. We were with the Indians more than five months.

My brother was owned by Eacanta. I cannot recall the name of the Indian who owned my sister.

We went back to Texas with our parents but in later years, after I was a grown man, I was quite friendly with many of these Indians.

Nathan J. McElroy, White Captive of the Comanches
Vol. 35, pp. 110–15

COMANCHES

In 1863 my mother, Mary Johnson, and her five children, and a widow with three children, who in later years married Judge Clifton, were captured by the Comanche Indians near Lawton and held in captivity for more than a year by these Indians.

I was born December 25, 1864, while my mother was in captivity; two of the widow's children died in captivity.

In 1865, my father, Britt Johnson, through a Mexican boy, an interpreter and guide, was able to locate his family with this tribe of Indians and to redeem them and also the widow and her child, by trading the Indians corn, ponies, blankets and calico, as a price for ransom.

My mother has related to me that in this trade, I was not included as Father was unaware of my presence in this world.

When the exchange was being made, an old Indian squaw who was my mother's guard wanted to keep me because I was born under her care, but mother refused to go without me, so I was bought from the Indians for twelve ears of corn. This widow took me in charge and kept me until I was eight years old. Then she returned me to my mother.

John Johnson, Cherokee-Comanche-Black

Vol. 31, pp. 261–63

COMANCHES AND KIOWAS

I remember when my parents first came to Oklahoma, Indian Territory. It was in about 1870. Several families traveled in covered wagons. Many times we were attacked by Indians. They were in droves and at a distance they looked like timber. Sometimes they took our horses, food, bedding, cows or goats. We usually had goats because they were less trouble to travel with. When the Indians robbed us, we had to travel on foot until we came to a farm house. There the many folks would work out for some horses and another place maybe some cows or goats. We then started on our journey.

I remember on the same journey, a white man by the name of Abe Lee and his family were traveling with us. Before dark we camped and made a big log fire. Just after dark a drove of Indians on horses came to our camp, there must have been three hundred of them. They rode around and around our wagons. Finally several of them got off their horses and came up to our wagons and walked around and looked at the horses, then at the women and children. They never said a word, even when our men folks spoke to them; finally a big Indian who must have been the Chief, shouted something and they grabbed me and Mrs. Lee and five children; they killed Mr. & Mrs. Lee and the oldest daughter and threw them on their horses. They then tied the other three children (Susana, Johnnie, and Francis Lee) on their horses and rode away shouting something. We never heard what become of the children, until I was about grown, that was in about 1880. Susana married and came to Jimstown and settled near us. It was then that she told me the story of her life with the Indians.

The Indians scalped her mother, father and sister and threw the bodies away. They put the scalps on sticks and tried to make the children dance across the Red River bed and carry the scalps high in the air. A squaw objected to this because everyone would have to walk. Instead, they were tied on the horses and made to ride across and carry the scalps on the sticks.

The squaws were good to them but the bucks were not. Susana was sold three times among the Indians. Each time she was sold, she was branded across the forehead and around the wrist. She still bore the three scars across her forehead and around her wrist. The children were with the Indians so long that they didn't want to leave them.

The Government cut off their food until they released the white children. I wish I could tell more of how the Government forced the Indians to give up the white children.

Mary Alice Gibson Arendell, Choctaw-Cherokee
Vol. 1, pp. 155–63

The 1874–1875 Red River War

COMANCHES

The Comanches and Kiowas were allies and Father was a friend and warring partner of Chief Quanah Parker; he was in the battle of Adobe Walls with him and he was in several battles in the early '70's. . . . The Comanches were a very wild tribe and were hard to subdue. They hated the white man because they killed all the buffalo, thereby depriving the Indians of their principal source of food supply. They made a vow to fight the whites and kill as many as possible, this being one cause of the Adobe Walls battle.

The hunters had a storehouse and Major Bent had a trading store and furnished hunters [with] ammunition.[11] The Plains Indians decided to wipe them out so they organized a war party and rode to the camp about eight hundred strong, Kiowas, Comanches, Cheyennes, Arapahos, and a few other of scattering tribes. There were not many hunters and they expected to catch them asleep and murder them but the tent poles broke before the Indians arrived and the hunters were not asleep, perhaps this saved their lives. The Indians surrounded the fort and Billy Dixon[12] and others poured the shot into them and killed several horses and wounded and killed several Indians. The battle kept up several days and only two white men were killed but over one hundred Indians were killed or wounded. Quanah Parker was wounded in the back of the head.

Father attended the Medicine Lodge Treaty, was a friend of Ten Bears, Comanche Chief, and Apeatone, Kiowa Chief, who was sent to Nevada in 1890 to investigate the Ghost Dance and came back and reported it a fraud. He went on raids into Texas with the Comanches and captured several white captives, among them the Smith boys, Herman Lehmann and others.

Herman Asanap, Comanche
Vol. 99, pp. 233–37

I have hunted lots of buffalo and was a fine shot with a bow and arrow, and I have seen thousands of buffalo in one herd. The white men killed them off and it made us Indians mad and we attacked some men at Adobe Walls in Texas and they killed some of us and we killed some of them.

Quanah Parker, my close friend (Chi Hoites), was wounded in the back of the head with a bullet. We fought all day and all night and several ponies were killed and several Indians.

I used to kill buffalo with an arrow while they were running. Some times I would shoot them a great many times. I never scalped any white men or woman or children. Never shot any that I knew of. I am a Jesus man and do not kill nor fight.

Quassyah, Comanche
Vol. 41, pp. 47–48

CADDOS

The [Anadarko Agency] Commissary . . . issued beef and groceries to the Caddos, Wichitas, and Delawares and a few Comanches. These Comanches had lived with the Caddos and Wichitas and Delawares for some time. In 1874 the government wanted the Comanches to move to the south side of the [Washita] river with the other Comanches and draw their rations at Ft. Sill. After they refused to move, the Government sent troops to make them move. When the Comanches saw the troops coming they got on their horses and fled. The troops set fire to the Comanches' tents and bed clothes. After the Comanches' return, they were forced to move south, with their own tribe, in order to draw their rations. A few days before this skirmish, some horse thieves from Texas had stolen some horses from Kunusky, a Caddo Indian, who lived about twelve miles east of the Agency. Jonathan Richards, the Indian Agent,[13] had asked my father to help trail the thieves and try to get the horses back. He did help and they trailed the thieves as far as some railroad town in Texas, where the horses had been loaded and shipped. The depot agent refused to give those following the stolen horses any information. So they returned without having caught the thieves.

While my father was gone trailing the thieves and stolen horses, the Kiowas went on the warpath against the white people. The Kiowas warned all the Indians that if they did not help fight the whites, they, too, would be killed. The Caddo chiefs issued orders for all Caddos to move to a big hill southeast of Anadarko, so that if the Kiowas attacked them (as the Caddos did not intend to fight the whites) they would all fight together. There were approximately three hundred Caddos at the appointed place. After we had been there about two weeks, we received word from the Government troops that several white men had been killed. (Frank Osborn [Osborne] and Ed Barrett were two of the men killed, I did not know the others) and that twenty-five or thirty Kiowas had been arrested, and the rest had all settled down. Later those arrested were tried, convicted, and sent to South Hampton, Virginia. They were kept there several years.

After receiving word that the Kiowas had quieted down, we all started home. My father had returned in the meantime, and when we got home our house was burned, our hogs and chickens had been killed, (as we shrewdly guessed, because my father was a white man, as none of the other houses had been burned.) They had also driven off our horses and cattle, about thirty head of each, which we never found.

Sara Ann Davis Smith, Caddo-White
Vol. 9, pp. 551–54

CADDOS AND DELAWARES

My grandfather on my mother's side was an old scout named Long Soldier, of the Caddo Tribe. After he died Grandmother married another old scout named Sam Slick, also of the Caddos.

Jack Harry, Chief of the Delawares, was my other grandfather. He helped the soldiers to capture the Kiowas. The soldiers couldn't get the Kiowas to understand that they didn't want to harm them but to bring them over to the other side of the river. The Kiowas were afraid and some of them, rather than to surrender, took their own lives by cutting their throats. Harry was a good interpreter, and spoke to them in Comanche as that was the universal language. He explained the reason to them and finally the soldiers accomplished what they were sent to do.

Jack Harry died with smallpox while in old Mexico; he was sent there on business. This was during Theodore Roosevelt's administration.

Sadie Bedoka, Caddo-Delaware
Vol. 53, pp. 14–22

Indian Diplomacy

COMANCHES

As to the Chickasaw and Choctaw and Comanche wild tribe of Indians, in the fall of 1868, after the Civil War, there was a band of Comanche Indians who came back into the Choctaw Nation and camped in what is now Atoka City in Atoka County, Oklahoma. The purpose of this band was for trading with the Choctaws and the Chickasaws, for permission to hunt, in what is now Atoka County, meat consisting of deer, turkey, squirrels, and fish. Game being scarce in the Comanche Reservation, Governor Allen Wright, Leon Harkins, and William Atoka, Choctaw Indians, Reverend J. S. Murrow, missionary among the Choctaws, Captain Hester representing the Choctaw and Chickasaw Nation met the Comanche band and their chief or leader at Atoka and went into an agreement giving the Comanche Indians privilege of hunting on certain grounds beginning at the mouth of McGee Creek and extending north to what is known as Brushy Creek in Pittsburg County, extending west to what is known as the mouth of Caney Creek, or middle Boggy, extending south to South Boggy to the mouth of Delaware Creek, and extending east back to mouth of McGee Creek. This was for ninety days for the privilege of hunting under certain agreements that they were not to bother or molest anyone in this certain district, and with the understanding that they were to establish their camp at Flint Spring. This spring was named for George Flint who lived at this place . . . northwest of Atoka City.

They had what is known as two light hacks that they had traded or gotten from the people of Texas. They also had pack ponies, camping outfits, or wigwams to live in while on a trip. They had bows and arrows pointed with flint, and stone arrowheads.

In those days the Creek Indians from Brush Hill west of Okmulgee, along the Canadian River were in the habit of coming into the northern part of what is now Atoka County and Pittsburg County for the purpose of hunting wild game without permission from the Choctaw and Chickasaw Government.

On August 2, 1937 there was a human skeleton discovered deposited in a crevice of limestone rock in . . . Atoka County, this location being within the boundary of the hunting grounds and which the Comanche Indians were permitted to use as their hunting grounds for ninety days. At the time permission was given, a band of Creek Indians was hunting in different locations in

Pittsburg County without permission, which caused some trouble between the Choctaw and Creek Indians. In all probability the Comanche Indians at their usual hunting season camped at this particular place. The human skull and skeleton shows that probably he was a Negro Indian type and indicated that he was shot with a bow and arrow, the arrowhead being the type the Comanches used. The point of the arrowhead entering the body extends into the back-bone, and the point of the arrowhead still remains in the backbone of the skeleton. Beads and other ornaments found with the skeleton show the type that a Creek Negro Indian wore in those days. This shows that probably there was a battle between the Creeks and the Comanche Indian hunters at this location. In 1934 there was a human skull found a short distance upstream from this location on Buck Creek.

John Ward, Choctaw-Chickasaw[14]

Vol. 67, pp. 3–6

CADDOS, KIOWAS, AND APACHES

I believe it was in 1870 and thereafter for several years that the Government tried to get all the tribes of the Territory together for a council. They met at Okmulgee.[15] I drove the "ambulance" that hauled the Sac and Fox chiefs to that council in 1870 and 1871. There was Miller, the Agent, Keokuk, Check-o-shuk, Potaquaw and several others of the tribe who were braves. Some of them rode horseback. I remember very well the first year that I was to meet them in a grove of trees just east of the Mission school at sunrise. Okmulgee was not much of a town at that time. There was only about seven stores. One of them was the Patterson Store.

The Kiowas, Caddos and Apaches didn't want to come to that council but they finally agreed. However, they went into camp on a creek just west of Okmulgee and refused to go any further until they had a feast and smoked a pipe of peace. So they were provided with a big barbecue and all joined in a big smoke. After they went into the Council. They hesitated to go to this Council because they had had trouble with the other tribes with whom they were going to meet.

Charles E. Guernsey, White Employee of Sac and Fox Agency

Vol. 4, pp. 200–07

COMANCHES

I went to Washington in 1921 with a delegation of Comanches, Kiowas, and Apaches to formulate a deal with Commissioner of Indian Affairs. The party consisted of Namsuawa, Comanche; Frank Moiti, Comanche; Apeaha Tone, Kiowa; Big Ben, Kiowa. I visited the White House and talked to President Harding. I wore my war bonnet and he shook hands with all of us and talked to us in his home, the big White House.

Quassyah, Comanche
Vol. 41, pp. 47–48

Chapter Two

◆ ◆ ◆ ◆ ◆ ◆ ◆ ◆ ◆ ◆ ◆ ◆ ◆ ◆

Southern Plains Cultures

◆ ◆ ◆ ◆ ◆ ◆ ◆ ◆ ◆ ◆ ◆ ◆ ◆

The word "Indian" or the phrase "Native American" does not do justice to the diversity and complexity of the traditional native peoples of Texas. In 1892, Dr. Charles R. Hume, a government physician to the Indian peoples around Anadarko, Oklahoma, saw this and commented upon it. "There are two distinct kinds of Indians," Hume said, "the Plains Indians and Timber Indians. The Plains Indians roamed the plains hunting buffalo and such. The Timber Indians have always cultivated their lands, raising mostly corn. The Kiowas, Comanches and Apaches are Plains Indians, while the Wichitas and Caddos are Timber Indians."[1] While differences existed between the Caddos and Comanches, differences also existed between the Caddos and Wichitas and between the Comanches and Kiowas. Each saw themselves at the center of the universe and each possessed their own unique way of providing food for themselves, building houses, dressing, marrying, burying and grieving for their dead, and worshipping the Creator. It would not be until the twentieth century, years after these peoples had been forced together on the reservations, that something of a distinct Southern Plains culture developed. Still, the uniqueness of these individual peoples continues to this day.[2]

Hunting

COMANCHES

My father, Asanap, lived to be ninety years old and was a great warrior and scout; he died in 1906. He could not speak a word of English and he wanted me to be educated and speak fluently so he sent me to school. He was a fine marksman with a bow and arrow, he was also a fine horseman and killed several hundred buffaloes. The Indians dried the meat, made clothing and shelter out of the hides, used the bones to make tools out of and the horns to make decorations. Father killed lots of deer; the Comanche Indians were great hunters and knew the art of tanning hides. They made robes out of buckskin and decorated them with elk's teeth. The one who had the most decorations was the best and recognized as the wealthiest. While father was a great warrior and fine marksman, he was not a savage. He was very kind and considerate, was a devout Christian and did a lot of good among the old Indians to get them to see the Jesus Road as they called it.

Herman Asanap, Comanche
Vol. 99, pp. 233–37

WICHITAS

I was too small to go hunting with my folks. At that time I was going to school most of the time. Sometimes when folks go out on hunt, be gone for a month or more. Don't know when get back. Maybe they steal horses and bring home. After my people go on hunts they would sit around the campfire at night and tell of experiences and what happened on hunts. I was just a little boy but I always listen to them talk. They would all sit around the campfire, they would make a little smoke first (meaning smoke cigarettes or pipe) and then they would tell where they had been. There was a smart man or medicine man in tribe and I remember them talking about when the soldiers try to fight them in Wichita Mountains. This man he get up on hill behind rock and wave shield. The soldiers saw the shield and thought there were lots of Indians. While he was waving shield the rest of tribe made get-a-way, and he still stood up on hill waving shield. After all my people get away, then he got on horse and got away. My brother-in-law say that man had power. He could tell when enemy come. He would make rain come. When he make rain come then my people would go out and get horses, no could track on account rain would wipe out tracks. He all time know what was going to happen and he would tell people. He set up all night and not sleep. I know he do this because my people tell me it is so. I no lie.

Jay Johnson, Wichita
Vol. 31, pp. 243–51

COMANCHES

I have been told a few things about our forefathers but not much. I think the Comanche Indians were known as the most expert horsemen the world has ever produced. In addition to the antelope, deer, elk and buffalo by the millions, wild herds of horses roamed the prairies and the Indians learned to capture and control them long before the white man appears. A Comanche Indian youth was taught to ride from childhood and for this reason the Comanches, because of their superb horsemanship, were frequently termed the "Cossacks of the Plains."

The Indian villages were more or less temporary affairs. They were moved from place to place as the season changed, following the wild game upon which the Indians depended for a living. Southwest Oklahoma, because of its abundance of game, was a favorite hunting ground for several tribes and frequently hunting war parties clashed. Sometimes there weren't any hard feelings but sometimes things would get serious.

The little Indian boys of early days were taught to ride horses very young. They were told to ride behind an older man and kill a buffalo with a bow and arrow. They must learn the exact location of the heart of the buffalo, then they ride in a circle around the buffalo and the boy shoots it, then he is taught how to skin and prepare it to eat.

Allen Mihecaby, Comanche
Vol. 36, pp. 259–61

CADDOS

The Caddo Indians always bred the best horses on the reservation. The Caddos were also great hunters. They would band together and hunt mostly on foot, as they were nearly all fast runners. I remember one time when a band of Caddos were going hunting down in the Wichita Mountains. They came into the store to buy the equipment they were going to take with them. Now the Caddos wore soft-soled moccasins and before they started on the hunt they came into the store to buy some extra soles to put on their moccasins. They each bought two pair of stiff soles so if one pair wore out in running down their game they would put on another sole. Their soft sole moccasins would not have lasted long on the rocks in the mountains. The way the Caddos would do they would run down their game on foot, and when they got the game cornered they would all rush in and make the kill.

R. L. Boake, White Merchant in Wichita and Caddo Territory

Vol. 90, pp. 403–10

COMANCHES

I was born in Texas and my parent died when I was a small boy. I came to western Oklahoma when a small boy, and the Comanche chief, Quanah Parker, adopted me and called me his son. I learned to speak the Comanche language and know it fluently now. I was interpreter for the Agency many years. . . .

Quanah Parker, my father, fed a great many Comanche Indians. He had a great herd of cattle and horses in 1890 and when he died in 1911, he did not have many left because he was so generous. When a person became hungry, he fed them. He could not stand to see anyone of his tribe go hungry.

I was a close personal friend of Herman Lehmann, a white boy of Texas, whom the Indians captured when he was nine years old and kept nine years. He and I had lots of fun together. We were about the same age. He wrote a book in 1900, entitled *Nine Years Among the Comanches.* He was allotted land in the Big Pasture near Grandfield and is now in Texas. I remember going on a big hunt into Texas with Quanah Parker, Herman Lehmann, and Tuck Locke, another white man who was raised with the Comanches. We killed a number of deer and buffalo, and the Comanches dried the meat and sold the hides.

Knox Beal, Adopted Comanche

Vol. 72, pp. 193–96

Farming

WICHITAS

We raise corn, pumpkin, sweet potato. I don't know where we got corn, probably given to my people four hundred years ago. Other Indians didn't know how to work, to raise corn and pumpkins. They would have to get this from Wichitas. Other tribes—Kiowas, Comanches, Apaches would trade us horses for corn. When we cut corn off the cob we would use clams for knives. Clams like you get out of river. We had no knives like we have now. I used to have all those things we used then, but since my wife died I have lost everything. We would cook corn with shucks on and when cool we would cut the corn off. Then let dry for three or four days, then put in cache and it would last for years. Funny how we raise pumpkins. We would take strings and seed out of pumpkin and plait and braid it and hang up for four days and let get dry. It would last about four years. When we had no meat we would eat pumpkin for meat. They would put it in corn and cook it. It was sure good. We also raise lots of sweet potatoes, great big long ones. We would make a meal out of corn. Put corn in a pot to boil to soften then take it out and wash it good. Then we would get long oak stick to use as pounder. Then we would make corn bread out of meal. It was better meal than we get now. This work was all done by women.

We would bury pumpkins, corn and sweet potatoes in the ground. We would dig a big hole in ground, small around the top but big at bottom. It was big enough in the bottom for you to lay down in. Then we would put stuff in buffalo hide made like a sack. Then we would bury this, and stick grass up all around and you could not tell anything was buried there. Sometimes leave it there for long time. Then when we go back to get it, it is just as good as when we put it in. No water can get down to it. One thing Wichita never do is to tell anyone but a Wichita where he hide stuff. For other tribes would come and steal it. One time in about 1901 or 1902 I come in to town in the spring and asked Mr. Hammert (local merchant) if he wanted to buy some sweet potatoes. He said yes. He didn't think I had any. I had them buried in cache in buffalo hide and they had been there for quite a while. When I brought them in he was surprised. He gave me $3.50 a bushel for them and said if I had any more, he would buy them. I took money home and give to wife, because she done the work.

Jay Johnson, Wichita
Vol. 31, pp. 243–51

WICHITAS AND CADDOS

The rations received by the Wichitas and Affiliated Bands were supplemented by the vegetables, field crops and some livestock. The Wichitas at that time raised small patches of corn, mostly squaw corn,[3] sweet potatoes, pumpkins, peas, beans, watermelons and some of the men had a few range cattle and many families had small herds of ponies. The Caddos and Delawares raised about the same kind of crops as the Wichitas but a few of the Caddos raised more cattle than the Wichitas.

The corn they raised was nearly all used by the Indians as food. Most of the Indian families dried some corn for winter use and stored some corn for bread. They pounded the corn with a pestle in the end of a round block of wood about three or four feet long set on the ground. In the top end of the round block, there was a basin about six inches deep, four inches at the top and about three inches in diameter at the bottom and by placing shelled corn in the basin it could soon be pounded to pieces or into a coarse meal which the Indians could make into the form of mush or bread. Most of the Indian homes were provided with the block and pestle to use in making the coarse meal out of their corn.

Pumpkins and squashes were important foods among these tribes and were used in the Fall as long as the Indians could keep them well and would dry a good supply for winter use. To dry the pumpkins, they would cut them into long strips and hang the strips on the poles, they usually were plaited into strips about one foot wide and twelve or fifteen feet long and wrapped in a cloth or put into a flour sack and stored away for future use. Corn was cut from the cob and dried and put away for winter use also and the Wichitas had a way of keeping sweet potatoes through the winter in good condition for food and seed. Most of the Indians raised squaw corn at that time and most of it was saved for food.

Walter Ross, a Wichita, raised a six or seven acre field of field corn of a very early variety each year. He plowed up his land and check-rowed his corn so that it could be cultivated two ways and he usually thinned the corn to one stalk in a hill. By the proper preparation of the land and thorough cultivation of his corn he raised a fair yield each year. There were a few of the Caddos and Delawares who did about as well as Walter Ross in farming at that time.

By far the larger part of the work that was done in agricultural work by the Indians was done by the women. In much of their planting, it was customary for the Indians to make a hole in the soil for the seed, with a stick or hoes and then drop the seed and push the dirt over it with their feet. Most of the Indians cultivated the small crops which they raised with a hoe.

In 1931, accompanied by my wife, I visited the home of Kih-Kih, a Keechi woman who at that time was seventy-six years of age and we found her planting a part of her garden. She had a small bucket with seeds in it and was digging holes with a hoe, dropping her seed in the holes and then pushing the dirt over them with her feet. We went into her home and she showed us a good quantity of dried pumpkin which she had stored away from the crop of the previous year, dried corn and a flour sack of acorns which she said she hulled and then pounded the kernels to a kind of a meal and made the meal into a mush or bread. Kih-Kih is the last of the Keechi tribe of Indians who speaks the Keechi language. The Keechi tribe has been absorbed by the Wichitas and the Indians who possessed Keechi blood, with the exception of this woman, speak the Wichita language, if they speak any Indian language.

Up until 1925 Kih-Kih had lived in grass houses and tepees but her home at that time was nearly ready to fall down and she lived alone for many years. She called at my office and informed me that she very much wanted a small house of the kind the white people lived in but she was thought to be too old to live alone far from her friends and relatives, so arrangements were made for the purchase of one acre of land from Hearty Stephens, a Wichita and distant relative of Kih-Kih, and a neat frame plastered house was constructed for her within about sixty yards from the home of Hearty Stephens. When the house was completed Kih-Kih moved into it and cultivated each year the acre of land, raising some corn, potatoes, pumpkin, squashes, beans, peas and so forth and she lived alone in her home which she kept reasonably neat for a woman her age and the rentals from her allotment provided her with enough to pay her living expenses.

John A. Buntin, White Teacher at Riverside Indian School
Vol. 89, pp. 319–53

Food and Cooking

CADDOS

I was born in the Chickasaw Nation, near Tishomingo, about 1884. My father died when I was about a year old, and when I was about five years old my mother died, and my grandfather came from the Caddo reservation and took me back there to live with him and my grandmother.

The next year or two after going to live with my grandparents, I started school at the Baptist Mission, near Anadarko. I believe Mr. Wilkins was in charge of the Mission at that time.

James Davis, my grandfather, and Molly Davis, my grandmother, were both Caddos and they drew their rations, at the agency in Anadarko. The

Agency is still there. We lived in a box house with a shingle roof. We carried our water from a spring not far from the house.

I have seen my grandmother roast corn over an open fire. When the corn was in the milk, an ear of corn would be laid next to the fire and when one side was roasted, the corn would be turned over, and the other side roasted. After the corn was done, it was shelled and put in a sack and kept in a dry place. The corn would keep indefinitely and was usually cooked with fresh meat or maybe boiled by itself. The corn had a delicious flavor from the wood-smoke used in roasting it.

My grandmother also made hominy and pa-sho-fa of corn. She burned green hickory wood and saved the ashes. These ashes were put into a pan and then water was poured over them, and the water was caught and used to boil corn in. The water contained lye out of the ashes and made the husk come off the corn. After the husk had boiled off the corn, the corn was washed, and cooked in a pot of fresh meat of some kind. The mixture was called pa-sho-fa.

My grandmother also made what we called roasting ear bread. When the corn was in the milk, she would grate it, and make it into bread.

We had a few neighbors that we divided our garden truck with or if our neighbors had garden truck which matured before ours, they would divide with us.

The Indians always divided with each other.

Aaron Hamilton, Caddo-Chickasaw
Vol. 27, pp. 223–25

COMANCHES

All Indian houses had tepees near them.... [T]he women built arbors which were made of poles and willow brush. Here the Indians lived through the summer. Their houses were clean and they were pretty clean with their cooking. The Indian women would cut beef in small pieces and dry it, then they would take a knot off a Post Oak tree which was called a bole. The dried beef was pounded until it resembled corn silk. This was called "tiho." Another way the beef was prepared was to cut the fat into small pieces, mix it thoroughly with sugar and a little flour, and fry it for a short while. Lots of Indians ate kidneys raw, but when cooked they wanted them cooked well done. Most of their bread was bought bread and they used crackers as bread some. Later they made bread from wheat flour called grease bread which tasted pretty good. Steak was cut in small squares, fried and gravy was made in with this meat. Indians are fond of fruit, cookies and candy.

Mrs. John Barnes, White Resident of Comanche Territory
Vol. 66, pp. 131–40

CADDOS, COMANCHES, AND KIOWAS

Beef was the main food. When steers were killed in the summertime, part of the beef was usually dried. The Kiowas and Comanches cut the beef in strips one inch wide and about an inch thick. These strips were then hung by ropes or in trees, in the sun.

The Caddos cut the meat they dried in big thin slabs, just as thin as it could be cut; for instance if they had a piece of beef eight or ten inches square, they would cut a slab the full width of the meat, then turn the meat over and cut a thin slab off that side, and in this manner the slab of meat would sometimes be one and half or two feet long, and eight or ten inches wide. This would then be hung on a rope, or sticks, and turned over once or twice a day. It usually took about three or four days to dry, depending on the weather. The meat would keep indefinitely when dried, and was good to eat raw. I have eaten lots of it raw. The Caddos usually roasted beef on coals of fire, then put it in a mortar and pounded it up with a pestle and it was then put into a cooking utensil with a little water and boiled. It was then called hash.

The Kiowas and Comanches usually ate the meat roasted. Sometimes fresh meat would be roasted on a green stick that was sharpened at both ends. This stick would be stuck in the ground so that when the meat was put on the other end it would be over the fire, and this would be moved several times so that the meat would be cooked thoroughly on both sides.

The Caddos would often gather summer plums a little while before they were ripe and dry them. Later, the plums were boiled and sweetened, before eating. They also gathered and dried wild grapes. These wild grapes would shrivel up until it looked like there was nothing to them but when they were boiled, the juice would come out of them and this juice was used to make grape dumplings.

The Indians made their spoons out of the lower part of the buffalo horn. It curved so that it made a very good spoon and there would be a notch cut around the handle part of the spoon and a string tied around it, so that it could be carried.

Mrs. Sarah Ellen Virginia Cannon, my grandmother, used to sew for the Indians, and in exchange for her work was given plates and dishes.

Fannie Hudson Crowell, White Resident of Caddo Territory
Vol. 30, pp. 56–58

COMANCHES

The Indians' principal food is beef. Not one of them would eat pork. Many times the older Indians came in to see me while they were in town. It was pretty hard for me to get acquainted with Indians but when I did make friends and learn to talk with them, they would come to my house and eat with us. Once quite a few Indians were eating at our house and I passed a dish to them, grunting, meaning it was hog meat. From that day every time I see Tamvanah, or widow, she will grunt like a hog and laugh. I have two nieces who married Comanche Indians, one Clinton Red Elk, and one Buster Work-a-wam. One of my nephews married Florida Nida.

Mrs. John Barnes, White Resident of Comanche Territory
Vol. 66, pp. 131–40

Houses

CADDOS

There are three different kinds of houses that were used by the Caddos. The log cabin, the grass house, and the bark house. All of the Caddo houses were oblong and all faced east. The log cabins were very much like a white person's with doors on any side, but always one in the east and west. The grass house differs from the Wichitas' by having a door in both the east and west, while theirs have only the one in the east and their houses were round. The Caddos also had openings rather high up on the north and south for air. The bark wasn't really made of bark but it was roofed with bark. The walls were made of split logs stood on end and plastered with clay and cattail reeds. These reeds were ground to a pulp and mixed with clay. On the top of the house there was a frame made of slippery elm and on this the bark was fastened.

The bark had to be well seasoned. It had to be kept flat while seasoning so it wouldn't warp. It usually took several months for the bark to season. These houses had doors only in the east and west. The doors to the houses were made of cedar if it could be gotten, if not they used dogwoods.

The beds were stationary. Four pronged sticks were driven in the ground for the posts, then four poles of cedar, if possible, if not then dogwoods were used for the sides and ends of the bed. After these were in place small poles about one and one and a half inches in diameter were used for the bottom of the bed. These were woven together with the slippery elm inner bark. When this was finished the whole thing was covered with buffalo hides. Sometimes the hide was so heavy and thick that it was as soft as if a mattress was on it. In the winter, sometimes, they would use hides as covers, turning the hairy side down. The pillows were stuffed with cattails, cotton from the cottonwood berries, feathers from wild geese, ducks, prairie chickens and other wild fowl.

Matting for floor coverings was made from cattail leaves woven together.

Mrs. Frank Cussins, Caddo
Vol. 21, pp. 376–88

KIOWAS AND COMANCHES

Every tent had its arbor. Usually this was in front of the tent. Sometimes there was one off from the tent. In warm, dry weather here was where you found the general activities of the Indian family. They would cook, eat, and sometimes sleep under these arbors.

The arbor was made of young willow limbs driven into the ground at intervals and drawn together at the top and fastened, then more brush was piled onto this until it was almost waterproof. The larger arbors were made with large poles set at the corners, and the brush piled on a frame work made on these poles.

A shallow hole was made in the ground where they made their cook fire. Over this fire a kettle was hung in which they cooked their meat or other boiled food. In olden times they had no ovens, so cooked their bread on top of Dutch ovens. They never rolled their bread and cut it. They patted it between their hands, sometimes flipping it back and forth until it was of the desired thickness, then laid it on the hot Dutch oven. Their early diet consisted mostly of meat. When they had a surplus supply of meat they dried it.

They sliced it in strips and hung it over a pole in the open air to dry. This is also called "jerked meat." The old Indians used to eat dogs. A nice fat puppy was a very delicate dish. Once in a while they ate a horse, but not very often.

They had no tables but spread an oilcloth or canvas on the ground and sat around that. When the weather was bad all these activities went on inside the tepee or tent, with the fire in the center of the tepee. The smoke escaped through the top of the tepee where there was an opening for this purpose.

Lillian Gassaway, White Daughter of J. J. Methvin, Missionary to the Kiowas and
    Comanches
Vol. 25, pp. 416–18

TONKAWAS

The Tonkawa Indians lived in cabins during the winter months and moved into tepees during the Spring and Summer months, in the early days in this part.

G. L. Gilkeson, White Resident of Tonkawa Territory
Vol. 105, pp. 367–74

WICHITAS

It was woman's work to build grass houses. They would pray before they start building it, and then pray when finished. This was to keep evil spirits away. All houses built facing the east. This way we can see enemy when they come and make get-away. Those grass houses sure fine to live in. Better than tent. My first wife she went to St. Louis in 1904 to build grass house at World's Fair.[4] There is only one grass house left in this country. It is over by Camp Creek or it was there the last time I was over there.

Jay Johnson, Wichita
Vol. 31, pp. 243–51

CADDOS AND COMANCHES

The Indian women built their houses and did all of the work while the men hunted. The houses were covered with bark. They would peel the red oak bark from the tree, let it dry, and cover the house with the bark side up. They usually traveled in wagons and sometimes the line would be five miles long.

When they camped, the men spread a blanket under the wagon and went to sleep, and the squaw would take care of the team, gather firewood and cook the meals.

Henry Beaty, White Resident of Caddo Territory
Vol. 14, pp. 126–37

CADDOS

There were quite a few Caddo Indians about three miles north of us on Boggy Creek bottom; they were good people and did not bother any one. I visited their homes several times.

The Indians' winter home, made of grass, was indeed very strange in appearance. They were round and the grass was closely woven; snow or rain did not penetrate; they were warm too. There was a hole in the center for smoke to escape. There was, also, a hole dug in the floor in the center of the room about three feet in diameter and one foot deep. This answered for two purposes—they heated the room and cooked here too. There were two good size limbs with forked tops about two feet high above the ground, on either side of this pit, with a pole across of iron. From this they suspended their pots in which they boiled their meat, corn and so forth. All that I ever saw were very neat and clean. I remarked to one of these Caddo women, "You do not have very much furniture," She replied in broken English, "We have all we need."

In the summer they lived out under brush arbors; their children always went to some Indian school; most of them, near us, would send their children to the Catholic Mission School, on the Washita River near Anadarko.

Mary Forgay Holmes, White Resident of Caddo Territory
Vol. 5, pp. 144–49

KIOWAS AND CADDOS

In 1903 and 1904, I picked cotton near Carnegie in the Kiowa country. The Kiowa Indians lived mostly in tepees. There were holes in the tops of the tepee to let the smoke out, and their fires were built in the center of the tepee. The smoke would drift out of the tops of the tepees without smoking the tepee at all. Just a small fire would keep a tepee warm. The Indians had blankets which they slept on and covered themselves with in the winter.

I picked cotton on the north side of the Washita River, in the Caddo country, late in the fall of 1903. The Caddos' homes were more substantial, and permanent, being made of small poles set up perpendicularly and the cracks between the posts were daubed up with clay. The roofs were of board shingles which were made with a frow.[5]

Nearly all the Indians who lived around us had small patches of corn and a few pumpkins and beans.

Lee Forest, Black Worker in Kiowa and Caddo Territory
Vol. 109, pp. 115–17

Dress

CADDOS

The women always wore their hair in two braids down their back and tied together at the end. The young girls and women wore the earrings of half moon shape. The old women wore flat earrings.

There were three general styles of dress. The one piece dress, the two piece dress for the younger women and the two piece dress for the old women. The one piece dress is what we used to call a Mother Hubbard. A full loose dress gathered onto a yoke across the shoulders, with long sleeves. The skirts are long, just barely missing the floor. Over these full, long skirts they wear a full, long apron tied around the waist.

The two piece dress for the younger women is a full gathered skirt on a narrow band. All skirts come to the floor, with a waist apron of the same length. The waist is made opened down the front with some kind of pins with fancy ornaments to fasten it. The waist hangs a little loose. This also has long sleeves. There is a deep round collar and around this is a ruffle. There are fancy ornaments around the edge of this ruffle.

The two piece dress for the older women is more simple. The skirt is the same as the other but the waist fits tighter and has no fancy trimmings or ornaments.

All dresses may have ribbon stitched around the hem, sometimes several rows. The young women wear lots of beads. A very long strand is roped around the neck several times, making a very heavy necklace. As they grow older they wear fewer beads until the old women wear only one strand or possibly none.

Every one wears leggings made of red flannel. The leggings for the women were made in one piece, with a flap about four inches wide down the side. These flaps were about two inches shorter than the legging, this is so the moccasin would fit over the legging at the ankle. Those worn for every day were plain, but those used for special occasions were decorated with beadwork. The leggings for the men were made just a little different. The flaps were made separate and sewed on. At the seam there were beads and the edge of the flap was fringed.

The Caddos used only buckskin for their moccasins. Other tribes sometimes used rawhide but the Caddos never did. They beaded them across the toe and up the seam at the back of the heel. The design on the toe is a formation of nine diamonds, and the design on the flap around the ankle of the moccasin is usually an oak leaf with an edging of beadwork. A simple design is on the back of the heel.

Mrs. Frank Cussins, Caddo
Vol. 21, pp. 376–88

CADDOS AND DELAWARES

Nearly all Delaware people are related in some way. There are only about two hundred of us left and a lot of us are mixed with the Caddo Indians. One reason we are so few is that so many of the Delaware Indians have intermarried with the Caddos and eventually went with the Caddo tribe.

My mother used to wear the regular Indian dress but we children kept after her to change to the white man's dress. My father also used to dress like the Indians and had peyote feasts, but have persuaded him to stop and now we live like the white people.

Leona Parton, Delaware
Vol. 93, pp. 54–58

COMANCHES

The Indian women wore dresses made with straight sleeves not sewed up at all and of two pieces, one on each side, sometimes the dress would be longer in front, sometimes longer in the back. One would never see an Indian baby out of his cradle board. This was something made of skins of animals, about two feet in length, made of round shape getting smaller at one end.

The Indian baby is placed on his cradle board, laced in tightly, which makes the baby think he is being held close in his mother's arms. Then the cradle board is strapped on the Indian woman's back and she can go about doing her work.

Mrs. John Barnes, White Resident of Comanche Territory
Vol. 66, pp. 131–40

COMANCHES

One Comanche girl made my little girl an Indian dress like the Comanches wore. It was very similar to the Kiowas and Apache dresses, except the square piece that is wrapped around the waist and called the apron was trimmed with ribbon, almost as narrow as baby ribbon. There were several rows of ribbon around the bottom of the apron and the bottom of the dress, also the sleeves, which were only straight strips the desired length and the necessary width, sewed into the very large arm hole. Sometimes there would be three or four rows of this trimming.

Mrs. W. R. Pulis, White Resident of Anadarko
Vol. 70, pp. 395–97

Household Arts and Crafts

CADDOS

The pottery was made from the different colored clays. The clay was mixed with pulverized mussel shells. There are several different colors of clay. Part of our colors come from these, others are from the different trees and roots. I don't know the names of them all, but I know some of them when I see them. Pokeberry and cottonwood were used for dark dyes, then there are different roots that I don't know the names of. Most of our pottery was used for cooking and carrying water.

The Caddo Indians always raised corn, pumpkins, and sweet potatoes. They also made their own by-products of corn. In making their meal they needed a sifter, so they make baskets woven so closely that they could be used for sifters. Then they made the coarser ones for heavier work.

Mrs. Frank Cussins, Caddo
Vol. 21, pp. 376–88

The different woods used to make baskets are: willow, hackberry, slippery elm, dogwood, cat-tail, swamp grall, soap weed or bear grass. Hackberry was used mostly for sifting corn and washing lye hominy. There were three standard grades. Each basket had a special purpose. The reason the hackberry is used most is because it has no bad taste. Most of the others have a bad taste, and baskets made from them are used as containers.

Dyes for these baskets are made from the bark of the slippery elm, blackjack, walnut leaves and bark, pokeberry, and elderberry. There are some roots, but I don't know them very well.

This is used mostly for cooking and containers. Many of these pots are lined with dipper gourds, the biggest used for dipping. Closely woven baskets are used for cold things. There is a filler of some kind but I never found out what it is. Some are filled with tallow, then fired. The dyes for this pottery are made from red clay, yellow clay, black clay, and blue clay, also white clay. All these clays are obtained from the river. Each clan had its own shape to make its pottery. One clan never thought of making anything the same pattern of another clan. You could tell who made the pottery by the shape.

After the clay is pulverized it is sifted through this fine basket, then crushed. Shell is added and a mud is made of this combination. Then it is molded and sundried and baked. But it must be polished before it is baked with a certain stone. Some baked them in ashes but the best results were those baked in buffalo manure.

There are two classes of beadwork, the patch and laid work. In the patchwork a few beads are taken on the needle at a time and fastened down to the material. The laid work is similar to our applique, it is done on thread and then laid on the material and appliqued on. It is lots more accurate than the patchwork. Laid work is used on moccasins, and patchwork is used on hand bags, hat bands, tobacco pouches, belts, leggings, moccasins, deer tail, and picture frames. The patterns were taken from nature, from the tree leaves and such things. Each family had its own designs. The best bead workers used both the patch and laid patterns and it was hard to tell which was which. On these they never used a coarse bead, always the finest they could get. It has been said that the Caddos never had buckskin suits. That is a mistake. They did have them and they were made in two pieces.

The Caddos used to have bead necklaces. After they stopped wearing necklaces they had lace collars made of beads. These ranged from one strand to sixteen inches wide. Each person had his own design. These were made of coarser beads, and were made for women to be worn for celebrations. Fewer beads were worn for every day.

Much of this beadwork had ribbons combined with it. And as a rule each family had its own design. No two blankets were alike, as in everything else everyone had his own design. A considerable number of beads were used on the edges of the blankets. These were of the coarser beads.

Ribbons were used on the soft soled flaps of moccasins which were made all in one piece. These were used only by the woods Indians, such as the Caddos, Delawares, and northern Indians. Among these tribes you can't tell the difference except in designs. It used to be that you could buy a blanket and suit complete for one horse in trade. Now a pair of moccasins will cost you $10.00.

The first thing after killing the animal the hide is stretched, with the raw side up, by stakes, stretching the hide tight, then all remaining flesh is removed down to the true skin, then taken down and soaked in ash solution. Later, after it is dry, it is laid on a clean log which is leaned up in two poles forming a fork, and is scraped with an instrument made out of a deer antler until all of the hair is off. Later, this tool was made out of bone or metal. Then it is taken and cleaned. Brains of a beef or buffalo are taken and boiled in water then strained, the liquid is used to clean the skin. Then it is hung on poles to dry, after which a rope is fastened to each corner and stretched on poles to dry. After it is dry and softened it is taken and the ends sewed together, making a bag. This is then slipped over three small poles, wrong side out, for it is the outside that you are tanning, over a hole about two feet deep, and smoked. Dead wood or cobs were used for the fire smoking, cobs giving the best results. This smoking gives the buckskin a dark finish. The Caddos never used the raw buckskin. After it is smoked it is ready for use. When the buckskin became soiled it was cleaned with brains boiled in water and strained. This solution gave the best results. Ash solution was used for moccasins. This keeps the buckskin soft.

The dyes are made by boiling the bark of certain trees in water and straining. The material is soaked in this water until the desired color is gotten.

The Caddos have their own silversmiths. They got their silver in Mexico. They made earrings, bracelets, etc. These also are made with designs of the clan that has made them. The Caddos are very particular about their designs. They never use one that another clan used.

Sadie Bedoka, Caddo-Delaware

Vol. 53, pp. 14–22

CADDOS

I have attended many Indian dances, a good many when I was small, and I always thought the Caddos' costumes, very beautiful. The women wore black wool shawls bordered with silk fringe, bright colored dress, beaded moccasin, silver bracelets, gold earrings with silver combs in their hair, and beads around their necks. Of course, all of the shawls were not black, but I thought them the prettiest.

The Caddo men wore beaded moccasins, pants made of black broadcloth, with a broad flange about six inches wide that stuck out on the side of the pant leg. This flange was beaded with different colored beads in different designs. Their shirts were usually of black calico, trimmed around the cuffs and down the front, with red or some other bright color. They also wore earrings and flat beaded necklaces about an inch and a half wide, tied around their necks. The beads of the necklace were always strung on horse hair as the horse hair made the necklace stand up straight, instead of wrinkling as it would have done if the beads had been strung on thread.

Some of the Kiowas and Comanche men painted their faces and breasts with powdered red and white clay. The white clay was dug out of the banks of rivers and creeks and the red clay was gotten at the edge of rivers. This red clay was usually in little round balls, about the size of a hen's egg. These clay balls were dried and beaten into a powder.

At the Indian dances a good many families would have brush arbors. These brush arbors were made by making a framework, the size of the arbor desired, out of forked poles, which was then covered with green boughs.

Mrs. I. V. Davis, Caddo

Vol. 31, pp. 395–98

CADDOS AND COMANCHES

The Caddos and Comanches made a perfume with a very strong odor that could be smelled for fifty yards. The older ones wore a silver ring in their noses and had holes pierced completely around their ears, with a ring in each hole.

Henry Beaty, White Resident of Caddo Territory
Vol. 14, pp. 126–37

COMANCHES

Tanning animal hides by the Indians was of great importance, as they used hides for so many different things. The Indians would take a new hide, let it dry a few days, then when it seemed to be drying through they would kill other animals and take the brains from them and rub them thoroughly on the underside after they had chiseled the hair off the other with a sharp, pointed rock. Working the brains over the hide was called curing it and this caused the hide to become soft. From this moccasins were made. They also cut the soft side in narrow strips, using these for string.

Bert Montague, White Resident of Comanche Territory
Vol. 108, pp. 368–75

Camp and Home Life

KIOWAS AND COMANCHES

The Indian dress was very suitable to their mode of living. Their narrow skirts with the extra straight piece of material, called an apron, wrapped around and tucked in at the waist line. This apron prevented the wind blowing their dresses into the fire.

Where there was a small baby in the family you would usually find an improvised hammock for it, made of a blanket or shawl wrapped over two ropes, hanging on two poles under the arbor or between two trees.

In the evening by the camp fire, the family gathered and told stories. This was when the legends were told. The Indians were great entertainers and story tellers.

The men were always considered the hunters and warriors; so never did anything around the camp. The women did all the work even to taking care of the horses, and putting up and taking down the tepees and tents.

Their early mode of travel was horseback, on foot, hauling their tepees and other things in a travois. Later there were wagons and two seated hacks.

Now most of the Indians have cars, and you seldom see a hack, but there are a few wagons yet.

Lillian Gassaway, White Daughter of J. J. Methvin, Methodist Missionary to the Kiowas
    and Comanches
Vol. 25, pp. 416–18

COMANCHES

The Indian women were known to do all the work. They made beautiful arbors but the men are taking more interest in the living affairs now-a-days. It was a common thing to see from one to ten dogs following behind an Indian's buggy or hack.

Little Indian boys were trained at an earlier age than girls. Both are taught to swim early and at about six years of age the boys are put on horses without saddles and with only a bridle made of dried skin and made to learn to ride real fast. The boys are taught mostly by their mothers to make bows and arrows.

Once in 1907 my husband and I went fishing west of Cache. Here we met some of our Indian friends. We were laughing and talking not noticing the children much when a little Indian boy fell into the deep water. I was sure he would drown but soon he came up swimming to the bank. He was about four or five years old and was wearing only a little long shirt such as little boys wore in the earlier days. Now this boy is married, has a family and a nice home near here.

Mrs. John Barnes, White Resident of Comanche Territory
Vol. 66, pp. 131–40

COMANCHES AND KIOWAS

The main trouble was that the Indians would take what the whites had to eat, as the Indians used Government supplies and they were always limited. However, the Indians never killed anyone. They felt that the white man was trespassing on their reserve and for that reason they took his supplies of food.

The mode of living of the Indians was to gather in small groups of seventy-five to two hundred in camps scattered over the reserve. Each camp had as its leader some chief, and at that time the Indians lived in tepees. Their women or squaws, as they called them, did all the work, such as getting wood for fuel, pulling grass for their beds, tearing down and moving tepees from one locality to another.

The Indian mode of travel in those days was by pack horses. Their tepees and tepee poles, which consisted of two or four poles to each tepee, were placed in equal numbers on each side of the pack horse and dragged along as shelves.

The only work done by the bucks, or men, was killing antelope or stealing beef. This food was usually eaten raw or partly dried in the sun. The Indians never wasted any part of anything they killed. There were times when they ate wolves and even their dogs. Indian bucks sometimes had from three to eight wives; the braves acquired their wives by trading horses for them.

In those days the Indians had what they called Medicine Men. If any of the tribe was sick the other Indians made music by beating drums. They drank much mescal and they would sometimes drink this mescal prior to making cattle raids.

The Indians were great gamblers, especially on horse racing and games of monté bank.

The bucks usually rode bareback and always mounted from the right side. The squaws used small wooden frames shaped like saddles, over which blankets were thrown. When the men hunted antelope, they used a trained horse to go in front with a red blanket on it. The attention of the antelope would be attracted by the red blanket, and the Indians taking advantage of the wind were able to get close enough to kill one or two antelope which before were out of range of their guns.

The Indians never had any trouble among themselves in their own tribes and it was the duty of the chief to give his tribe names in their own language for all articles such as wagons, horses used by the whites, as the chief was the supreme ruler and guide of his tribe.

The fact that Indians believed in a Hereafter was shown in their mode of burial. Indians were buried in the mountains among large rocks. All the Indian's earthly possessions, such as saddles, blankets, beads and trinkets were buried with them. I have a number of times found skeletons of Indians beside which were remnants of saddles, guns and other things which had been placed there so that the departed Indian might use them in the Happy Hunting Grounds to which he was supposed to go after death.

Newt Stroud, White Cowboy in Comanche and Kiowa Territory
Vol. 68, pp. 148–56

Games

CADDOS

The girls played very little after they got old enough to begin to learn to work. They only played shinny once in a while with the boys.[6] But they must learn to work, and do everything about the home.

The boys played a great deal like boys of today. They played marbles, only they had to make their marbles out of clay. Tops were made out of the little yellow briar berries. A stick is pushed through them and the point sharpened. These would spin very nicely. The boys had a game where each boy would get so many sticks, then the boy whose top would spin the longest got a stick from each of the other boys. The boy winning all the sticks won the game. There was a game very similar to the polo that is played now, only the mallets were longer. They played shinny. It was played with a ball made of buckskin and stuffed with cattails or the cotton from the cottonwood berries. The shinny sticks were something like golf sticks, but were small branches of trees or bushes cut so that the base of the limb forms the club. The boys would choose sides and each side would try to put the ball across its goal. They had all kinds of sports: broad jumps, foot races, horse races and so on. These were the amusements when the Indians from different localities were gathered together. At these gatherings each band would camp to itself, keeping the band intact. In these contests the loser had to give a feast for the winners.

When the boys reached early manhood they had to stop playing or taking part in the sports. He had to begin to learn how to hunt and make crops. All boys and girls are trained to make homes, so they will make desirable mates. When a boy makes his first kill, he never gets it. He must give it to the oldest man in the crowd, even if it is just a rabbit.

Mrs. Frank Cussins, Caddo
Vol. 21, pp. 376–88

COMANCHES

A few of the games in my girlhood were, for the women, "Kicking ball." The ball was kicked from the toe to the opposite knee, then to the toe, from that toe to the opposite knee while the girl or woman was walking. The person kicking the ball the farthest distance without dropping it, won the game. Some could kick the ball about one hundred and fifty feet without making a mistake.

For the boys and men, shooting arrows, making bows and arrows, and foot racing.

Emily Riddles, Comanche
Vol. 82, pp. 41–44

WICHITAS

Shinney they call it. Played with crooked sticks, stick like white man play golf with. We use round balls. Always have big crowd at shinney games. Before they would start the game all players would get out in center of field. There would be a man to talk to them. He was the umpire. I don't know what he say. Then he would throw ball up in air and game would start. One side would hit the ball one way and the other side would go the other. All us kids would get together at the end of field and watch game. Everybody would yell. We no play game dirty. We no hit one another on shin. Sometime they make mistake and hit another player, but they don't mean to do it. Women also played games but I forgot what kind of game they played. We would also have lots of foot races when the hunters came in from hunts. Then we also had to run twice a month. The men would run five miles and the kids two miles. We would always run at day-break. We run these races so that if some other tribe attacked us we could make get-away and save our lives. Old Indians would tell us kids that "Indians who can't run is dead Indians." Sometimes I get awful tired but father tell me keep on going, maybe so get second breath. Sometimes my legs sure sore, but I keep on running. We never know when we run whether it is practice or real. They would just give a signal at day-break, and we would all jump up and start running. We no wear many clothes then. Just a breech-cloth, and our bodies were painted bright colors. The real old men would ride behind us on horses, and tell us to keep running. The last run we has was in 1908 about two miles from Camp Creek.

Jay Johnson, Wichita
Vol. 31, pp. 243–51

WICHITAS

Mrs. Gladys Miller is an intelligent Wichita Indian, she has a good education for an Indian. The family lives in a frame house and while they do not have much furniture in their home, they cook on a range and can fruit and vegetables. This is what she told regarding the game (see last illustration in photo section):

◆ ◆ ◆

Mrs. Miller called this the dice game for want of a better name. There are two players and they always bet something. It could be money but Mrs. Miller said that usually it was corn bread. There may be four players; in that case, two play as partners. The players each have a bunch of either the purple or orange sticks. There are twenty of each and these are to keep track of the points made by the players. No. 1 takes the four bamboo sticks; holds them tightly together and drops them with some force on a small rock and the way they fall decides the points made by No. 1. If he does not make any points the dice or bamboo sticks go to No. 2 and she tries her luck.

The points are as follows:

Three pink up and blue down .... 10 points
All four sticks falling color side down .... 5 points
The blue up and pink down .... 10 points
One pink up and rest down .... 0 points
One pink and one blue up, others down .... 0 points
All four sticks color side up..................................... 5 points

The sticks are made from tamarack as it has such straight, smooth sticks. The bark is peeled from the branches and the surface colored with some of the paint known to the Indian tribes. The game furnished in this case were painted with water colors as paint is hard to find.

Gladys Miller asked $3.50 for this game saying that the Wichitas are not supposed to give away the knowledge of the tribe.

Gladys Miller, Wichita
Vol. 36, pp. 286–88

COMANCHES

My grandmother was a very fast foot racer. She was the fastest runner in the Comanche tribe. They used to have races and she would run against horses. She could beat all the horses. Of course, these races were not very long races. But the Indians were noted for their endurance. She went with the warriors on a raid one time where there were several killed. She was buried for dead along with the others. In those days they buried the dead in caves and covered them with brush and rocks. Also they buried all the personal possessions along with the body. She had a knife with her, in her clothes somewhere and when she regained consciousness, with the aid of this knife she came out of her "grave" and went back to camp. She had been gone three days and the Indians thought she was her own ghost. She got a spear wound in a raid once that she carried for the rest of her life. My grandmother lived to ripe old age of one hundred and fifteen years. She was known by the name of To-see.

William Karty, Comanche-Spanish
Vol. 78, pp. 164–66

COMANCHES AND KIOWAS

The Indians played many games. They also had many foot and horse races. One of the games played by the Indians was to put a rock or ball like object in one of their hands, and have the other side guess which hand it was in. In case they guessed right they would gain a man; but if the guess was wrong, they would have to give one of their men to the other side.[7] They also had another game in which they used a big hoop. They would throw this hoop in the air and men would try to shoot their arrows through the hoop before it hit the ground. They played many other games which I do not remember.

W. H. Darnold, White Resident of Comanche and Kiowa Territory
Vol. 21, pp. 461–64

The American Indian Exposition[8]

CADDOS, COMANCHES, AND WICHITAS

The American Indian Exposition in Anadarko opened August 18, 1937, with a parade of Indians in full Indian regalia. The Mayor of Anadarko led the parade followed by Jasper Sankeah, the president of the American Exposition Association. Sankeah was in Indian dress with his war bonnet almost reaching the ground in the back, his blanket and moccasins. He was followed by the princess of the Exposition on horseback. She was accompanied by four attendants also on horseback.

The Princess had been chosen a few nights before the fair; there were twenty-five contestants. They were all in beautiful buckskin dresses except one girl who was Wichita. Her dress was of dark material, made after their own tribal costumes.

The women of the Plains Indians were all dressed in buckskin dresses, beaded and fringed. The everyday dress of the Indians is cut similar to the old butterfly pattern of the white women except that the sleeves are straight pieces as long as the sleeve is desired, about eighteen inches wide. These are sewed around the armhole leaving the under arm seam open. Then over this dress is worn a straight piece of material just wrapped around and tucked in at the side front. This dress is always of some dark material, either red or blue and usually calico or print.

The buckskin dresses are beautifully beaded and do not need the apron.

The Caddo women wore their two-piece dress, which consisted of a full skirt with a full length apron, the waist made a deep collar with a ruffle around it. On this collar were ornaments placed around the ruffle. The sleeves were long. These Caddo women wore in their hair a German silver roach comb, which was a circular comb reaching almost around the head with ribbons about four or five inches wide fastened to it. These ribbons reached below the knees of these Caddo women.

Some of the men were in their buckskin suits but most of them were in their dance costumes. These costumes were mostly made of feathers. The men wore feathered headdresses, were bare to the waist with feathered shields tied to their arms about half way above their elbows. Then they wore a shield at their backs. I suppose these shields must have been fastened around the waist. Their legs were bare. Among all the feathers were small sleigh bells.

Augustine Campbell, a Kiowa girl, was chosen princess. She rode a painted pony in the parade as did all her attendants. In fact, almost all the horses ridden by the Indians were painted white with black or brown markings. The horses all had their manes and tails braided and tied with bright ribbons and around their necks there was a strand of small bells.

On the fair grounds are a Kiowa tepee, a Caddo bark house, and a Wichita grass house.

The tepees are made of ducking stretched over a frame work of cedar poles driven into the ground to form a circle. These are brought together at the top and crosses in such a way that they will support each other.

There is an opening at the top of the tepee to let the smoke out, for that and the door are the only openings the tepee has. At this opening there are large points of ducking that are used to control the air circulation. They can be adjusted as desired as they are controlled by long poles outside the tepee. There is an extra piece of ducking fastened over the doorway. A person never knocks for admittance; he or she just raised the flap and walks in.

In the center of the tepee is a hole in the ground for a fire. This is used both for heating purposes and for cooking. Around the sides of the tepee are placed the beds. These beds are made similar to the beds of the Caddos, with four pronged sticks for the legs and corners of the bed with small poles woven together and with the inner bark of slippery elm as the bottom of the bed. The head of the bed was about three feet tall and slanted a little. This was also woven like the bottom.

The bark house is made of logs, standing upright, and the cracks are filled with mud and grass. The house is covered with grass, though the olden houses were covered with bark that had been cured for a season. There was a hole in the center for a fire and the bed was made like the beds of the Kiowas except that it had no head pieces. There was a door in both the east wall and west wall and a little cover over the east door.

The Wichita grass house is round with a door in the east and the hole in the center for a fire and a very small opening near the top for ventilation. All Indian tepees and houses open toward the east, to face the rising sun.

The whole Exposition is being carried out in real Indian style and almost everything is typical of the old Indian custom.

Lillian Gassaway, White Daughter of J. J. Methvin, Missionary to the Kiowas and
    Comanches
Vol. 25, pp. 421–25

The Indian International Fair

PLAINS INDIANS

The Indian International Fair Association was organized in Muskogee, Indian Territory in 1875. . . . At the time the association was organized, the intention of the officials was to make it an enterprise for the eastern part of the territory; but encourage by the interest manifested in the new venture, they decided to make it an international affair and include the western tribes or "Plains Indians. . . ."

The Western or "Wild" tribes of Indians came bringing their herds of ponies with them.[9] The tribes represented were: the Sac and Fox, Comanches, Arapahos, Cheyennes, Shawnees, Osages, and Delawares. The first years they camped on the outside of the enclosure but one night almost all their ponies were stolen and had to be paid for by the Association and that almost bankrupted the treasury.

The Indians brought their own tents and tepees and set them up inside the enclosure as they refused to camp on the outside again. They were a picturesque group with their gaily colored blankets they had woven and their imposing headdress. The headdress of the chief was made of eagle feathers but no one else could wear eagle feathers. Several beeves were always prepared for them, furnished by the association. One beef was slaughtered each morning and divided among them and cooked over their own camp fire. As they all seemed to like their meat rare they never waited until it was well cooked but would eat it was the blood still running out.

The Indians always welcomed visitors to their tepees and it was my delight, as a small child, in company with my little cousins, the Ross children, to wander among their camps. . . .

The women of the "wild" tribes were in a class by themselves as they rode bare-backed and astride. On one occasion when a woman was awarded the prize, she refused to accept a woman's saddle but took a man's saddle.

One of the most attractive things to me was the silver ornaments the men of the wild tribes wore, particularly the chiefs. Crescents, stars, all kinds of emblems cut from pure silver as thin as a knife blade securely attached to a long cord that fastened to their headdress of eagle feathers and hung almost to the ground. I do not know where the silver came from, from which their ornaments were made, but the paints they used on their faces and bodies came from the paint rocks in their own reservations.

They adopted the white man's clothes by degrees. I remember of meeting a big six-foot Osage chief after a hard rain one evening. He was clad in a beaded shirt, black broadcloth trousers, a long linen duster, was barefooted, with a gorgeous string of ornaments fastened to his eagle feather headdress that nearly reached the ground, and with his trousers rolled up, he splashed through the mud.

Ella Robinson, White Resident of Muskogee, Creek Territory
Vol. 52, pp. 396—04

PLAINS INDIANS

The Indian International Fair held in what was then the small town of Muskogee, in 1879, attracted large numbers of people from various sections of Indian Territory and from beyond its borders. . . . There were present at the Fair more Indians than were ever afterward seen on a similar occasion. Besides numbers of Indians of various tribes in the Indian Territory, there were many Indians from distant states and territories, wearing their usual costumes and headdresses. Some of the Indians had paint upon their faces.

On one occasion two Indian women, not members of any of the Five Civilized Tribes, wished to compete in the Ladies Riding Contest and insisted on riding astride; which desire was granted. White women at that time used side saddles in riding.

One of these squaws won the prize which was a side-saddle, which she at once refused and demanded a man's saddle. The committee in charge began taking up a collection of money with which to purchase a man's saddle which was bought and presented to the Indian woman. Immediately, the other Indian woman rider declared that she too deserved a prize as her riding exhibition was equal to that of the rider winning the saddle. Again a sum of money was collected and given to her. To this contestant, during the night following, a daughter was born and was given the name of "Muskogee Fair."

One night during an early Fair the visiting Indians had gone to bed leaving their ponies in the inclosure of the fair-grounds. During the night some horse thieves cut the fence and stole the whole herd of Indian ponies. The Indians were amazed and angry. A sum of money large enough to purchase horses for the Indian's return home was subscribed. The Comanche chief, Toshuway, borrowed a spirited iron gray saddle horse belonging to Joshua Ross, Secretary of the Fair, on which to return home, with the agreement that the horse would be returned to the owner, but Mr. Ross never saw his horse again.

Joseph Martin, White Resident of Muskogee, Creek Territory
Vol. 60, pp. 295–300

Fairs, Celebrations, and Feasts

CADDOS AND COMANCHES

July 4 was always a time of celebration among the Caddo and Comanche tribes and the Indians and white people came to Anadarko for miles to attend this celebration. Every occasion was celebrated with a dance and a feast; after the parade the feast started and in the evening they danced. In 1901 I attended the celebration and one Comanche covered himself and his horse with mud and rode in the parade. I do not know what this custom represented and they celebrated it only occasionally. The Comanche men did not wear trousers, but wore long white shirts reaching their knees.

Henry Beaty, White Resident of Caddo Territory
Vol. 14, pp. 126–37

COMANCHES AND KIOWAS

For amusement we had roping and riding contests in 1889–1890. . . . The Kiowa and Comanche would come to the races and trade beads and moccasins and blankets for goods. They camped around close and stayed until everything was over. Then they would give a war dance. If someone gave them a beef they would kill it and dance around with their shakers for noisy rhythm, and beat on a drum they had made of rawhide. Some of the old Indians would give a war whoop. They called a match a "tido."

L. A. Crabtree, White Resident of Old Greer County[10]
Vol. 21, pp. 134–41

COMANCHES

In 1910 there was a time when we didn't have much to do. Many Indians would come to our house and we would sit on the floor telling jokes. The Indians seem to be quite serious, but when they are in large groups they joke and have lots of fun. Among this circle of Indian friends each one in turn would tell a joke. One said, "Once when they were at church, the preacher asked Mr. Paddiaku if he didn't want to go to Heaven." He replied, "Yes, but I want to go home now," thinking he meant to ask where he wanted to go just then.

Mrs. John Barnes, White Resident of Comanche Territory

Vol. 66, pp. 131–40

COMANCHES

We had what we called a Peanut Carnival up east of Duncan which sometimes lasted for several days and sometimes for a week or two. The Comanche
Indians would come down and camp maybe a hundred in one bunch, they
would put up their tepees all over the place. They were very interested in
learning to plant the peanuts and in the many ways in which peanuts could
be used. The motive of the Peanut Carnival was to try to teach the Indians
the many uses of the peanuts.

Sidney Alonzo Bullard, White Resident of Comanche Territory

Vol. 66, pp. 465–80

Caddo Village. Courtesy Western History Collections, University of Oklahoma Library.

Home of Tawakone Jim, a Wichita Indian chief, northwest of Anadarko, Oklahoma Territory, 1901.
Courtesy Archives and Manuscripts Division of the Oklahoma Historical Society.

Grass House interior. Courtesy Archives and Manuscripts Division of the Oklahoma Historical Society.

Red Horns' summer camp near Anadarko, Oklahoma Territory, c. 1895. Courtesy Archives and Manuscripts Division of the Oklahoma Historical Society.

Wichita sweat house on the Wichita dance grounds. Tepee may be Cheyenne or Apache. March 3, 1900. Courtesy Western History Collections, University of Oklahoma Library.

Caddo Indians skinning beef, c. 1895, near Anadarko, Oklahoma Territory. Courtesy Archives and Manuscripts Division of the Oklahoma Historical Society.

Tso-Tuddle and Red Bone, Kiowas, cutting meat after beef issue, May 1902.
Courtesy Western History Collections, University of Oklahoma Library.

Kiowa Indians receiving rations at Anadarko. Courtesy Archives and
Manuscripts Division of the Oklahoma Historical Society.

Comanches and Kiowas waiting for payment at Agency, January 28, 1901.
Courtesy Archives and Manuscripts Division of the Oklahoma Historical Society.

At the Wichita payment, February 1899. Courtesy Western History Collections,
University of Oklahoma Library.

Apache women with gifts for Comanche guests. Courtesy Archives and Manuscripts Division of the Oklahoma Historical Society.

Tonkawa Indians with their arbor at Anadarko. Courtesy Archives and Manuscripts Division of the Oklahoma Historical Society.

Kiowas at prayer, pre-1910. Courtesy Archives and Manuscripts Division of the Oklahoma Historical Society.

Wichita Indians playing monte. Courtesy Archives and Manuscripts Division of the Oklahoma Historical Society.

Two Presbyterian missionaries visiting an aged Apache woman, November 3, 1898.
Courtesy Western History Collections, University of Oklahoma Library.

A class at Riverside Indian School. Courtesy Western History Collections,
University of Oklahoma Library.

Comanche baby in coonskin-lined boy's cradle, February 2, 1901.
Courtesy Western History Collections, University of Oklahoma Library.

A council of Comanche, Kiowa, and Apache chiefs, probably around the turn of the century.
Courtesy Western History Collections, University of Oklahoma Library.

Quanah Parker on balcony of his home near Cache, Oklahoma, c. 1904. Quanah is the large man,
fourth from left. Courtesy Archives and Manuscripts Division of the Oklahoma Historical Society.

Quanah Parker and his favorite wife, probably Too-Nicee. Courtesy Western History Collections, University of Oklahoma Library.

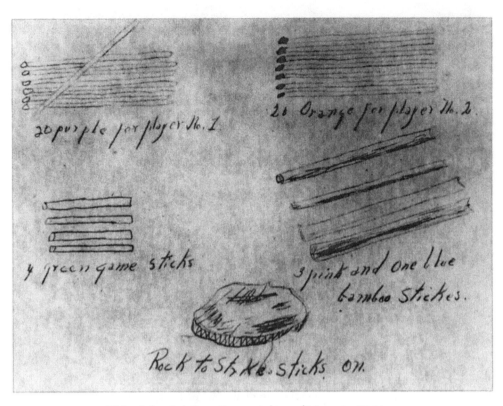

20 purple for player No. 1.

26 Orange for player No. 2.

4 green game sticks

3 joint and one blue bamboo Sticks.

Rock to Strike sticks on.

Wichita Indian Stick Game. Courtesy Archives and Manuscripts Division of the Oklahoma Historical Society.

Chapter Three

◆ ◆ ◆ ◆ ◆ ◆ ◆ ◆ ◆ ◆ ◆ ◆ ◆ ◆

A Spiritual Life

◆ ◆ ◆ ◆ ◆ ◆ ◆ ◆ ◆ ◆ ◆ ◆ ◆ ◆

The Southern Plains Indians are very spiritual people. The agricultural peoples, such as the Caddos and the Wichitas, traditionally practiced a religion based on the Earth Mother and the Corn Goddess, with priests conducting religious ceremonies. The hunting peoples, such as the Comanches and Kiowas, practiced a religion that usually revolved around animals, such as the buffalo, with shamans providing spiritual guidance. As these two different types of peoples came together, especially after their confinement to the reservations, they began to share their spirituality and adopt practices and beliefs from one another. Compounding this was the influence of Christianity as expressed by the many missionaries of the various denominations who tried to convert these peoples during the latter part of the nineteenth century. Some of these traditional Indians of Texas wholly adopted Christianity; some tried to remain true to the old ways; and in many instances, a mixture of Christianity and the old ways melded to create whole new belief systems. Still, a spiritual life remains vital to these traditional Indians of Texas.

Ceremonies and Beliefs

APACHES

There were many customs which to us appeared strange and unnatural. The giving of gifts was an important part of every ceremony and event of importance. When a child was born, the father gave away one of his ponies. At the ear-piercing ceremony, which took place when the child was nine months old, the father always gave a gift to the ear piercer. This habit of giving away belongings was carried to extremes among these people. It was not unusual for an Indian to give away almost everything he owned, leaving himself poor, and feeling himself well rewarded for his good deeds among the tribe. I never knew any of its members to be in actual want, for others would always provide food, shelter or whatever was needed.

William D. Hargraves, White Teacher and Missionary
Vol. 27, pp. 390–96

COMANCHES

She-wickey was my best friend, her husband was Black Wolf. They lived near Cache in 1907 and '08. The drums beat for days until it rained. I believe this was 1906, '07, '08, '09, and 1910 the drums never did stop beating at night or day. The Indians always believe in drum beats. They would beat drums making medicine for someone who was sick and the sick person would be taken out of the house and placed in a tepee. I have had some sick Indian tell me that the beat of the drums would ease the pain and was good music to them. Then there was the drum beat for wars.

Mrs. John Barnes, White Resident of Comanche Territory
Vol. 66, pp. 131–40

KIOWAS

The Quo-dle-quoit was a privileged class of Kiowas. It was an honor that was transferred from one to another. One can be a Quo-dle-quoit for only four years, then he must choose his successor. A person chosen to be a Quo-dle-quoit dare not refuse and must submit to being painted and decorated after the manner of the Quo-dle-quoit: around the forehead at the edge of the hair are parallel streaks of black, these are continued around the face, on down under the chin. On each cheek bone is the picture of the moon very far in crescent. On the center of the chest is the picture of the sun and on each side of the chest a little lower down is the crescent moon which is painted green and light green on the open side of the moon. The sun on the chest is also light green, while the whole body is yellow on a background. He wears a jack rabbit bonnet, ornamented with ears of jack rabbit and eagle feathers. Instead of being painted, some had the sun and moon cut into the flesh.

When a man is selected to be a Quo-dle-quoit by a friend and is painted up and ornamented he must pay his predecessor well for it, and each year as his predecessor paints and ornaments him he is obliged to pay additional installments of ponies, blankets and robes. At the end of four years he in turn selects some friend as his successor, then he begins to receive remuneration.

This sometimes works a hardship, but none selected dare refuse to become a Quo-dle-quoit. Many things are denied him. He never looks into a mirror of any kind. He dare not see himself. He is denied the privilege of eating dog or polecat, or of being around the fire where cooking is done, or entering a tepee where a dog is. There are many other things denied him, but he enjoys security in war. No weapon can hurt him.

Rev. J. J. Methvin, White Missionary to the Kiowas and Comanches
Vol. 36, pp. 108–109

Marriage

WICHITAS

Always tell when Wichita was not married. All boys wore a string on wrist, and when they got married they cut this string off. They usually took a wife when they were twenty-five years old. Up until time they get married they were boys, when married they were men. The folks of girl who was going to be wife of boy would watch this boy all time and see if he was good hunter and good farmer and could take care of her. If he was all right, then they got married. Wichita Indian would not marry outside of tribe. We believed in marrying in our tribe.

Jay Johnson, Wichita
Vol. 31, pp. 243–51

KIOWAS

The Kiowa Indians of the past conducted marriage of their daughters in this way. The brother of a girl would arrange with the young brave who wanted his sister. If she had no brother, then an uncle would make the marriage arrangements. The brave's parents would present to the girl's parents as many ponies, arrows or any other thing of use and value as they could spare and the girl would go to live in the boy's home. At the end of six months the girl's parents would make a return gift to the boy's parents. This was one way of getting married. If for any reason the boy did not want to go through this ceremony the young couple would simply run-away but this sometimes caused a lot of trouble in the family.

Robert Onco, Kiowa
Vol. 107, pp. 284–92

CADDOS

I don't know whether you would call the marriages religious or not. The parents usually made the marriages. The boy's parents would look for a girl who knew how to do everything about the home. She must know how to cook, make her own clothes as well as her husband's, make meal from corn and all other by-products of corn, nothing must be overlooked in her training. In turn the boy must know how to provide for his wife. The girl's parents, too, have been looking for a well trained boy for the girl. The boy's parents always ask for the girl. If the boy meets with the approval of the girl's parents, they give their consent. When the wedding day arrives the boy's parents bring presents to the girl's parents, such as ponies and such. After the presents have been given then the Headman comes and takes the young couple off to one side a little way and performs a ceremony, uniting them as man and wife. From the time the boy's parents have asked for the girl, she isn't seen until the day of the wedding. The boy has a home ready for his bride.

Mrs. Frank Cussins, Caddo
Vol. 21, pp. 376–88

COMANCHES

Years ago when I was small the Indians did not go through a marriage ceremony as now. The father and mother would decide if the man that was to marry their daughter was honest, would treat their daughter right, and that he had enough to provide a good living for her. If he suited the parents, he could take the daughter and live with her. He didn't have to pay for her.

Adeline Apauty, Comanche
Vol. 99, pp. 186–88

Funerals

CADDOS

The Caddos were great mourners. When a person died they mourned for six days. The procession was led to the grave by the oldest daughter carrying the fire. When my mother died my oldest sister carried the fire in a pot my mother had always made her medicines in. If there wasn't anything to carry the fire in then a torch was carried. When she got to the grave she marched around it four times, stopping at the foot of it. There she stood until the body was buried. A fire was made at the foot of the grave and it must be kept burning for six days. The belief is that the spirit hovers around for six days then it leaves. During this time no one must leave the place. The last thing before the fire goes out my mother's things were brought and opened. They had been tied up in bundles until now. If anyone wanted anything that belonged to her they could have it, and the rest were burned in the dying fire. When this was over everyone washed his face. The spirit was gone now, and the tears must be washed away, as we will meet again some day. The pot that my sister carried the fire in is now in the possession of Father Aloyisius Hitta of the St. Patrick's Mission, southwest of Anadarko about a mile.[1] When a woman is prepared for a burial a grain of corn and something else, I can't think what it is, are tied in a rag and tied around her right wrist. A bow and arrows are placed in the right hand of a man.

In olden times there were no coffins. There was a rack made like the beds, a pronged pole was placed in each corner of the grave and a bed was woven on this. The body was placed on this and covered. Over the body another bed like rack was made and this was covered with a buffalo robe. This served as a casket.

Mrs. Frank Cussins, Caddo
Vol. 21, pp. 376–88

CADDOS AND DELAWARES

Our burial ceremonies are very similar to the Caddo rites. I can only tell this as my folks have told me for I have never really seen a burial like it. They march around the grave four times, dropping a little dirt in the grave as they go around. Then they must return to the grave every day for six days; this is because the spirit is supposed to linger around for that time.

Leona Parton, Delaware
Vol. 93, pp. 54–58

KIOWAS

The Kiowa Indians usually buried their dead in some cave or between rocks, piling rocks and earth over the body which had been wrapped in blankets and clothing. Their custom was to place every article belonging to the person in the grave and often their ponies and dogs were also killed. This was done not because it was thought by the Indians that these articles would be needed in the Happy Hunting Ground, but because they did not want to see these things which belonged to their dead. The Kiowas believed that there was a place of peace and happiness to which the good would go after death, also a place of punishment to which the evil would be consigned by the Great Spirit. . . .

In times long past it was the custom among the Kiowas that if a wealthy Indian had a son or daughter to die, they would put up a tepee, placing everything owned by the child in it with the body and go away never to return. I have often wondered why they did not know that the body was eaten by animals with which the country was then filled.

The Kiowa Indians have some members who are trying to preserve the memory of their ancient customs but as the older people die I fear there will be no person to take their place in teaching these.

Robert Onco, Kiowa
Vol. 107, pp. 284–92

TONKAWAS

When an Indian died, the whole tribe would be heard in lamentation of great agony and immediately the hair of the deceased would be cut off and the face painted yellow. Internment was invariably made on the day of death if possible.

The graves were dug to the width of an ordinary bed mattress and were about six feet deep and all members coming to the home of the deceased would bring some gift to be buried with the dead. The manner of preparing the dead for burial was to begin wrapping the body with blankets, at the same time placing all the gifts as well as his entire earthly possessions which were not too large nor too bulky in blankets. These articles were wrapped until the roll contained all that could be placed within it or until it was about three or four feet in diameter. Then it was placed in the grave, and all cooking utensils, pans, buckets and other possessions that were not rolled in the blanket were placed in the grave beside the body, with the sole exception of feathers. If the deceased owned feather pillows, they would be emptied and cloth deposited in the grave. When all this had been deposited in the grave, someone, usually some old member of the tribe would advance to the west end of the grave, while all others would step back a few steps and after making a talk this person would reach down and get a handful of dirt and throw it across the grave, then to the east end of the grave and repeat the throwing of dirt across the grave, all the time talking to the dead person. This was a touching ceremony.

Three days of mourning after the burial must ensue and on the morning of the forth day the tribe all came to the home of the deceased bringing gifts of clothing or bedding, cooking utensils, or other things to replace such things as had been buried with the dead after which the Chief made a talk to all members formed in a circle who were then dismissed, and they never again mentioned the name of the deceased.

The Tonkawa tribe of Indians, owing to the number of enemy tribes which they had, made no mounds to mark the graves of their dead: after burial the earth was filled in level and a bunch of weeds were broken off and used to sweep the earth free of all tracks or evidence of burial that was possible. No stone or marker was used in the early day burials of the Tonkawas to designate the places where their dead lay.

It has been said that enemy tribes of the Tonkawas would scalp their dead when they were found.

The Tonkawas all worshipped the "Great Spirit" and younger one took part in singing songs and were attentive listeners to Bible reading and explanations of such.

Bertha Brewer Plummer, White Daughter of Agent to Tonkawas
Vol. 40, pp. 162–71

CADDOS AND KIOWAS

I attended a Kiowa funeral with [a friend] once and this was very interesting. They drove all the stock belonging to the dead man, to the grave, shot them, and buried them with the man.

I remember a full blood Comanche Indian named Arco, who died with consumption. After he was buried, he came back for food. He was riding an old horse and they supplied him with food and a fresh horse. They cooked the food and gave it to him on the end of a long tepee pole. They were superstitious and were afraid to get close to him. After he received the food and horse he never came back. When Arco died, his wife tried to shoot his buckskin pony and blue roan horse, but they got away. She burned all of his blankets and saddle near his grave and cut deep places in her arms to show the pain of death.

The Caddos buried their dead west of the camp, for they claimed the spirit would not go east toward the sunrise.

The Delawares wrapped their dead in a buffalo hide and placed them in a tree.

Henry Beaty, White Resident of Caddo Territory
Vol. 14, pp. 126–37

KIOWAS AND COMANCHES

How well I remember the old graveyard on top of the highest hill north of Anadarko, a little over a mile. The slow, tortuous climb up that long hill to the bleak graveyard. Bare of everything except scrub oaks, very few of the graves having headstones. It was horrible to see the self-inflicted punishment the wife and mother tortured themselves with. They would cut off the end of a finger for each member of the family that died, cut their hair, which is usually kept long, to shoulder length. Then they stripped their bodies to the waist and slash their arms and breasts with a razor-sharp knife. This is only a part of their mourning. At night the relatives meet at the home of the bereaved family and spend the night wailing. This wailing lasted a certain period of time, I have forgotten just how long.

Lillian Gassaway, White Daughter of J. J. Methvin, Missionary to the Kiowas and
    Comanches
Vol. 25, pp. 407–14

WICHITAS

Dirty Face, a Wichita woman, sister of Sallie Hunter, was so sick that they thought she was going to die. She was living just east of the little creek that flowed from the small lake into the Washita River in . . . Caddo County.

The family loaded her into a wagon and hauled her to the old Wichita burial ground . . . and they dug the grave with Dirty Face lying in the wagon beside it. But when she did not die by evening, they took her up to the house of her sister, Sallie Hunter, just about 200 yards south of the burial ground. She got well and lived for three years after that.

Several years later, Jimmie Hunter lost a little child, while they were living on the other side of the Washita. I asked him where he was going to bury the child and Hunter named a burial ground on that side of the river. When asked why he did not bury the child in the old burial ground on Sallie Hunter's place, Jimmie Hunter replied, "We do not take the bodies of our dead across running water."

That explains why they hauled Dirty Face to the graveyard before she was dead, so they would not have to cross the little creek near her home with her dead body.

O. P. Downing, White Resident of Wichita Territory
Vol. 83, pp. 354–55

COMANCHES

In 1897 I was in the Indian country, in Comanche County, and was present and saw an Indian man die, and watched all the minute details of how the body was prepared for burial and the actual putting away of the corpse. This man had called in his friends and relatives and told them, "at noon I go away." This was early in the morning, and they immediately began to make all preparations for the funeral. They gathered up his bedding, guns and all other personal belonging, caught two horses and hitched them to an almost new wagon, left them standing nearby and waited. About noon this man ceased to breathe. They immediately bent his feet back up to his hips, securely tying them in this position making a short pack. Then he was placed on his bed of blankets, rolled up inside them and securely tied. Then placed in the waiting wagon with his squaws and his sister, starting their journey not far distant up into the mountains on the south side of the Wichita range.

They carried in this wagon besides themselves and the corpse, all of his clothing that they could not get into the pack or bundle with him, an ax and a butcher knife. On reaching the foot hills of the mountains, there was a gradual slope up to, or near some ragged cliffs. They drove as near this point as they possibly could, using force on the team of horses. This being accomplished, they dismounted from the wagon, lifted the corpse out and laid it out to one side on the ground or rocks, took the butcher knife and cut the harness off the horses, cutting each piece of leather many times. In earlier days they would kill these two horses, but the Government forbade their doing this so they would take the butcher knife and disfigure the horses by cutting the hair on the neck down to the hide as close as possible, also shaving the tail close to the hide. Then they would leave the horses to die, or to hunt for food and water. Most always there was plenty of grass and water, and this treatment very seldom worked any hardship on these dumb animals. The immediate family did not want to see these animals any more, so by the time the hair was grown out they were then usually sold or given to some of their friends in the tribe. Then the Indians took the ax and chopped each spoke of the wagon wheels into two pieces, cut the tongue, single-trees and double-trees in two, and busted up the body of the wagon as much as they could, broke the handle out of the ax and left it with the rest of the wreck. Then they proceeded with the corpse up into the cliffs, placing it in under the rocks and completely covering it. This accomplished they took the butcher knife and cut or haggle about one half the hair out of their heads, hacked their arms from wrist to shoulder in a number of places, fully believing that by shedding some of their blood, that the wrath of the "Great Spirit" who had just taken their loved one from them, would be appeased. They then threw the knife away and bleeding profusely from their self-inflicted wounds, started afoot the homeward journey back to camp.

On reaching camp the entire village would break out anew into wailing and crying and beating their chests. The dead man's name was very seldom spoken again in the presence of his loved ones.

I have counted as many as twenty hacks or wagons on top of the mountains which have been destroyed when some Indian man was buried in this same vicinity.

Dick Banks, White Resident of Comanche Territory
Vol. 72, pp. 118–22

COMANCHES

At Post Oak Mission I have attended many funerals. When one Indian cries they all cry; then there is a quietness, then the crying is repeated. They want to bury their blankets, clothes, and their most precious belongings in their graves. The Post Oak Mission Cemetery was very small until 1907, but now it is a large cemetery. On each Decoration Day the Indians always decorate the graves beautifully.[2]

Mrs. John Barnes, White Resident of Comanche Territory
Vol. 66, pp. 131–40

KIOWAS

I kept riding for the [Kiowa] Indians until 1901, when this Kiowa Country was opened [to white settlement]. In the meantime, I had made lots of friends with the Indians, most all of them knew me and they wanted me to take claim with them. I think now I was foolish not to, but I didn't.

In later years I learned that the tribe had a belief of faith among the tribes that if a newborn baby died, the mother would have to go through a purgatory of punishment. I happened to ride into camp on one occasion of this kind. Before this, I had been there and had broken some stock for [the family]. [The wife] had a beautiful two-year old pony she wanted broke and they had sent me word to come. When I got there, she was crying and her arm was bleeding from wrist to shoulder. It looked like she had just taken the point of a knife and stuck in enough to bleed a little. Although I had rode some of their ponies before and they wanted to know what to call me, I said, "You won't remember me by name, so I'll name this pony Daisy, and you call me Daisy." She didn't know me and as all the men were gone, she asked me in sign who I was. So I asked her if she savvied crazy pony by my making signs and she said, "You Daisy" and she ran up and grabbed my hand and patted it and hugged my neck. But she told me that her baby had died and they had gone to Anadarko to the funeral. I dressed her arm with some kind of oil she had. But I know that she had punished herself or her buck had for the loss of her baby.

C. S. Webber, White Cowboy in Kiowa Country
Vol. 11, pp. 299–304

Dances

I have attended stomp dances conducted by the Creeks, Seminoles, Chickasaws, and Choctaws of the Five Civilized Tribes and those of the Osages, Iowas, Kickapoos, Shawnees, Comanches, and the Kiowas of the wild Indians.

In summing them all up, I would say that in every case it amounts to practically the same. Parts of these dances were religious ceremonies and times of feasting; others were dances of joy and happiness over what they had accomplished or over abundant crops.

The most exciting dance among any of them is their War Dance, working themselves up to a fever heat and ready to do or die for what they think is right.

There was a dance near Anadarko in which several tribes participated, and which lasted for about five weeks. At the designated time, Indians began to come to the Stomp Grounds, and brought with them provisions to last for weeks. The dance got underway and was conducted as all stomp dances, including the medicine men, barbecue, roasting corn and dancing different dances pertaining to religion, according to their old tribal customs. Men, women and children for miles and miles came and camped at the grounds. Measles broke out among them, and away from the grounds some quarter of a mile they erected a tent and confined all their measles cases to this tent while the others continued in their festivities. The result of this stomp dance was that sixty died with the measles, mostly infants, before the Indian Agent was notified. Upon the receipt of notice by the Agency, men were sent to the Stomp Ground, causing the dance to be discontinued.

Mrs. A. Avery, Choctaw Resident of Western Oklahoma
Vol. 13, pp. 7–21

COMANCHES AND KIOWAS

My father traded a lot with the Indians, and I was practically raised with them. I played with them, ate with them, and danced with them. I slept with them in their tepees. The Kiowa and Comanche Indians lived around us. When I was about 11 years old I went to their dances. The Indians would paint and dress me up so I looked like one of them. I can dance their Indian dances today. They held their dances in the tepee. They would build [a] small fire in the center of [the] ground. Fixed with long weeds lined up in straight row, encircled about the fire. Both old and young male Indians danced about the fire and occasionally the squaws would dance, but not very often. They would wait on the men. They would make a tea out of the mescal beans, a yellow fuzzy bean. I would drink tea with them, and then we would dance some more. The tea tasted kind of funny, and would make one crazy drunk. They would also make coffee out of green [coffee] beans issued to them by the Government. They had small bowls about six inches in diameter and two inches deep made of solid rock, and a crusher about three inches long and two inches in diameter that they used by pounding into [the] bowl to grind coffee and corn.

For music they used the tom-toms. It was a stick with a large ball on the end, and they would take a cowhide that they tanned and stretch the hide over a hollow log, and beat on the hide with this stick. You could hear the tom-tom beats for miles around. The Indians would get out in the warm sun and take sunbaths for hours at a time by lying in [the] hot sun. When they ate they would come up around the pot, and each would have a cup or hand-made bowl, and each would dip food from [the] pot with a dipper serving themselves and sit down and eat.

Bert Buxton, White Resident of Comanche Territory
Vol. 1, pp. 466–69

COMANCHES

The Comanches held stomp dances every summer. They would get together and stay maybe a week at a time, just eating and dancing. They would dance any time they felt like it. I have seen them dancing at all times during the day and night. At night they would build up a big fire and dance around it.

There was a leader, usually an older Indian. He would lead the dance in a circle at night around the fire. He sang a sort of song or chant in the Indian tongue. The other Indians would dance after him, some of them shouting and prancing louder and higher than others. A stomp dance was usually pretty noisy and also pretty exciting. I liked the dances; I have danced with the Indians lots of times.

Morris Brown, White Traveler through Caddo and Comanche Territory
Vol. 17, pp. 52–57

The Green Corn Ceremony

CADDOS

The Caddos have very few ceremonies. Sometimes in the spring when the corn is planted, there will be a field that almost everyone has a part in. Before planting this field the Caddos would gather and go around the field stopping at every corner to offer a word of prayer. The corners representing the four corners of the earth. When the corn was harvested they had the Green Corn Dance. This was a dance of thanksgiving.[3]

Mrs. Frank Albin, Caddo
Vol. 12, pp. 178–82

CADDOS

In August the Indians celebrated what they called the Green Corn Dance. I understand this dance is given at this time to show their thanks for being taken care of through the winter. They danced around the camp fire, smoked the peace pipe made of corn cobs, and played games. The women played a game similar to our present game of shinny.

Henry Beaty, White Resident of Caddo Territory
Vol. 14, pp. 126–37

CADDOS

We attended part of the ceremony in August of the Green Corn Feast or dance. This celebration usually lasted about three days. The first day, we attended and it seemed to be a thanksgiving day to these Caddo and Shawnee Indians, as the feast was opened with prayer by the Chief. This ceremony seemed to be very sacred and was unlike any gathering I ever saw. There was a big square of ground cleaned off and a fire built in the center. The bucks were gaily decked with war paint, feathers, some in native costume, others had short buckskin jackets and breeches on, or blankets wrapped around them. The women had gay colored dresses and bright colored shawls of various hues and strand after strand of bright colored beads around their necks and gold earrings in their ears and shell combs in their hair. Some of the younger women had their hair braided down their backs. The men had their hair wrapped and hanging down on the sides of their shoulders. Their hair was long, too, and they had small gourds cleaned out and filled with small stones, these gourds were hung about their person some way. When they danced the gourds would make a noise. After they prayed the bucks and the squaws assembled around this fire in a circle, and began a weird chanting in their native tongue, accompanied by the tom–toms, the rattling of gourds, and chanting; then they would have a big feast.

Barbecued meat, bread and different kind of Indian dishes. I think this ceremony lasted three days and each day was different. The days had different meanings.

Ella Evans, White Resident of Caddo and Wichita Territory
Vol. 3, pp. 393–95

The Ghost Dance [4]

KIOWAS

My brother, A-peahtone, was born in 1856. Our grandmother was a Royal Sioux and Father was a brother to Lone Wolf, Kiowa Chief; he lived in Kiowa County near Mountain View, Oklahoma. A-peahtone was appointed chief solely on merit; usually this position is hereditary, but he was a man of keen intellect and good judgment, therefore, he was selected Chief of the Kiowas.

There is a small town southwest of Walters in Cotton County named for A-peahtone. He was loyal to his tribe and he and Chief Quanah Parker made frequent trips to Washington in behalf of their respective tribes. The Kiowas loved this chief; he was a personal friend to the Reverend J. J. Methvin of Anadarko and also of Andrez Martinez, the Mexican captive who lived in Anadarko.[5]

In 1890, the Plains tribes in New Mexico, North Dakota, Arizona, and Oklahoma Territory all began a dance which they called the Ghost Dance. The dancers would dance until they became exhausted because the one who danced the longest was to be chosen the leader, to lead the Indians after the white men had been destroyed and the buffalo had returned. The Agency at Anadarko appealed to the dancers to cease their dancing but they said it was a religious dance and the government could not stop them. So they danced on and the dance went on night and day for several months. The Kiowas, the better element of them, decided to send A-peahtone to find out what started this craze which was spreading fast. The teacher in every camp was requiring the Indians to pay him ponies and blankets and he was making a lot of money out of it for the longer the dance lasted the more ponies and blankets he collected. He told the Government officials that the laws of Oklahoma Territory protected religious dances and the officials were powerless to stop it.

A-peahtone traveled to Pine Ridge Agency in Utah[6] and tried to find the self-styled Messiah, but was informed no such person was there. However, they told him they thought he was on the reservation in Nevada, so he traveled far on horseback with the aid of some friends in other tribes who were also interested in finding out about this craze which was sweeping the country.

He finally arrived at Pyramid Lake among the Utes and their Chief, Sitting Bull, was finally located.[7] He was in seclusion and the Indians told A-peahtone they could not find him, but he told them he was also a Chief and wanted to learn the dance and its secrets so he was finally admitted, after hours of delay. He found an old ignorant Indian who had preached that the Messiah was coming soon to destroy the white man and put the Indian back in charge of the country and that the buffalo would return in great herds.

It was an easy matter to make believers of thousands of Indians, but A-peahtone soon saw that it was a hoax so he returned home and called a meeting at Anadarko for all tribes. They exposed Sitting Bull and forced the teacher to return all the ponies and blankets and leave the country, thus ending the Ghost Dance craze. A-peahtone did something that the Government officials could not do—ended this craze.

A-peahtone was honest, kind, very dignified and proud. He visited in Lawton on several occasions and visited Chief Quanah Parker often, for they were working together for the good of their tribes.

Mary Ma-Na-Ka, Kiowa
Vol. 106, pp. 486–88

CADDOS, DELAWARES, AND ARAPAHOS

I am an Arapaho Indian who came to Colony in February 1891. . . . My home is located on Cobb Creek which runs by my house, and sometimes we would find a hundred wild geese in a bunch on the creek.

We would meet and have Ghost Dances. The Arapaho, Delaware and Caddo Indians would be there and we would dance all night. At the Ghost

Dances we wore blankets and our paints and feathers. When we got tired we would sleep awhile and get up and dance some more.

Joe Creeping Bear, Arapaho
Vol. 100, pp. 385–91

Joe Creeping Bear, Arapaho
Vol. 100, pp. 385–91

COMANCHES

We never feared the Indians very much. In the winter of '91 when Minco was still the terminal of the Rock Island, the Indians of the Bad Lands of Dakota, who were transferred to Western Oklahoma, went on their famous horn and ghost dances. Their ceremonies were elaborate and their dances frenzied. They broke away from the reservation and were creating a great deal of excitement, so the Government sent troops from Fort Sill and Fort Reno to round them up and take them back to their reservation.

Later on, the "Wounded Knee" Agency had quite a bit of trouble in which a number of Indians were killed before they could conquer them. During this period the Comanches, who were blanket Indians out west of us, staged a big Ghost Dance which made us more or less nervous, however, before the United States Troops could be returned from the "Wounded Knee" Agency, the Comanches had quieted down and everything was peaceful.

M. B. Louthan, White Resident of Chickasaw Territory
Vol. 78, pp. 348–54

The Sun Dance[8]

KIOWAS

The Kiowas were polytheists and animists. They deified all the powers of Nature and prayed to them in turn according to occasion. The old Indians did not believe in Heaven or Hell, but believed in transmigration. All night birds were animated by souls of the dead. They thought then and do yet that a person can be bewitched by making medicine.

The Sun is the greatest god of the Kiowas. They made sacrifices to him and each year a Sun Dance was held. The buffalo, too, was held in reverence as was the peyote. The buffalo as an animal symbol of strength and the peyote as a representative of the sun in its shape and because of the button in the center.

Inside the medicine lodge the medicine was exposed during the whole time of the dance, which was four days, though the preparation for the dance took several days. The hunt for the buffalo, the women securing the center pole of the medicine lodge. Then the four days dance in which they neither ate, drank nor slept.

The center pole must be cut down by a captive woman, usually a Mexican, and the "tiame" was held in so much dread and has so many taboos attached to it, that a Mexican, captured when a boy, was given to it for the special purpose of unwrapping it and setting it in place; then if anything went wrong the punishment would fall on the captive instead of the tribe.

T. C. Battey who was with the Kiowas in 1873 and was a witness to the Sun Dance at that time, describes the medicine lodge as follows:[9] "The medicine lodge is situated nearly in the center of the encampment; is circular in form, and about sixty feet in diameter, having its entrance towards the east. It is built by support; around this and at nearly equal distance, are seventeen other forked posts, forming the circumference of the building. These are from twelve to fifteen feet in height and all of cottonwood. Small cottonwood trees are tied on the outside of these in horizontal position, with ropes of rawhide, having limbs and leaves on them.

Outside of these small cottonwood trees are placed in an upright position, thus forming a wall of green trees and leaves several feet in thickness in the midst of which many hundred spectators afterward find a cool retreat, where they can observe what is going on without making themselves conspicuous. Long cottonwood poles extend from each of the posts in the circumference to the central pole, and then limbs of the same are laid across these forming a shady roof one-third of the way to the center.

The central pole is ornamented near the ground with robes of buffalo calves, their heads up as if in the act of climbing it. Each of the branches above the fork is ornamented in a similar manner with the additions of shawls, calico, scarves, etc., and covered at the tip with black muslin. Attached to the fork is a bundle of cottonwood and willow limbs firmly bound together and covered with a buffalo robe and with head and horns so as to form a rude image of a buffalo. To this were hung strips of new calico, muslin, shrouding, both blue and scarlet, feathers, shawls, etc., of various lengths and qualities. The longer and more showy articles were placed near the ends. This image was so placed as to face the east. The lodge of the encampment are arranged in circles around the medicine house, having their entrance toward it and the nearest circle being some ten rods distant.

The ground inside the inclosure had been carefully cleared of grass, sticks, and roots, and covered several inches deep with clean white sand. A screen had been constructed on the side opposite the entrance by sticking small cottonwoods and cedars deep into the ground, so as to preserve them fresh as long as possible. A space was left two or three feet wide between it and the inclosing wall, in which the dancers prepared themselves for the dance, and in front of which was the medicine. This consisted of an image lying on the ground, but so concealed from view in the screen as to render its form indistinguishable. Above it was a large fan made of eagle quills, with the quill part lengthened out nearly a foot by inserting a stick into it and securing it there. These were held in a spread form by means of a willow rod or wire bent in a circular form; above this was a mass of feathers concealing an image on each side of which were several shields highly decorated with feathers and paint. Various other paraphernalia of heathen worship were suspended in the screen among these shields or over them, impossible for me to describe so as to be comprehended. A mound had also been thrown up around the central post of the building two feet high and perhaps five feet in diameter. If at any time during the dance there was any bloodshed, even accidentally, it was considered an evil omen and the dance was discontinued."

In 1890, the Kiowas made preparations for the old Sun Dance, but the Government had forbidden it because it was so barbarous, and was a prelude to the warpath. The agent had given his consent for the dance to go on if they would omit the objectionable part of the performance, but Washington officials ordered the dance stopped. Big Tree, the chief, declared that they had gone too far with the preparations to stop but was told that he would either stop it or fight. He said that he would fight and that night troops were ordered to Anadarko, and the next morning the Agency was full of soldiers. The dance was called off and no attempt has ever been made to have another.

J. J. Methvin, White Missionary to the Kiowas and Comanches
Vol. 107, pp. 24–28

COMANCHES AND KIOWAS

While at [Ft. Cobb] I witnessed my first and last attempted war dance by the Comanches, Kiowas, Apaches, Cheyennes, and Arapaho Indians. Such dances were prohibited by the government.

They were to have held this dance northwest of Fort Cobb, in a bend of the Washita River. They had everything complete except a buffalo head to be placed on top of the medicine pole. They found out they could get a buffalo head from Charlie Goodnight, near Clarendon, Texas, for eight hundred dollars.[10] This sum of money was made up and an Indian was sent for the head. The Indian Agent got the news and ordered Charlie Goodnight not to make the sale. This made the Indians mad, so they went to the Indian Agent at Anadarko and told him they were going to dance or fight. The commanding general was called from Fort Sill by the Indian Agent of Anadarko.

The Chiefs of each tribe were at the Indian Agent's office demanding they be given food or they would fight. Just at that time the Commanding General stepped in and told them to disperse and go to their homes or he would call out the soldiers and confiscate all of their belonging and make them prisoners the rest of their lives. The next morning at nine o'clock there wasn't anything left at the dance ground but the medicine pole, which was decorated with shells, tin cans, bows, arrows, ropes, bridles, spurs, and many other trinkets, which they had left behind. This was about the middle of July 1890, and was the last war dance ever attempted by the Indians.

Charles Oman, White Cowboy in Kiowa Country
Vol. 7, pp. 558–66

The Peyote Road

CADDOS AND COMANCHES

The Caddos and Comanches made a liquor by soaking mescal beans in water. Once a month they would celebrate and get drunk on this liquor. They called it "Jesus Talk" for they claimed when they drank it they could hear Jesus talk.

Henry Beaty, White Resident of Caddo Territory
Vol. 14, pp. 126–37

CADDOS

The Indians here in the Creek Nation, and many other Indians in many other nations, have what is known as a Peyote religious worship. It is called the Union Native American Church. This religious worship was handed down to the Euchees here by the Caddo Indians. This Indian church is put up by the Indians. They worship God, our Creator, in a tepee. They put up 21 poles and put a canvas tent over the poles and they have their church house built. When they have finished putting up the tepee, they build a moon out of dirt for an altar. They cut wood to burn in the dirt moon in order to keep light and warmth in the tepee.

They worship and pray all night in the tepee. They have a man to conduct the Peyote religious meeting. The Peyote is an Indian herb that has been in use for many years. Apaches were the first ones to find this herb. Lots of people call this Peyote the bitter herb.

The Indians use this herb for many kinds of sicknesses. It will also teach a person more about the good ways of God. The Indians eat of this herb for their health.

Jacob Rolland, Euchee[11]

v.9, pp. 32–33

COMANCHES AND KIOWAS

I have dealt with the Indians since I was 13 years old. In fact, in the early days I was known as handy man among the Indians, and was well known among the different tribes. I have had many dealings with them, and they were always fair and aboveboard. The Indians at that time did not drink. There was very little alcohol in the country. However, I have seen them at their religious councils when they indulged in peyote. They would all gather around in their tents, wrapped up in blankets; they would sit this way for hours under the influence of this drug. One of the Indians would beat the tom-tom, and this slow monotonous boom of the tom-tom would go on continuously. This worship would sometime last for two or three days.

W. H. Darnold, White Resident of Comanche and Kiowa Territory

Vol. 21, pp. 461–64

KIOWAS

I am forty-nine years old. I was born here on Polecat Creek right near Heyburn, the old Indian trading post, and I have lived here all my life. The Kiowa Indians had given the Euchees here what is known as a bitter herb that the Indians call peyote. The Kiowa Indians had used it for sixty years or longer and this herb is for the Indians to use to build up their body and mind toward God Almighty. The Indians used this herb to heal sick people among Indians. In later years there are a few white people who use this herb, also. The white people have advanced in this peyote religious worship.

Our white brother has taken up the peyote religious worship among the Indians and there are a few white people who conduct themselves the way that the Indians do, and also our white brother can sing the song of the Indian language and make it good.

This peyote herb has helped many a person in health. The Indians usually put up a tepee tent to worship their God and also eat of the bitter herb, for the good of their bodies and mind and also to thank God for this herb. It is in cactus form and looks like a radish when it is green and when it is dried it looks like a dried peach.

Kelly Yellowhead, Creek
Vol. 94, pp. 482–83

COMANCHES

There is some herb called peyote. It first originated in Mexico. It has some effect on people like dope. Years and years ago I have heard that they had Peyote ceremonies. This was used as medicine.

Allen Mihecaby, Comanche
Vol. 36, pp. 259–61

KIOWAS

The way they would have their Medicine Dance was they would eat a bean that was called the mescal bean and this bean would make them drunk. Then they would begin to dance and would dance all night and up into the day or until they fell exhausted then they would go to sleep, and whatever the Chief dreamed while asleep they would do after they waked up. That is, if he dreamed that they would go and kill an Indian family that is what they would do.

After they had danced and slept and wakened from sleep they would go and get a cattleman to give them a beef and then they would have a feast and would prepare it as I have told you before.

The way the Kiowas would make a drum was to take a willow stick, bend it into a ring and stretch a green hide over this, tie it and let it dry. These drums were what the Kiowas would make their music on and you could hear this music for two or three miles.

Manda S. Evans, White Resident of Kiowa Territory
Vol. 79, pp. 480–92

Christianity

APACHES

In 1894, near Cash [Cache], Oklahoma, I held several revival meetings among the Apache Indians. They would come into camp on Sunday morning and stay until Monday evening. They always brought their food. They killed a beef or two and hung it out to dry. This was known as jerked meat. During these meetings, a man by the name of Ross interpreted my sermons to the Indians. While in camp, everyone cooked on an open fire. All were Indians except three white men. The Indians put so much pepper in their food and cooked it so raw, that it was almost impossible for us to eat it. We usually built a camp fire and cooked, but we always gave them some of the food that we cooked and took some of their food, so as not to break the social circle. The Indian women made good cornbread.

William D. Hargraves, White Teacher and Missionary to Indians
Vol. 27, pp. 390–96

THE PLAINS INDIANS

[The narrator is telling a story that was related to him by John McIntosh, a Creek Indian missionary to the Plains Indians.]

"In 1874, the Baptist Convention of Texas requested me [John McIntosh, Creek] to go to the Wichita Tribe and undertake a Mission work. For a long time I had cherished a burning desire to preach the Gospel to these wild tribes, yet when the way was opened I hesitated. I began to count the cost of such an undertaking, the long journey from my country to the Wichita tribe. There were no roads, in fact I did not know how far it was, I only knew they were somewhere on the Western plains. Besides these were days of notorious outlaws and horse thieves.

"After much prayer, I was convinced that this was God's call and summoning all the courage and faith I could, I determined to go and trust to my Savior to give his blessings upon the effort.

"I had heard much of the wild Indians animosity toward the white people and feared my little bit of white blood might prejudice them against me. Then too, I wore citizens clothing and my hair was short. With all these things in mind, preparations were made for the trip. A good horse was selected, food for the trip was prepared by my wife, which consisted mainly of dried beef, sofkey[12] and blue dumplings (a mixture of cornmeal, beans and hickory nuts pounded up together, rolled into a round ball and then boiled), these would keep fresh for days, two canteens of water. Early in July 1874, I bid my family good-bye and started on the hazardous journey of more than two hundred miles.

"I passed the last settlement the second day; as I left the borders of the Chickasaw Nation, trackless plains lay before me.

"The weather was extremely hot and dry, very little water for man or beast. . . The fourth day and no water, it seemed that horse and man would perish in the heat; I happened to run my hand in my pocket and found there one of my bullets of lead. I put this in my parched mouth and soon the saliva came in to moist my tongue and I did not suffer for water any more. Finally when I reached the Ouachita [Washita] River, it was to us a real oasis in the desert.

"At the Wichita Agency at Anadarko the government officials and soldiers gave me a cordial welcome and ministered to my needs by sharing their ration with me. There were but few Indians around the Agency, I learned that they were encamped some four miles north of the Agency. I soon contracted one of the very few Indians that could speak English and act as Interpreter. I engaged him (Black Beaver)[13] to go with me to the camp as Interpreter, fortunately he could speak several of the dialects that were spoken around the Agency. The camp covered several hundred acres, tepees, and grass wigwams in groups along the creek banks and around Rock Spring.

"We did not receive a very hearty welcome as they seem to regard me as just another government official who had come to dictate to them, however, every camp we visited we were expected to eat. My Interpreter said that this is the Indian way, you must eat. Black Bear [Beaver] seemed to be able to eat everywhere, but I soon found that I had to only mince, I did not know what kind of food I was eating much of the time, menus peculiar to this tribe.

"At each of these visits I would tell them that I was not a government man but that I was sent by the Great Father above to tell the Indians how to worship him. When we visited the Chief we found him very bitter and un-relenting. He said his people would continue their warfare against the white people until they had killed them all. I told him it was useless for the small Indian tribes to fight against the powerful white race, that I had traveled many hundreds of miles toward the rising sun and that every where I see great throngs of white people more than all the buffalo on the plains. He showed little concern until I picked up a handful of sand and said this little handful of sand is like the Indian people and that big mountain of sand is like the white race, if you continue to fight these armies will come and kill all your people even your women and children. I saw his countenance change and that I had scored a hit with that illustration. He seemed willing to listen to me after that and my message seemed to interest him.

"Late in August 1874, the Chief sent his camp callers through the camp and called the Indians to come together and hear the man who had come to them from the Great Spirit. It was Sunday morning, a scene I shall never forget. Indians with human scalps hanging to their belts as trophies, the men with guns and bayonets, faces smeared with the war paint, long neatly braided hair hanging across each shoulder, squaws dressed in gaudy blankets and little or nothing except the blankets, crying babies, all seated flat on the ground. They signed for me to proceed. I standing up with Black Bear [Beaver] by my side, I opened the Bible and said to them this is the word from the Great Spirit Above to all his children, then waited for Black Bear [Beaver] to inter-pret it into their language, then I read John 3:16 and this was interpreted to them and so on for two full hours. I gave to them as best I could the revela-tion of God to man; frequently I was interrupted with the acclamation: Oh-Oh. This approval and response encourage me. This was the beginning of mission work among the wild Indians of the plains. So far as I know this was the first sermon ever preached to any of the wild tribes. Thus a start was made and the Spirit gave life to the seed that were sown.

"On my next visit to them, I was accompanied by Dr. A. J. Holt, and a church was later established, called the Rock Spring Baptist Church."

[*Phelps now speaks his own words*] During all these years the Creek Associ-ation has sent a missionary to minister to this church. The older members have passed on to their reward and younger people in large numbers are carrying on the work. Thirty-five years have passed away since I made this first visit to the home of John McIntosh. His body sleeps in the family cemetery near his beloved church (Big Arbor).

This year, 1936, Rev. Job McIntosh, the youngest son of the pioneer father . . . is the missionary to the Wichita and Caddo people. Thus the work goes on from one generation to another.

G. Lee Phelps, White Missionary in Indian Territory
Vol. 8, pp. 213–22

WICHITAS

There was a school for Indian girls out in Wichita country and the Indian agent there thought it would be a good idea for the girls to visit a camp meeting in the Choctaw Nation. They decided to come to High Hill [south of Alderson], and the mothers and fathers came along with their daughters, sometimes bringing whole families.

At that time I was living at Brazil, later to be called Calhoun, north and east and not very far from Skullyville. A crowd of us went to High Hill in a wagon. There was a good-sized church building at High Hill, but this camp meeting I am telling you about was held under a big arbor. Then there were a lot of small arbors for people to camp under and there were lots of people present.

Not many of the Wichitas showed up. We called them wild Indians, or the "wild bunch," and they really were pretty uncivilized. There weren't more than thirty or forty of them; I heard that about a hundred planned to come but two-thirds of them refused to ride on a train. You see, none of them had ever ridden on a train before.

They held services three times a day; at eleven in the morning, at three in the afternoon, and at night. I don't remember any of the Indians' names except the name of one deacon who seemed to have charge of seeing that the arrangements were all right, that people had plenty to eat and a place to camp. He lived there at High Hill, and his name was Jimmy Nature. Everything went off fine; the Indians were deeply religious, friendly, and very hospitable.

There was plenty to eat for everyone. We cooked mostly on stoves set up under the arbors, but some of the cooking was done on fires. There were cake and pie and almost anything you could think of and we had beef and pork and cornbread and biscuits. One little boy who had come with the

Wichitas wouldn't eat any cake or pie, or drink the coffee; he didn't seem to know how. We had some "Tom Fuller," the old Indian dish made from soaked corn, and I gave the little boy some of that. He lit right into it and ate three bowls full.

We had preaching and praying and singing, all in Choctaw, and some of the more important Indians made speeches. One of the Wichitas, an old gray-haired fellow, made a long talk. "We have not come to rob or steal, but to extend you the right hand of fellowship." He was a wild looking figure. He had on leather leggings and moccasins, a calico shirt and a vest, but no trousers. And his hair was long, down to his shoulders.

Monday morning when the Wichitas started to leave, everyone shook hands with them, and the Wichita women got hysterical and began to shout and dance. The Choctaws took the Wichitas to McAlester. There they boarded the train for the Reservation.

Mary Cole, Choctaw Freedman
Vol. 20, pp. 202–208

COMANCHES AND KIOWAS

My father traveled in a buggy. He would be gone two and three months at time, enduring many hardships. . . . The wild Indians had great respect for him and would never bother him. He went among them freely and never felt afraid. He preached through an interpreter. The Kiowas, Comanche, and Cheyenne Indians would camp at the foot of Mount Scott,[14] and hold meetings which would last two or three weeks.

At one of these meetings at Mount Scott an Indian woman got up and made a talk. We could tell something had moved her. The interpreter told us her son had been very sick; that the Medicine Men had been called in and made Medicine over him. She had climbed up on Mount Scott and offered her prayers to the Great Spirit, praying all night. Early the next morning the Great Spirit answered, and told her the boy would get well. Sure enough, when she went back her boy was better and later recovered. He was at the meeting with her.

Albert N. Averyt, Jr., White Minister among the Comanches
Vol. 13, pp. 30–39

Reverend [Elton] Deyo would hold a camp meeting once a year at the Fort Sill Agency.[15] His congregation was composed chiefly of Comanches. Between services the Indian women assisted by Mrs. Deyo, would hold quilting parties and make dozens of quilts for themselves.

The popular method of calling the righteous to worship was for old Kicking Bird, one of the pillars of the church, to stand outside the tent, and scream at the top of his voice: "Come to Church, Come to Church." And everyone within hearing distance had to go in self-defense, for he never let up yelling until they were all there.

H. M. Fullbright, White Interpreter at Deyo Mission
Vol. 103, pp. 61–65

Chapter Four

◆ ◆ ◆ ◆ ◆ ◆ ◆ ◆ ◆ ◆ ◆ ◆ ◆

Education and Health

◆ ◆ ◆ ◆ ◆ ◆ ◆ ◆ ◆ ◆ ◆ ◆ ◆

Once on the reservation after the Red River War of 1874–75, the societies of these traditional Indians of Texas underwent tremendous change. The U.S. government, backed up by eastern humanitarians and church groups, instituted a policy of "civilizing" the Indians in which they felt they must "kill the Indian to save the man." Education was the cornerstone of this policy. Indian children were forced to attend reservation day schools or far-away boarding schools, some run by the government and some by church denominations. Given little choice in the matter, Indian children were torn from their families and sent to these schools. Officials and humanitarians did not believe that Indian children were capable of becoming doctors, lawyers, or academics, so instead they taught them industrial and domestic arts, American history, and English. At the same time, the old problem of disease still stalked the Indians at the schools and on the reservations. At a time when their old ways were being crushed out of them and new ways forced upon them, Indian peoples tried to cope with this changing world and the problems it brought in the best way they could.

The Government Indian Schools

KIOWAS AND COMANCHES

There were four Government Reservation schools: the Wichita, the Kiowa, the Rainy Mountain, and the Comanche schools. In the Medicine Lodge Treaty, provision was made for Government schools for a period of twenty years. No school was established until 1871 when T. C. Battey, a Quaker teacher, came among the Caddos and took over the school started by A. J. Standing, who had only been teaching about three weeks. This school was first held in the old commissary building in the old Agency, north of the Washita River. It opened with five or six pupils, all boys. There were no dormitories and the boys slept on the ground behind logs or against the bluff or behind any kind of wind break that could be found. When winter came the boys slept in one room of the commissary. The pupils were provided two meals a day and these were cooked by a Cherokee Indian woman. This was called the Wichita School and was the beginning of the well-equipped River Side School of the present day.

T. C. Battey stayed with the Caddos for about two years when he came to the Kiowas. His school was not very successful but his influence here was lasting. During Hunt's administration,[1] 1878, the Kiowa School was established on the south bank of the Washita River, a mile west of the Indian Agency. . . .

The Comanche School was located near Fort Sill and is known now as the Fort Sill Indian School. This school was founded about 1892. It started with only forty boys the first year. The buildings were all ready but because of the inability to secure ready-made clothing for girls, there were only boys in the school. The next year there were forty girls. Mr. J. W. Hadden who had been superintendent of the Wichita school had been transferred to the Comanche school and Mr. Pigg took his place at the Wichita School.

When the Rainy Mountain school was established in the course of a few years, Mrs. Dunn, who had been an employee in the Wichita School, was recommended as superintendent. She filled this place until the school was closed. This school was located just south of the present town of Mountain View.

The Catholic school had been established for many years, with Father Isadore Ricklin in charge. At his death, Father Aloysius Hitta was put in charge. This school was, for many years, supported by the Government.

Pupils were gathered from different schools over the reservation and taken to the non-reservation schools that were supported by the government for higher education. The Carlisle school at Carlisle, Pennsylvania, was the most prominent. This school was closed down about the time of the World War and converted in the U.S.A. General Hospital No. 31.

The Chilocco School was at Chilocco, [Oklahoma]. It is now an industrial school. Haskell Institute is at Lawrence, Kansas. Most of the Indians from Oklahoma go to Haskell at the present time.[2]

J. J. Methvin, White Missionary to the Kiowas and Comanches
Vol. 36, pp. 157–62

CADDOS

I was born near what is now the little town of Verden, Oklahoma, located on the south side of the Washita River. At that time the land on the south side of the Washita River was claimed and controlled by the Caddo Indians, but later they were moved to the north side of the river.

At that time schools were few and far between. There were two government schools near Anadarko for the Indian children. One on the south side of the Washita River for the Kiowa, Comanche, and Apache children, just west of the town of Anadarko (The Indian Agency) and one located on the north side of the Washita River for the Caddo, Wichita, and Delaware children.

These schools were in charge of white men and women. The superintendent was usually a married man, but a number of the teachers were single men and women.

The Government schools were full of children. The accommodations were good, the food was supplied by the Government, and in abundance, such articles of food as meat, flour, beans, potatoes, rice, sugar, coffee, and sometimes dried fruit. The food was prepared by the older girls, under the supervision of a teacher. The girls were taught to cook, sew, mend clothing, and do housework. The boys were taught such work as is done on every farm, also carpenter work and blacksmithing. The discipline as well as I can recall was extra good, considering the fact that the Indian children did not understand the English language. The Government schools have been and are a grand success and they are more popular today than when first established.

The denominational schools were located near the town of Anadarko also, and it is an evident fact that their precept and example was and still is a wonderful power for good, and their influence is still bearing evidence among the Indians today. The Methodist, Baptist, and Presbyterian Churches, each supported a mission school, for the benefit of the Indian children, and many white children took advantage of the opportunities offered by these good schools, without detriment to either. Since statehood these Protestant schools have diminished and it seems to me a lamentable fact that we need them now more than ever. The Catholic Church has a school near Anadarko, known as St. Patrick's Mission and is still carrying on.

My first school was a subscription school in Anadarko. I was about five years of age. I boarded with Mr. and Mrs. Pat Pruner, good friends of my family. Mr. Pruner was a carpenter in the Government service. The school was held in the building known as 'Masonic Hall.' My first book was a McGuffey Primer. . . .

The Methodist Mission was in charge of J. J. Methvin. The Baptist Mission was in charge of G. W. Hicks.[3] S. V. Fait was in charge of the Presbyterian Mission, and a fine institution it was.[4] Dr. Graves was the Indian physician for a number of years, and then Dr. C. R. Hume[5] served the tribes for many years.

Jim Deer and Anco were Indian Police. It was their duty to catch whiskey peddlers, and to keep farmers and cattlemen from intruding.

Mrs. Frank Albin, Caddo
Vol. 12, pp. 178–82

COMANCHES

My first school was the Kiowa Indian School. Then I went to Carlisle College. Six of the girls from near my home went away to this college together. I was the only one to return. People from this dry climate couldn't live there very long because of such damp climate.

Emily Riddles, Comanche
Vol. 82, pp. 41–44

COMANCHES

I attended school at Fort Sill Indian School and finished the 7th and 8th grades at Bacone, Muskogee, Oklahoma. In the school I didn't have a chance to make my own money as the boys and girls do nowadays. But for pastime the girls learned to make beads and different kinds of bead work.

Sometimes I make my pin money by making bead belts. The ones I make over I get $5.00 and the ones I make I get $3.00.

I was married to George Apauty. He is 38 years old and is a full blood Kiowa. We have seven children. Four are in the Fort Sill Indian School and three at [the] house. All of the children speak English well.

My husband works for white people some. We have taught our children to "take care" and "work." We try to raise turkeys to help make a living. We have our own home, but all have to work and save.

In the school our boy and girls have their own crops, gardens and poultry. When any money is received from their work they are given checks. This encourages the children lots.

Our method of doctoring was with herbs my aunt would find but she never would show us younger children. Now we go to doctors at the Fort Sill Indian Hospital.

Adeline Apauty, Comanche
Vol. 99, pp. 186–88

COMANCHES

I was born and reared in this country many years before the Opening.[6] In the days of long ago my mother (as well as the other Indians) did not know how to tell the dates, but they counted by the seasons of the years, so my birthday was sometime in December near 1882.

My first school days were spent in a little school near Fort Sill called Cache Creek School. Then I went to the Kiowa Indian School. The school terms, when I was a boy, were very short. I did not like to go to school.

My father had large herds of cattle and horses. It was the duty of the boys in our family to herd the cattle and horses and the girls went to school.

At my first school each morning we were taught to pray, each night before we went to bed we must say our prayers. We had very good teachers. I didn't want to go to the Kiowa Indian school because the boys fought there very often. I never did want to go to school, I'd rather be home with my parents.

My people told me that if I went to Carlisle Indian School I would die. Lots of our boys and girls died there with a kind of lung trouble. I reckon because of the damp climate and people who didn't know how to handle this sickness.

Andrew Perdasophy, Comanche
Vol. 39, pp. 437–39

I was born here in Comanche County, 28 November 1905. My father and mother are full blood Comanche Indians. They were born here many, many years ago. I am the mother of five children. I received my education here at the Fort Sill Indian School. My children go to the Lawton public schools. They like to go there. When they don't study their lessons, to punish them, I tell them I'll have to send them to the Indian school, then they sure to study. When I was but a small girl, I remember coming up to the Red Stores,[7] about two and one-half miles north of Lawton. I believe there were four or five little stores there and this was the trading post of the Indians. We do our cooking, use the medicine like white people do. Our church services are about the same as those of the white people.

Elsie Chatt, Comanche

Vol. 19, pp. 427–28

TONKAWAS

Tonkawa Indian School was organized January 1, 1891, at Oakland Agency, Oklahoma Territory. The original enrollment comprised six (6) adults and eleven (11) children. Of the adults, four were male and two were females. Of the children, eight were male and three were females. All being below the age of twelve years. The total enrollment was these seventeen scholars, eleven of whom had never attended any school before.

There was no schoolhouse on the reservation but there were two houses for employees; one of the houses was unoccupied, accordingly it was fitted up with some old benches formerly used by the Nez Percé who once owned and occupied this reservation. The teacher, with the aid of a few friends, dressed the children in clothing such as white children wore, borrowed a few dishes, knives, forks and spoons from the Ponca School, also, books, charts and chalk; teacher furnished slates, pencils, pens, etc.

At the time the school was opened beef, flour, coffee, sugar, and beans were issued to the Tonkawas every Saturday, also salt, baking powder and soap once a month. The children had one meal a day (dinner) at the school.

The scheme of having a school at home greatly pleased the old Indians, for they had sent some of their children to Chilocco to school, where one had died. In some cases some were taken sick and had died before the old Indians knew of their sickness. In order to secure a school at home the Indians were glad to give a part of their rations toward the support of the school.

The first six months of the school were from January 1st to June 30, 1891. On September 1, school reopened, with an enrollment of thirteen scholars; a large part of the adults having to attend to their farming and other work could not attend school. At this time there were no rations issued to the tribe, so the teacher fed the scholars until late in September. She afterwards furnished them with potatoes, milk, etc.

A boy died October 1891 of paralysis and dropsy; another boy died, age eleven years. He had been to school at Chilocco for three years; he came home ill and entered the day school, where he remained until his death, in February 1892. Another boy died in March 1892, aged nine years; at this time only one adult attended school; he withdrew on account of sickness and died in April 1893.

Supplies for the school arrived late in September 1892. These consisted of flour, sugar, and coffee; later a good supply of books, slate pencils, crayons, erasers, tableware and slating for blackboards were received.

Flour, baking powder and a supply of clothing, consisting of hats, pants, flannel shirts, suspenders, some very small stockings, twenty-three yards of cotton shirting, twelve yards of mosquito bar, and five boxes of spool cotton came at the same time.

In December of the same year, 1892, a supply of soap and sixteen cords of wood. Before this time the wood was furnished by the teacher. The beans that the Nez Percés left in the commissary and a little salt were turned over to the school. These are all the supplies the school had up to June 30, 1893. In September 1893, school opened with ten scholars. The supplies consisted of coffee, sugar, beans, baking powder, soap and salt. One box of shoes and one bolt of gingham were received. The school was in a flourishing condition; all the scholars contented and learning fast, but in October 1893, the school was discontinued and all children over five years old were sent to Ponca School, except one, who went to Chilocco.

Bertha Brewer Plummer, White Daughter of the Agent to Tonkawas
Vol. 93, pp. 353–62

COMANCHES

When I was fifteen my father sent me to the Indian school called Chilocco. At that time Indians and whites attended the school though now only Indians attend. In this school all kinds of vocational training was in operation. The school was established in 1882 by an appropriation by Congress. W. J. Hadley was the first superintendent. I learned to be a stone cutter in the quarry at this school.

Quanah Parker's daughter attended Chilocco at the time that I attended. I admired her very much and when the students were instructed to set out trees I named the first tree planted for Miss Parker, whose name was Hester and I called the tree Hester Parker. We planted a line of trees from the Campus to the Kansas line north, a distance of two miles. The first tree on the west side of the road going north is Hester Parker. An old school chum visited me lately and told me the tree is now eighteen inches in diameter. The trees are maple.

The rock quarry was three miles from the school. All the rock for the buildings were obtained from this quarry.

The students also did the milking and worked in the vegetable gardens and in the fields. A boy or girl could learn almost any kind of vocational work.

We answered roll call three times daily. The school was only five miles from the Arkansas River and as there was a creek that ran nearly all the way from the school to the river we boys when we could get away would skate to the river and sometimes for miles on the river. We were almost always punished for this, but we skated again if we could slip away.

Joseph Esau, a full blood Pawnee, was my pal and also the leader in most of our entertainments. We killed rabbits by making a circle of boys on the prairie. The noise we made started the rabbits and we closed in the circle and killed the rabbits.

J. J. Farris, White Student at Chilocco Indian School
Vol. 105, pp. 205–207

TONKAWAS

I went to school at Chilocco seven years, and worked at harness making about two years after coming out of school.

John Rush Buffalo, Tonkawa
Vol. 77, p. 332

When I was twelve years old, I went to stay with my aunt, and she put me in the Chickasaw Orphans school at Madill. I went there for two years. Then I went to the Indian school at Sulphur Springs for a year. Both schools are now gone.

After I quit school at Sulphur Springs, I went to school at Tishomingo, and from there to Ardmore, where I took a Commercial Course.

Aaron Hamilton, Caddo-Chickasaw
Vol. 27, pp. 223–25

The Riverside Indian School[8]

KIOWAS

When I reached the [Riverside] school plant, which was about two miles northwest of the [Kiowa] Agency Office, I found four white ladies and two Indian men employees, the two Indian men being carried as laborers. One of the Indians was a Seminole of the name of John Wolf who was married to a daughter of the Wichita Chief, Tawakonie Jim, and the other was a full blood Wichita of the name Philip Hendrick; both deceased at this time. A part of the duties of these two men was to work on the school farm and to look after the school stock.

I immediately made an inspection of the school farm, crops, stock and the school plant and found that some of the school cattle were getting through a wire fence into the school corn and doing considerable damage and that the place where the cattle were getting through the fence into the corn was in a thick growth of timber at the rear side of the field well hidden from the school. I instructed the two Indian men to hitch a team to a wagon, and get the necessary material and tools, and I would go with them to fix the fence. After we got into the thick timber, I began to recall reading of many raids which the Kiowas, Comanches, Apaches, Cheyenne and other Indian tribes had made into Texas and other states, the captives they had taken, murders they had committed, stock they had driven off, etc., and I became slightly alarmed. Furthermore, after looking John Wolf over quite carefully in the dense timber, I though he had the appearance of being a vicious fellow. I took charge of the work and took the hatchet they had brought along to use in driving the wire staples to secure the wire on the posts and had them to do all the other work while I drove the wire staples and chopped small brush that was in the way, and held on to the hatchet. After I became well acquainted with the two Indian men, I found them to be absolutely harmless. . . .

In 1893 when I entered on duty as Industrial Teacher in the Riverside Boarding School, . . . the capacity of the school was sixty pupils, thirty girls and thirty boys. The brick building contained two dormitories for pupils, two school rooms, a dining room, kitchen, two play rooms and quarters for eight employees. There were also two small wash rooms one for the girls and one for the boys. There was no basement and the building was badly overcrowded.

The school plant was located about a hundred and fifty yards north of the Washita River from which stream the larger part of the water for the use of the school was taken, being hauled from the river in barrels. There were also three cisterns but they supplied only a small part of the water used by the school. The school was heated by wood stoves and the wood was purchased from the Indians.

The pupils up to and including the second grade were kept in school all day but after they completed the second grade work they were kept in school in the classroom work only half of the day and assigned to industrial work the other half. There was a one hour classroom session each for four nights in the week where the pupils received literary instruction. The girls were given industrial instruction in housekeeping, sewing, cooking and laundry work and the boys were given instruction in gardening, farming and a little instruction in raising livestock and in dairy work, there being sixty-five acres of land in cultivation.

The Indians would be notified in advance of the time when the school would open and would be invited to bring in their children to the school, but not more than from twenty to twenty-five per cent of the parents would bring their children promptly.

Notwithstanding the fact that the Government provided free schooling for the Indian children, including quarters, board, clothing and medical attention, at least seventy-five per cent of the Indian parents of the Wichita and Affiliated Bands opposed having their children attend the school so it soon became a part of my duties within two or three days after the school opened to hitch a team to a wagon or hack and to visit the homes of the parent of pupils who had not returned their children to school. In some cases the family would be away from their homes and even away from the Reservation and such things caused unavoidable delays in getting some of the pupils in school on time. Sometimes to get pupils started in school where the parents were opposed to having their children attend was a difficult task. However, in most cases about all I had to do to get children back to school who had been previously enrolled was to drive to their homes and inform them that I had come to take them back to school. Usually the Indian children would begin to get ready by taking off their Indian summer clothing and dressing in the clothing they had worn home from school. The Indian clothing worn by the school children through the summer at that time was a long shirt; they went bare headed through the summer, also. It would usually require three or four weeks to get the school filled after the opening of the term.

Where the parents would not consent for their children of proper age and health to be put in the school it was customary to withhold issuing the regular allowance of rations that was being issued to the family or to withhold the payment of funds to the parents who would not put their children in school.

John Buntin, White Teacher at Riverside Indian School
Vol. 89, pp. 319–53

CADDOS

At the age of six, I started to school in one end of the old Commissary building, located a short distance north of the Washita River, near the Anadarko Agency. There were approximately twenty children attending this school, all of them Caddos and Delawares. The teacher's name was Alfred Standing. This was a boarding school, and the girls' matron's name was Hattie Sheron. Her duties were to teach the girls to wash, iron, and sew. Emma Sheron was the dining room matron, her duties were to teach the girls to sweep, mop the floors, etc. Polly Keyes, a Cherokee Indian woman was our cook. Our beds were made of cottonwood lumber, and the mattresses were made of brown muslin, filled with hay.

Sara Ann Davis Smith, Caddo
Vol. 9, pp. 551–54

The Church Schools

The first school that I attended was Fait's Mission, located three miles east of Anadarko. This Mission was in charge of S. V. Fait and his wife. They were Presbyterians, and Mr. Fait preached every Sunday at his church in Anadarko.

There was a hack and team kept at the Mission for the students to use in attending church. There were so many students at Fait's Mission, both Indian and white children, that we couldn't all go at once. Each student took his turn, and would get to go to church about once every three weeks.

Mr. and Mrs. Fait and the teachers and matrons were very kind to all the children. We had milk cows and chickens at the Mission to furnish the school with milk, butter and eggs. We had other food such as rice, potatoes, beans, beef and canned fruit.

The Mission was not very far from the Washita River and in the Fall, we would have school picnics and gather wild grapes, of which the older girls made jelly. We gathered plums and black walnuts.

The school rooms were heated by a wood furnace. The Mission had a cook employed, but the older girls helped set the table and wash the dishes, and at the same time learned to cook. The girls were also taught to sew and mend. They did most of the laundry work.

In the Fall of 1889, one of the children, a Caddo boy named Johnny Green, broke out with the smallpox. Mr. Fait notified my mother and father that we had been exposed to the smallpox and they came after my two sisters and me. All three of us had the smallpox, but we got over it, and returned to school.

Dr. East from Chickasha was our doctor and he said that all could be done was to take heart tablets, to strengthen the heart.

Mrs. I. V. Davis, Caddo
Vol. 31, pp. 395–98

I was born on the Caddo reservation, ten miles northwest of Chickasha, in 1889. At the age of six years, I started to a Catholic Mission school at Anadarko, Father Isadore [Ricklin] being in charge of the school. The school was a two-story building; our sleeping quarters were upstairs and we girls, as there were eighteen or twenty to the room, were put in the care of the Sisters, Tranquilla, Milliana, and Becarty. These Sisters were all young, and were very kind to us. One of our daily studies was Catholic Catechism. Every Sunday when Father Isadore held services, several Indian men and women would come to hear.

In the Fall of 1896, I started to Fait's Mission, located about three miles east of Anadarko. My book studies were taught to me by Miss Mahan, and our Matron, Miss Langalier, taught us to sew and darn. Each child had a sewing bag, which contained a tape measure, needles, thread, pin cushion, thimble, and darning needles and thread. My mother bought goods and made my clothes, yet it was exciting to see the boxes and barrels of clothes opened that were shipped to us from the East.

There were approximately fifty pupils going to school there, and as many of us as could went with Mr. Fait to Anadarko every Sunday to hear him preach at the Presbyterian Church. Two of the songs we sang then were "Sweet hour of Prayer," and "Anywhere with Jesus."

During school term the Indian children's parents would camp on the creek, close to the school, and visit their children; sometimes they would stay two or three days, and it was a real treat to the children to go to their parents' camp and eat with them. I have attended many Indian dances when I was a child, and have found the Indians to be very kind hearted, and generous to a fault. . . . I attended the Washita school, in Grady County taught by Miss Eloise Bell, one year; went to Almeta Bond College at Minco, taught by Mrs. Sager, for two years; went to Haskell Institute at Lawrence, Kansas, three years, and finished my education in a business college at Chikasha, Oklahoma.

Mrs. Cragg Goetting, Caddo
Vol. 105, pp. 405–408

KIOWAS, COMANCHES, CADDOS, AND APACHES

On September 8, 1891, Reverend Isadore Ricklin, O.S.B. arrived at the Kiowa agency to establish himself as a missionary among the Kiowas, Comanche, Caddo, and Wichita Indians. An offer had been made by the Department of the Interior to various denominations of a land grant on condition that they would establish a school for Indians. A site of 160 acres was selected by

Reverend Isadore on a high plateau southwest of the Kiowas and Washita Agency. This grant, for the foundation of a Catholic Mission, was approved and confirmed by the Indian Agent, Charles E. Adams.

Five months after the arrival of the missionary his work among the Indians was so well appreciated that the Comanches in formal council of the chiefs adopted him into their tribe.

In 1892, a two-story frame building was erected for school purposes and in November some teachers were sent from Philadelphia, being financed by Miss Catherine Drexel who also had contributed to the expense of the erection of the first buildings.

On November 25, 1892, thirty-five Comanches, Apaches and Kiowas were enrolled as boarders; fifteen boys and twenty girls.

Keeping down the expense of the missions was greatly helped by receiving rations issued by the government to Indians at regular intervals.

Soon after the opening of the school when the Bishop of Oklahoma first visited the new mission, a larger number of Kiowa, Comanche and Caddo Indians gathered around the school. It was on that occasion that old Chief Lone Wolf, standing before a cross, "Thanked the Great Spirit for sending a great spiritual man among them to teach them to love rightly and to live Jesus." Walking Bird made his invocation in Comanche and implored the Great Spirit, "To help the Pale Face Medicine Man heal the sick, to procure abundant food and to grant them better luck with their ponies and pastures. . . ."

The curriculum of the institution corresponded to curriculum of other Indian schools. Farming, gardening and stock raising were emphasized. Indian laborers were employed as much as possible in all the work done around the mission and oftentimes a large group of Indians would come to take lessons in agriculture and horticulture from the expert gardener, Michael Wack, who was at the head of the agricultural activities.

Mrs. H. C. Rooney, White Resident of Anadarko area

Vol. 42, pp. 279–85

KIOWAS

Few persons now living know there was ever an Indian Mission school at Missions Spring because, although the springs remain, no trace of the building is left. The spot upon which the early Kiowa Indian Mission School was located, lies between what was then two large springs of fine water, each flowing out from the south side of a small mountain of the Wichita Range. The water from these springs flowed away down the valley forming a small lake. The grass grew in abundance and until this time numerous wild plants and flowers are to be found in this locality. There were also many trees growing in the valley; mesquite with great cotton-woods, elms, and hackberry trees growing near the river. The North Fork of Red River flows one mile to the west. The mountains, Mount King, Flat Top and Soldier Peak are to the south. ... The picket house used for a school and the teacher's house [was] located ... south of Lone Wolf. At that time a large number of Kiowa Indians were living in this vicinity. They had been moved by soldiers sent from Fort Sill by the Government, away from their camp on the west side of the North Fork of Red River and located in the vicinity of the present village of Lugert on the Kiowa side. Lone Wolf, Komalty, Kiowa Bill, Loud Talk and many more Kiowas with their families were very friendly with us. Loud Talk's squaw was the best housekeeper and the cleanest Indian I ever saw. She was smart and always wanted to know how I did my house work and cooking and when I told her she would try to do things that way.

Many of the young Indians were sent away to school but when they came back they would put on their Indians clothes and seem glad to get back. Roasted dry land terrapin was a favorite food among the Indians. I remember one young Indian girl who had been away to the Carlisle Indian School who came home and right away put on her blanket, took a sack and went out and captured a whole sack full of terrapins, brought them in and built up a big fire in front of the tepee and poured the terrapins into the fire alive just as they were. With a long stick she kept them in the fire until they were dead and then when all were roasted, she seemed to like them as well as we do oysters and they all had a feast. I never feared any of these Indians and we lived among them until they were moved to Rainy Mountain and farther east on Elk Creek. ...

Hattie Parrish, White Resident of Kiowa Territory
Vol. 79, pp. 456–60

WICHITAS

I was born north of Anadarko, in the Caddo country, in 1886, at which time my father was freighting supplies for the Government, from Gainesville, Texas.

In 1891, I started to school at what was then called the Wichita school, north of Anadarko. There they furnished us clothes and boarded us. There were between forty and sixty Indian children going to school there at that time.

In 1893, I started to school at the Catholic Mission at Anadarko. Father Isadore was the priest. There were seventy or eighty girls and about fifty boys going there.

The most of the Indians at that time didn't trust the white people, but the Catholic sisters were very kind to the Indians. A good many Indian men and women had sore eyes and the sisters doctored them. This made the Indians love the sisters and they would come to the Mission in time of sickness instead of going to the agency. They also ate so many meals at the Mission that the Government issued beef and other supplies to the Mission.

Most of the Catholic sisters were of German descent.

My teacher's name was Osmonda. We studied Benziger Brothers school books.

A good many Indian men and women came to the Catholic Church. The Indians had an interpreter to preach to them and several of them were baptized.

At Christmas time we always sorted names and presents so that each one we thought would be there would receive a present.

In 1898, I entered the St. Elizabeth Convent at Purcell. My teacher's name was Teresa, and Father Williams was the priest. Music was taught there, but there was a small charge for the lessons.

The Government issued one beef for three families, usually the beef was eaten fresh, but sometimes the beef would be cut in strips, and hung in the sun to dry. It took about three days for the beef to dry.

The Kiowas and Comanches didn't bury their dead very deep, but nearly always killed the best horse belonging to the party who had passed away and put the saddle and other belongings in the grave. It is my supposition that the Kiowas and Comanches thought that those who passed away would need their horse and belongings in the happy hunting ground. Relatives of the deceased would come to the grave a sunup and mourn all day for seven days.

Martha Holt, Chickasaw Resident of Wichita Territory

Vol. 29, pp. 348–50

School Discipline and Runaways

COMANCHES

In the early days here when rations were issued, after schools were established, the Government wouldn't issue any rations if the Indians didn't send their children to school, and they were punished if heard speaking the Indian language. This was to bring them closer to civilization, causing them to forget their Indian ways.

Ella Wer-Que-Wa, Comanche
Vol. 49, pp. 178–80

COMANCHES

The first days of September were always sad for the Indian mothers. We could see the white men taking their children to school. They had to leave off their shawls and dress as white children dressed even though they were in Indian schools. Just as soon as some Indian children had a chance they ran away from school. But when school was out they came home very happy to get into their Indian clothes.

Mrs. John Barnes, White Resident of Comanche Territory
Vol. 66, pp. 131–40

KIOWAS AND COMANCHES

I came in January 1891 as an employee to the Kiowa Indian School at Anadarko, I. T. At the time, Minco was the end of the railroad. A day or two prior to my arrival three boys had run away from the school, a blizzard over took them & they were frozen to death. Indians were dancing the Ghost Dance at that time and collected around & threatened to burn the school. Employees were instructed to never let but ½ of the children out of the building at a time thus preventing the burning of the building. One old Indian gave the Supt. G. V. Gregory a whipping with his quirt. I was at the meeting of the Dawes Commission with the Kiowas and Comanches in 1894. . . . Had an epidemic of measles, saw the mothers of dead children cut off points of fingers, cut faces & breasts & hair & heard them mourn all night long and dance the ghost dance etc., etc. Have seen Indian bucks with blankets wrapped round them exposing only one eye and heard them play their mournful sounding flutes, standing by the hour at the fence surrounding the school to catch a glimpse of a girl sweetheart. Heard Joshua Givens, a full blood Kiowa, graduate of Carlisle, called the Silver Tongued Orator of the Indians.[9] He was in the Presbyterian Mission . . . five miles out from Anadarko.

Mary Elizabeth Daly Ware, White School Teacher at Kiowa Indian School
Vol. 73, pp. 310–11

KIOWAS

In 1891, Mr. Wherritt, a teacher in the Kiowa School whipped a boy of about fourteen years old. This boy and two others determined to run away and go home down among the mountains, about thirty-five miles to the south. During the night a blizzard overtook them when they were almost home, and they froze to death. This almost caused an outbreak among the Indians. Captain [Hugh L.] Scott saw no reason for calling out the troops. However, Mr. Wherritt stayed hidden until he could get away, when he left the school, and further trouble was averted.

J. J. Methvin, White Missionary to the Kiowas and Comanches
Vol. 36, pp. 157–62

CADDOS

Since many of the Wichita Indian families lived within five or six miles of the school it was a common practice for a number of the children to slip away from the school and go home, which practice was called "running away." Many of the parents would try to keep their children from running away and this kind of cooperation, with a mild form of punishment, was sufficient to reduce the runaway to a small number. However there were usually a few pupils in the school who would run away.

Several years after I became an employee at the school, there was a very bright, active Caddo boy of the name of Aloysius French about twelve or thirteen years of age who would frequently run away. His parents opposed his running away and did all they could to cause him to stop it but the boy would not obey them in this particular. Just to the rear of the home of the parents of this boy was a thick growth of timber and if Aloysius saw anyone coming to their place whom he thought wanted to take him back to school he would run into the woods and hide out until the suspected party left. His home was about twenty miles from the school. One time soon after Christmas he ran away so I secured a Santa Claus face and some wearing apparel that was used with it at the school during the Christmas school exercises and drove a team of Government school horses which Aloysius well knew to an Indian's home about one mile from where the boy lived. I secured a gentle pony from the Indian and put a blanket on the pony which was so large that it nearly covered the pony and made him hard to recognize. I then put a saddle on the pony and mounted him and rode close to the home of the boy and dismounted and walked up to where the boy and his parents were and started to shake hands with them and saying "I am hungry, give me 'wa-haw'"; nearly all the Southern Indians knew that "wa-haw" means beef. When I got Aloysius by the hand I took off my false face and informed him that I had come for him. He offered no resistance and in a short time we were on our way back to the school.

About four months later in the same school year, two of the large girls ran away early one morning and went to the home of one of them about sixteen miles from the school. I had a team hitched to a hack or spring wagon and went after the girls and I found them about one o'clock at the home of one of the girls eating dinner. I told them as soon as they were through dinner, I would take them back to the school. Aloysius, who had recently run away from school, was in camp with his parents in a thick timber about a mile away and I knew if he saw the school team or saw me coming he would run off in the woods and I could not catch him so I asked the girls to get two long, colored Indian dresses and put them on and instructed them that we would drive as near the camp as we could without the boy or his parents seeing us and then we would get out and the two girls would walk abreast close together and that I would walk in a crouched posture close behind so they might not see me until I got near enough to the boy to get him. We marched up to the camp as planned and since Aloysius had caught some young owls for which he was fixing a little box he did not see me. Because the girls had their camp dresses on instead of the school dresses when they approached the camp, they boy and his parents most likely thought that some of the neighborhood Indian women were coming to pay them a visit. When I instructed Aloysius to get his owls fixed and then to get ready and we would be on our way back to the school, it did not take him long to get ready and the four of us were soon on our way. We talked considerably on our way back to the school but never mentioned a thing about any of the children having run away. Of course, after we got back and supper was over the children were talked to and reprimanded and lightly punished for running away.

John A. Buntin, White Teacher at Riverside Indian School

Vol. 89, pp. 319–53

Disease and Illness

KIOWAS

In 1892, an epidemic of smallpox broke out in the [Kiowa] school and instead of caring for the children in the school, the superintendent sent the patients home, thus scattering the disease among the other Indians. That winter about fifteen percent of the Indians died. The school was closed during Frank D. Baldwin's administration in 1894.

J. J. Methvin, White Missionary to Kiowas and Comanches

Vol. 36, pp. 157–62

COMANCHES, KIOWAS, AND APACHES

In the winter of 1899, and the spring of 1900, I witnessed a smallpox epidemic among the Indians. At this time I was working as a clerk in the Indian Trading Post, one mile west of the present town of Cache.

There had been an Issue Day in December and there were some five hundred Indians—men, women, and children—camped at this place. Some of them lived quite near this post while others lived twenty-five miles or more away, but this place was their trading post. When there was to be an Issue Day, the Indians would begin to come into camp, some two or three weeks ahead of time, bringing their tents, stoves, and general camping equipment and would visit with their neighbors. The men would play monte and gamble and they usually spent every cent from one payday until the next for when an Indian has any money or anything to trade he is not long in disposing of either. He is always a free spender and a good trader.

While the Indians were encamped at this time, smallpox broke out among them and spread like prairie fire. It first broke out, however, in a railroad grading camp on the Frisco right-of-way, about a mile distant from this trading post. A number of workers in the grading camp were Mexicans and were no cleaner in their mode of living than the Indians.

When this disease broke out it was not long in reaching the Indians in camp and with the same ferocious destruction as is made from a wild prairie fire, was not long in thinning out the ranks. Many of the Mexicans would come over and gamble with the Indians, bringing the germs with them, and the toll of deaths was heavy throughout the Indians camp of Kiowas, Comanches, and Apaches.

Medical aid was almost impossible to obtain. One doctor, located at Fort Sill, came twenty miles distant, had more patients there than he could possibly wait on by going day and night, so the Indian Medicine Men proceeded to doctor the patients in their own crude way. They tried several ways to cure them, one way being to plunge the patient (with high fever) in the creek. This was a quick and very effective way of "stopping" the disease, a number of them dying before they could be taken out of the water.

In February, 1900, some two hundred Indians died like rats, within almost a stone's throw of this trading post. Their crying and wailing was plainly heard all day and throughout the night, but it only meant to us in the store that another one of our Indian friends had gone to his "Happy Hunting Ground."

In those days sanitation was something unheard of among the Indians, neither did they know of the white man's way of doctoring and it took years of preaching and teaching from the white missionaries before the Indian would consent to our way of doctoring and sanitation. It was pitiful and horrifying to see this scourge taking so many lives and little or nothing could be done about it. They would come into the store in many different stages, some could not be recognized by their looks and the ones we knew best could only be recognized by their voices, their features being entirely obliterated from swelling. None of us in the store took it for we kept disinfectant out all over the store and after waiting on a customer would always wash our hands.

One young man and his wife, with a year old baby girl, were camped quite near the Post. They were in the store trading late one afternoon and both were found dead in bed the next morning. The baby, sleeping between them, survived and lives today near Cache.

Dick Banks, White Storekeeper in Comanche Territory

Vol. 99, pp. 437–42

Tuberculosis, malarial fever and scrofula were very common among the Wichita and Affiliated Bands in 1893 and for several years thereafter. There was also a number of cases of typhoid each year among these tribes and trachoma and other eye diseases were quite common among the members of these tribes. Their homes, sanitary conditions, unbalanced diet and the great number occupying the same room made it very difficult to prevent contagious diseases from being spread among them. I estimate that nine out of ten would not accept the treatment of a licensed physician but preferred that the Medicine Men should treat them when they were sick. None of them had any way of protecting themselves against flies and mosquitoes. Their drinking water was unsanitary and of a poor quality, the water was usually being hauled in barrels from some distance and it might stand in barrels for a week before the supply would be replenished. Their birth and death rates were very high and the population was slightly on the decrease. They seemed to have gotten the superstitious idea that to be afraid of a disease greatly increased your likelihood of contracting the disease. Their Medicine Men used some herbs, peyote, the sweat bath, cold water, cutting and scratching, rubbing and so forth.

I remember that some months after I entered the school service [1893] I went out to see a boy who was sick in his home. The boy was on a bed on the ground in a grass house and the Medicine Man, who was well painted up, was sitting on the ground near the boy. There was a fire in the center of the grass house around which four or five members of the family were sitting on the ground and on the fire in a vessel there was a dark colored liquid which I was informed was the boy's medicine. I talked with the members of the family and the Medicine Man about getting the Government doctor to aid the Indian doctor in treating the boy but the whole group strongly objected. These Indians informed me that they knew of one Indian in their settlement whom the Government doctor had treated and who had died and they said they did not want this boy killed. While I was in the grass house I started to walk between the fire on which the medicine was being prepared and the sick person and was told that it would result in death to the sick one. The boy got well and was back in school in a few weeks.

On one occasion at an Indian gathering, in connection to other things, I endeavored to explain to the Indians that tuberculosis, typhoid fever, sore eyes and practically all other diseases were due to disease germs. I tried to explain to them that the germs were like a great number of worms so small that you could not see them with your naked eye. One of the men had very sore eyes and I explained that the sore parts of his eyes were alive with these little worms or germs. One of the old Indians immediately went over to the man who had the sore eyes and looked his eyes over very carefully and turned and informed me through an interpreter that my statements about the germs or little worms being in the man's eyes making them sore was false. This old Indian further claimed that he had good eyes and he had looked and could not see them and if the germs were so small that they could not be seen that they would be too small to do any harm. The other Indians agreed with him and I lost the argument.

John A. Buntin, White Teacher at Riverside Indian School
Vol. 89, pp. 319–53

CADDOS, COMANCHES, AND KIOWAS

In the spring of 1892, an epidemic of measles broke out among the Indians camped around the [Anadarko] agency. More than three hundred children died before the treatment of the medicine men could be stopped, for their treatment killed more than it cured. The medicine man would make medicine over the patient, grunting like a hog or bellowing like a bull, trying to scare the evil spirits away. Then he would apply suction with his mouth on the child's throat, chest, and bowels. He also would place them in a sweat house and when the patient was perspiring profusely he would either pour cold water over them or taken them to the river and dip them into the river.

The sweat house was made something like a small arbor, bringing the boughs together at the top, then covering the whole thing with canvas in such a way as to make it almost air tight. Hot stones were placed in a pit in the center of the hut and water poured over them making a steam. Under this treatment hundreds of children died and the wailing of the Indians was heard constantly for two or three months.

The wailing and the tom-toms could be heard all night, and at each death the wailing increased. Their self-inflicted punishment was pitiful. The women would strip their bodies to the waist and slash their arms from the shoulder to the wrist, and their bodies and breasts with a sharp knife. They smeared the blood over their faces. Many of the women cut the end of their fingers off, and cut their hair. There was a great deal of property destroyed, and the graveyard had the appearance of a junkyard, with all the broken wagons, chairs, and toys.

In the early days, the Indians didn't have regular burial grounds, but buried their dead in very shallow graves. They would take the body to some hole in a canyon and dig a very shallow grave, place the body in it and cover it with the dead person's personal property, then half cover the grave with dirt, finishing with brush; leaving the body easy prey for the wolves and coyotes. After the grave was covered, the man's horse was led up close and killed. Sometimes as many as ten horses were killed, owing to the wealth of the deceased.

The son of [Kiowa] Chief Stumbling Bear was the last person to be buried in the old graveyard on top of the hill north of Anadarko. The Indians wanted him to have a Christian burial, but they wanted the old way, too, and wanted us to combine the two. I told them no, that it would have to be one or the other. They then told me to go on with the Christian burial, then go away. I did, and on looking back I saw them put in all of the boy's things, blankets, bridle, saddle and many other things. The saddle was a new cowboy saddle and the boy had just paid fifty dollars for it. After the grave had been covered they led the boy's pony up and cut its throat, and let bleed to death on the grave. Thus the boy had his horse and saddle in the Happy Hunting ground. Either that same night or the next some white men dug the saddle up and took it away.

J. J. Methvin, White Missionary to Comanches and Kiowas
Vol. 36, pp. 103–106

COMANCHES

Years ago there were many cases of typhoid fever in our neighborhood. Two of my children had it. When my little girl had fever and was so sick this Indian man came to our house. He thought it was so bad and wanted us to feed the child as she said she was so hungry. When this Indian man went home in the evening, he went by town and bought things for the little girl. Next morning he came back riding an old mule with a barbed wire for a bridle bringing popcorn, candy, peanuts, fruits, cookies and crackers. He came in, pouring all these things out on her bed, saying, "Now help yourself Betty, you can have something to eat." Most Indians are free hearted, and this man had never forgotten what I did for his family when they were in need of someone to help with their sick.

Mrs. John Barnes, White Resident of Comanche Territory
Vol. 66, pp. 131–40

Treatment and Remedies

CADDOS, KIOWAS, AND COMANCHES

The Indians of my acquaintance used little medicine. Balmona, the little plant with the bell-shaped flower, which you see growing all over this part of the country in the Spring, was the main medicine used by them.

It was gathered by the squaws when it was in bloom and laid out to dry. When it was thoroughly dry, it was crumbled up and usually placed in a leather or buck-skin bag ready for use when needed. The dried leaves were made into a tea and given as a purgative.

The most usual way of treating the sick was by sweating. This was done by hollowing out a hole in the ground, according to the size desired and digging a small trench leading into it from one side. Then a number of small stones something like the size of a man's two fists would be gathered and heated very hot in a fire close by. The hole would then be filled with water and the sick laid beside the hole and all covered with a buffalo robe which would be staked down over all except the person's head which would be left out. The hot stones would be rolled down the little trench, into the water under the cover and this, of course, would cause a great steam, which would sweat the sick as much as the Medicine Man desired.

When the sweating was finished, the patient would be taken out and dipped in water, usually the creek. Then he would be rolled up in blankets and made to lie down several hours. This was done until the fever was broken and the patient generally got well.

Nathan J. McElroy, White Resident of Western Oklahoma
Vol. 35, pp. 106–107

CADDOS, WICHITAS, COMANCHES, AND KIOWAS

In 1892 or 1893, I can't remember which, we had an epidemic of malarial fever. The Indians would take the patients while they had high fever and dip them in the river as treatment. It was in the summer time and so did little harm. A few years later we had an epidemic of measles. We kept the children in the schools, so we could care for them, but the parents were camped all around the Agency and they would slip them out, and take them to their tepees. They tried the same treatment for the measles as they did for malaria. This caused a great many to die. Then later still we had the smallpox to break out among the Indians. There was no way to keep them quarantined. We tried to get them to stay away from those who were sick, but they had to go to see their sick people. This caused the disease to spread fast, and many people died. We began to vaccinate the children in the schools, and had very few cases there.

In those days, when a child was born, there were no men to care for the woman, just a bunch of ignorant women. If any unusual case occurred, the patient usually died. One case especially I remember. My assistant came in one day and told me that there was a sick woman in camp. It was issue day and more Indians than usual were camped near. I went to see her. One child had already been delivered but another, a twin, was in an unnatural position and if she did not get the proper care she would die. I made the delivery and the woman got well. When the woman's sister saw that the woman was going to get well, she threw her arms around me and said that I made good medicine. I told the Indians that if they would camp close when any of them were to be sick I would help them if they had any trouble.

One man married a woman and lived with her for years and they never had any children. The wife told him to take her sister also for a wife. This younger sister had been going to the Methvin Institute to school. He took this sister and raised a large family. The older one of the women helped to take care of the children as if they were her own. When the older woman died, the usual custom of lamenting began. The sister began with the rest of the family, but I told her she mustn't work herself into such excitement; it wasn't good for her; that she had these children to look after. She said: "We have lived together and I have had all these children. She has helped to care for them and has never spoken a cross word to me as long as she lived."

When Cynthia, an Apache woman became sick, Mrs. Pruner, Black Beaver's daughter, came and told me, and I went to see her. The girl was having a rather tedious time and the woman didn't want me to come in. I told the woman that if they didn't let me alone I would send for the patrol wagon and put them all in jail. They left at once, and I took care of the girl.

Dr. Charles R. Hume, White Government Doctor for Kiowas, Comanches, Caddos, and Wichitas

Vol. 30, pp. 222–28

CADDOS

One time Mr. Stone wanted me to go with him near Fort Cobb, to see about buying some saddle horses he said. We came upon a group of Caddo Indians, on the Washita River near Fort Cobb. They had some kind of fever and the measles. The Indians were going in the river to cool the fever and in five minutes after one would come out of the water, he would die. We stayed there about one hour and I counted about 25 dead Indians. I could not understand them but Mr. Stone could. They talked with their hands mostly, would point and wave their hands around. Mr. Stone told them that going into the water was what was killing them. Mr. Stone finally got them stopped and we went on. Mr. Stone told me that if he hadn't got them stopped, everyone of them would have died.

John R. Gott, White Resident of Comanche Territory
Vol. 4, pp. 119–20

CADDOS, COMANCHES, AND KIOWAS

I know they used herbs of different kinds for all ordinary sickness. I learned about herbs from the Indians and my family do not have a doctor unless we cannot cure ourselves. One herb called butterfly herb is used for stomach trouble. Shoestring herb and bloodroot are used for diarrhea. They mostly used roots and made a tea. I think the reason that the herbs are growing scarce is that they dig up so many roots. If the leaves were used the plant would not be killed.

C. L. Ray, Black Resident of Caddo Territory
Vol. 113, pp. 238–42

COMANCHES AND KIOWAS

The Medicine Man, when calling on the sick, would have all leave the room. They would then take a rattle from their Medicine kit which was decorated with feathers and wave it over the patient, saying strange words. Then they gave them medicines made from herbs. The Indians would not talk about the

Medicine Man. They were sacred to them. All Medicine Men wore a peculiar painting on their faces.

Albert N. Averyt, Jr., White Minister among the Comanches
Vol. 13, pp. 30–39

KIOWAS

The persons whom the white people call the Medicine Men went to places which they would select and there they would fast and pray until they felt that their prayers had been heard and answered by God. Two miles west of the town of Gotebo in Kiowa County on Highway No. 9 stands a small teepee-shaped peak in the gypsum formation. Upon this peak my uncle, the oldest of our family, spent four days and nights in fasting and prayer at one time, for the purpose of receiving from the Holy Spirit knowledge of the use of medicines and other gifts which are the faith of the Kiowa people.

I do not propose to say what this gift is as I have never experienced it, but honesty forces me to state that my uncle, known as Sam, has at his advanced age wisdom which I do not comprehend. For example:

Some years ago my only daughter, a girl of fourteen, became ill with pneumonia. I called the white physicians and they did all in their power to restore her to health, but she grew rapidly worse. At last the physicians told me that they could do no more and that she would be bound to die, they thought by four o'clock the next morning. I decided to go for my Uncle Sam who lives near Carnegie which I did and asked him to do anything he thought best for my child.

He went willingly, taking along some herbs and other things and when we reached my home, he said to me in Kiowa, "I am afraid you have waited too long." But he asked for a newspaper and spreading it upon the floor, placed the herbs upon the paper, then told me to bring a coal of fire from the stove in the shovel. I brought the burning coal and he placed it upon the herbs, then began to pray. I listened closely for I was anxious to understand what he was saying. It was this, He was asking God to hear his prayer for my child, telling Him that it was my only girl and if God was willing to spare her to me, that he might have the wisdom to know what to do for her. He prayed a long while and the smoke from the herbs was filling the room.

When the child began to breathe easier he took out a quill or feather, which was sharp on the point and after baring the child's breast, he made incisions with the quill over the child's lungs and the blood which came out was perfectly black. He continued to work over her until she showed that she was better and fell into natural sleep. The next morning she was conscious and asked for food, but Sam said she should not eat yet. Under Uncle Sam's treatment the child recovered and is yet living. I do not understand what he did, but I give you this as a testimony to his work among the Kiowa people.

Robert Onco, Kiowa

Vol. 107, pp. 284–92

Chapter Five

◆ ◆ ◆ ◆ ◆ ◆ ◆ ◆ ◆ ◆ ◆ ◆ ◆ ◆

Life on the Reservation

◆ ◆ ◆ ◆ ◆ ◆ ◆ ◆ ◆ ◆ ◆ ◆ ◆ ◆

The Indian peoples living on the Comanche and Kiowa, the Wichita and Caddo, and the Tonkawa and Apache Reservations found themselves forced into close proximity of white peoples. These whites often had their own agenda and usually wanted something from the Indian people. Cattlemen wanted to graze their cattle cheaply on Indian land. Cowboys wanted to drive their herds across the reservations, with their cattle eating Indian grass and drinking Indian water, all for the cost of a cow or two. Farmers wanted Indian land to settle upon. Settlers outside the reservation boundaries wanted Indian wood or ponies. Merchants wanted their money. Missionaries wanted to convert them to Christianity. Teachers wanted them to learn a skill. The Army wanted them to remain peaceful. And government officials wanted them to give up their Indian ways and disappear, as an Indian ethnic group, into the vastness of mainstream society. Despite all these pressures, these traditional Indians of Texas faced these pressures as they always had, sometimes keeping within the old ways, sometimes adopting white ways, and sometimes changing by creating a wholly new and Indian way.

Agencies and Reservations

WICHITAS AND COMANCHES

With P. B. Hunt's appointment to the office of [Wichita] Indian Agent in April 1878, the Quaker Administration was brought to a close, and the politicians took over the management of Indian affairs at the Wichita Agency.[1] Hunt adopted some very progressive rules in the management of the affairs at this agency. He first induced the Indians to work for wages. They were taught to harness and drive double teams and to cut wood, which was always before considered woman's work, and haul the supplies for the agency and government schools. So after taking office Hunt organized an Indian police force. San-ka-do-te was made Captain with two lieutenants, four sergeants and twenty-two privates. There had been a lot of trouble with horse thieves, and Hunt authorized the Indians to follow them. This they did with much vigor. They have been known to follow as far as one hundred and fifty miles, recovering the stolen horses.

It was in the summer of 1878 that the Florida prisoners were returned.[2] Some of the prisoners died while in Florida, and some had been taken by people from the east, who had become interested in them, and educated them in the eastern schools.

In 1879, the Kiowa and Comanche Agency at Fort Sill was consolidated with the Wichita Agency at Anadarko.

The cattlemen gave the government a lot of trouble by letting their cattle wander over on the Indian land. The Indian police with the aid of the soldiers at Fort Sill were sent to patrol the borders of their land. When cattle were found the cattlemen were forced to drive them off, but in a short time the cattle were back again.

In 1881 it came about that something had to be done for the Indians were not getting enough beeves to eat and they were hungry. They became angry and threatened to kill everyone at the agency. Hunt made an agreement with the cattlemen. They could graze their cattle on the Indian land if they would furnish a certain amount of beeves for the Indians. The Indians were so mad they were ready to go on the warpath. Hunt called for troops from Fort Sill. They were sent to the agency and stayed until the Indians quieted down. Although Hunt's agreement with the cattlemen were not official, and he was rebuked for it, nothing could be done about it. The Indians had more to eat.

It was during Hunt's administration as Indian Agent that the old Kiowa school was established. This school was closed during Major Frank D. Baldwin's administration as Indian Agent.

Hunt was removed from the Wichita Agency in 1885 at the election of a Democratic president. Lee Hall followed.

Lillian Gassaway, White Daughter of J. J. Methvin, Missionary to the Kiowas and Comanches

Vol. 80, pp. 129–31

West Cache Trading Post was located on West Cache Creek, four miles south of Chief Quanah Parker's home and one mile west of Cache. It was a government licensed post; license was granted to G. M. Harris and E. L. James in the year 1896. There were about five hundred Indians who traded here regularly and were on the rolls at the subagency, located nearby. There were two payments made to Indians annually, usually in June and December. About $100.00 per year per capita divided into two $50.00 payments. The Indians all had plenty of cattle and horses and were able to live in a very comfortable manner.[3]

The store carried a line of general merchandise, from high-class silks and satins to fast colors of calico, all-wool blankets, and shawls, and imported Lisk-cloth. The store carried beads of all descriptions, bells, spangles, silver rings, and bracelets, all of which were in great demand. This trading post store was 75 x 125 feet and was well-filled with first-class merchandise, including fresh and cured meats. The merchandise was bought in eastern markets, shipped to Marlow and then freighted to the store in wagons, a distance of fifty miles.

Indians are good customers and very easy to please. If their credit is good, or if they are paying cash, they do not quibble or try to "Jew" you on the price. They are very fond of watermelons and I've seen them pay $1.50 for a twenty-five pound melon without a murmur. An Indian is honest at heart, if he makes you a definite promise you can depend on his fulfilling that promise. Somehow each Indian kept accurate accounts of the bills he owed, also the amounts he drew, and tried to be able to balance these accounts each payday. Some of the greedy Indian Traders would encourage the Indians to buy more merchandise than they had money to pay for, and in this way a great many of them were led into financial difficulties, thereby breaking down their good intentions.

At this time the older Indians did not speak English and the children who had the benefit of schooling wouldn't talk it so the personnel of the store naturally had to understand and talk their language. The Indians would give all the white people in or connected with the store Indian names. For instance, E. L. James was named Hoke-a-to-nits (Running in the Woods), so named because the first time he was seen by some of the Indians he was running. G. M. Harris was Pie-won-ard, meaning, Tall and Slim. And I was name Toah-vista, Nad-I-mo, Young Store-keeper.

Dick Banks, White Storekeeper in Comanche Territory

Vol. 99, pp. 437–42

CADDOS AND COMANCHES

I used to drift around a lot when I was young, and I have seen stomp dances in western Oklahoma. Up along the Washita River was Comanche and Caddo country. The Caddos and Comanches were pretty wild and fierce. The Choctaws seemed liked civilized people in comparison to them. The Caddos and Comanches wore their hair long, usually braided like little girls do and they nearly all wore blankets.

These Indians were not much account to work. They drew blankets, rations and sometimes horses from the Indian Agency at Anadarko and they would trade anything they had. And they usually got cheated when they traded with white men.

If they made any kick to the agent about a trade that did not suit them the agent would come and make the white men give the Indian back whatever had been traded. If you traded a gun to an Indian for a horse, for instance, and the Indian decided he was sick of his trade or if his wife was dissatisfied, the agent would come and make you give the Indian back his horse and you could not get your gun back, either.

I have been riding over the plains lots of times and a band of Comanches would come by. They had been to Anadarko usually and had blankets and stuff that they wanted to trade. The would come riding up like they meant to scalp a fellow and then they would say "Howya John." They called everyone John.

Then they would ask, "Where you from?" If you said that you were from Arkansas, they would say, "Good man!" But if you said you were from Texas, they would call you a name that I will not repeat; they hated the Texans. We got so we always told all the Indians we were from Arkansas.

Morris Brown, White Traveler through Caddo and Comanche Territory

Vol. 17, pp. 52–57

TONKAWAS AND APACHES

In 1886, the Tonkawa Tribe, which had some Lipan Indians and one Iowa Indian, moved to the Nez Percé Reservation which the Government had then set apart for use of the Tonkawas. Owing to a war that other tribes had made upon the Tonkawas previously, there were but few who moved to this new reservation—about seventy-five in all.

In 1889, Mr. Brewer came to act as agent or rather sub-agent under the White Eagle Indian Agency for the Tonkawas. His residence and office were located on Government land which had been set apart for use as Agency headquarters, on the west side of the Chikaskia River, two miles east and one mile south of the present town of Tonkawa. This was called the Oakland Agency.

Mr. Brewer instructed the Indians in the work of farming and assisted them in every way to become a self sustaining and independent people. The Government furnished their first horsepower threshing machine to thresh their grain. Wheat and corn were the principal crops raised.

The Tonkawa Indians were given an allotment of a hundred and sixty acres of land each. Helen Clark, an educated Blackfoot Indian lady, refined and intelligent, was sent from South Dakota to assist in the allotment of lands for the Tonkawas and to Mr. and Mrs. Brewer was given the task of assigning names for any of the Tonkawas who had Indian names that could not be written in English. Their allotment showed a total of seventy-two members of the Tonkawa Tribe—a mere remnant of a tribe which a few years previous had numbered over three thousand.

Bertha Brewer Plummer, White Daughter of Agent to Tonkawas
Vol. 40, pp. 162–71

COMANCHES

I am the reservation manager for the CCC-I at Anadarko.[4] My father's name was Buffalo; he died in 1931. My mother, Tarsarer, was born about 1880 and is still living. My grandmother, To-see, was born in Mexico, in 1809; died in 1924. I was born on West Cache Creek in September, 1909. I am of Spanish and Comanche blood. My grandmother on my mother's side was a Spanish captive. She was captured in Mexico when she was only eight years old.

My father was a Comanche and a member of the Indian Police force at Fort Sill before the opening of the country. As you see, my name is not like the name of my family. They used [to] never have family surnames. I will tell you how I got mine. One time when I was a very small boy, Buffalo Bill (Bill

Cody) came to the Fort to make a motion picture and I was in that picture with him. When he left he gave me his name but in going through the government offices it became Karty instead.

William Karty, Comanche
Vol. 78, pp. 164–66

COMANCHES AND KIOWAS

When I first came to Anadarko there were Indian tents stretched clear out to the Indian school north of town (Riverside Indian School, which is located two miles north of Anadarko). I have seen under some of those elm trees, along the banks of the river, more silver money stacked up than anyone could ever dream of. This silver money was brought here in wagons, guarded by government troops. It was called grazing money or grass money. The government always paid them in silver.[5]

At the old agency building north of town there was a cannon which was used by the government as sort of a curfew. The cannon was called the Break-of-day-gun and Sunset-gun. When this gun was shot all the Indians had to be in camp, and any Indian found outside of camp after this gun was shot was punished. . . .

I also remember the Indians would hold Court or Council, when one of the tribe had disobeyed the rules of the tribe. It was much like our present court system. They would hold this court or council once a month. When an Indian was brought before the court the Chief would send a man for him and this Indian would get the accused Indian by the braid and bring him in to answer to whatever offense he had committed. He was allowed council among his tribe. One of the punishments inflicted on them, if found guilty, was to be dismounted. He was not allowed to go on hunts, but had to stay in camp with the squaws and take care of the camp, keep it clean, etc.

W. H. Darnold, White Resident of Comanche and Kiowa Territory
Vol. 21, pp. 461–64

COMANCHES AND KIOWAS

There was a spring in Council Grove and the Kiowas and Comanches would come to the grove and camp for a month at a time. They did a lot of pony trading and dancing at night, too, and they bought quantities of groceries from me for nine years. I couldn't speak much of their language but could understand enough to wait on them. When I first began selling to them they would buy sugar by the dollar's worth and if I put in too much sugar and would take some out, they would shake their heads and walk out and wouldn't take it. I soon learned to guess pretty close and if it was too much I would just let it go, as I didn't dare to take anything out of any measure I sold them, but if they thought I was giving them something, that was all right. I never had any trouble with the Indians and I bought many pelts of wild animals from them.

John Abernathy, White Store Keeper in Western Oklahoma
Vol. 99, pp. 14–20

CADDOS, COMANCHES, AND KIOWAS

I was an Indian trader for sometime before the opening and then opened a store in the new Anadarko. . . . There were no laws except those made by the Interior Department. We had strict orders and had to abide by them. There could be no firearms or ammunition sold to the Indians without an order from the agent or with his permission. No whiskey could be sold to the Indians. The reason we could not sell firearms and ammunition to the Indians was that the Government was afraid that the Indians would go on the war path and use these firearms. Though through the government orders we could sell the Indians firearms, we were not allowed to buy firearms from them, no matter how they had secured them. I could never understand why this was so. It would surely have been less guns on the Indians' side. When the Indians were issued beeves they would bring the hides to the traders. The traders had a buyer to look after the hides. The Indians could trade most anything for groceries but the traders had to pay cash for the hides. We would give the hide man (the man who looked after the hides) the hide checks and he would go to the hide yard and if the hide was worth $2.00 he would give the Indians a hide check for $2.00. The Indian would come to the store and get the silver for it. Many times he would spend it right there in the store. But it was his to do what he wanted to with it and he had to have the cash. Though the laws for selling firearms were so strict, in later years the agent became more slack in enforcing it, saying, "Oh, go ahead and let the Indian have it; the Indians are not going on the war path any more, that has all been taken out of them." But as long as I was on the reservation I never sold an Indian a gun or ammunition. During Col. Frank D. Baldwin's time as agent here the Indians were issued cattle for breeding purposes.[6] One, one year old heifer was given to each man and one male to every twenty-five cows. These cattle were shipped in here from Louisiana and were unloaded at Chickasha. Those sent to Fort Sill were unloaded at Rush Springs and Ninnekah. These cattle were shipped double decked which was the first time I ever heard of shipping cattle double decked. Jack Stilwell was the inspector of these cattle. He would throw them and thumb them. He would run his thumb over the front teeth to see if the heifer was one or two years old. If it was two years old he would refuse to accept it. After the inspection the cattle were taken to the slaughter pen, or issue pen, in Bill Deitrich's place and issued to the Indians. These cattle were branded with the Indian's individual roll number and tribe initial. If the Indian was a Kiowa and his number was 120, his brand would be K120. These cattle could not be sold and if one of them was found where it should not be it could be returned to the rightful owner. If the Indians had taken care of these cattle they would have been rich by the time the country opened but this was hard to do as the cattle would not stay in one place. The Indians ate part of the cattle I suspect and then when they would come to the Agency some of them were stolen, maybe by their own tribe for food. Earlier than this though the Caddos had raised cattle and horses. The Caddos were more progressive than many other Indians but all the Indians had plenty of horses. When the country opened two Comanches had quite a nice herd of cattle but had to sell them for lack of range.[7]

R. L. Boake, White Merchant in Wichita and Caddo Territory
Vol. 66, pp. 248–52

Reservation Crime and Law Enforcement

COMANCHES

When the Kiowa-Comanche country opened for settlement in 1901, the Governor appointed Mr. Painter sheriff of Comanche County, which at that time was a large county comprising what is now Cotton and part of Tillman counties. Mr. Painter appointed five Indian policemen, two of whom I remember, Clark Che-u-quer and Post Oak Jim, who resided near Cache, Oklahoma. Painter told the Indians to buy themselves both a good gun and holster.

I remember when Post Oak Jim came to Cache, very proud to display his star and gun and he was happy to make people behave. He could talk some English and was a pretty good Indian; however, he liked his whiskey. He had not been appointed very long when he rode into Cache about 9 P.M., rode to Charlie Yahn's saloon and went in and shot a few bottles off the shelf. When he began shooting, the bartender jumped under the counter; John Passmore and a Mr. Brooks were gambling and Mr. Passmore jumped under the table or counter, and Brooks ran through the back door. Post Oak Jim filled his pocket with whiskey and went out the front door and when he got on his horse, Brooks shot him in the mouth with a .45 Colt's revolver, knocking out two front teeth, which retarded the force of the bullet, thereby saving Post Oak Jim's life. The bullet lodged in his throat and he fell off of his horse. Brooks thought he had killed him and started to pick him up but Post Oak Jim jumped up yelling at the top of his voice, and yelling the Comanche war whoop as loud as he could, got on his horse and rode to the reservation one mile west. Waking all the inhabitants up in Cache, he reached the reservation and told Jim Simmons, agent, what had happened. The Indian Agent took him to Fort Sill to the Government physician, Dr. Shoemaker, who thought he would die. He did not get the bullet out and Mr. Pachall told me later, when I worked for him in his store, that Post Oak Jim sent his wife to his store the next day and that she took Post Oak Jim two knitting needles, some silk threat and a pair of scissors. Post Oak Jim tied the silk thread around the needles and had his wife push them down his throat. Then pushing the thread down his throat, he clamped the needles against the bullet and extracted it. He had two gold teeth put in and he is living today. He weighs about 235 pounds and lives two miles west of Cache on his farm. It is needless to say Sheriff Painter concluded that Comanche Indians were not capable peace officers. The Sheriff took their commissions from them because of this rash act of Jim's. Jim told me: "I am glad I had extra large teeth, for they save my life."

Robert B. Thomas, White Resident of Comanche Territory
Vol. 112, pp. 112–14

KIOWAS

On August 29, 1891, I had been elected Sheriff again. A boy of the name of Jake Booher was herding cattle for Bill Mann, a white man, on the North Fork of Red River near the place where Lugert is now located, and he and

Bob Poline, a Kiowa Indian, fell out over a steer. The boy thought the Indian was going to shoot him, so he shot first and killed the Indian. This caused a terrible commotion among both the whites on the Greer County side of the river and the Kiowa on the Territory side. The Kiowas gathered, had war dances and said that they were going to fight the whites as they felt that the whites were imposing upon them. The whites in turn were excited and some of them as unreasonable as the Indians but the greater number of white people thought that more trouble could be avoided. However, many brought their women and children to Mangum and began to arrange to protect them. The boy, Jake Booher, hastened to Mangum and surrendered himself to me, telling me what he had done. I placed him under arrest and in jail, then with John Byers, Walter Pendergraft, Judge Slavens, Judge Huling and fifteen or twenty others, set out for the Engleberger's farm where many other men had gathered near the seat of trouble. Here J. N. McElroy, who could talk the Indian language, and two other men who could also, volunteered to go over into the Territory and talk to the Chiefs, Old Lone Wolf, Komalty, Little Bow and a number of others. The four of us went and had a long talk with the Indians, assuring them that Jake Booher would be tried by the white man's court and asking them not to fight. When we convinced them that Jake would be tried, they agreed that they would not make any more trouble as Bob Poline had a bad record among his own people.

Sam Houston Tittle, White Sheriff of Greer County
Vol. 112, pp. 256–61

COMANCHES AND KIOWAS

It was just two miles from my school (known as Little Hope) to the line of the Kiowa and Comanche Reservation. That reservation had not been opened to settlement but was in much the primitive state of any unsettled country. The prairies and distant blue of the Wichita Mountains lay away to the south. It had considerable groves of mesquite timber, looking much like an orchard. The trees were about as high as full blown peach trees and the foliage about as thick. This timber is extremely crooked but it is of a nature of hardwood, and it lasts well, and it was about the right size for posts for wire fences. The settlers in Washita County needed the timber very much for fuel and posts, and to make sheds and corrals and to brace their dugout homes, so they raided that Reservation with little molestation from the Government agencies. I am sure that a thousand loads of that timber were hauled out of the reservation by my schoolhouse during the three months I taught there. This was only one road leading into the reservation, and no doubt many others were used as much.

Thomas A. Edwards, White School Teacher near the Comanche and Kiowa Reservation
Vol. 23, pp. 283–89

KIOWAS

I was down on the creek one day cutting some green oak posts out of a green tree. I wasn't supposed to do this. I always said they wouldn't take me in if I got caught unless just by force. So I was working this day and along comes Jack Dayto, a police for Indians under Komalty Tribe which was in Chief Lone Wolf's territory. He was riding a pony and leading a horse. He rode up and looked me over. At that time I didn't know him and I asked him "Where you sit down?" Mean where do you live? "Me no savvy," said the Indian. I asked him what his name was? "Me no savvy." I thought I had done about everything I could do, anyway he had caught me getting wood but he was going to have a battle if he tried to stop me, so I went on getting my posts. So after a short time he says to me, "Where you sit down?" I told him the same then, "Me no savvy." But I saw he wanted to talk so I stopped my work and said "Where catchem pony. Maybe so, crazy pony." I made the signs with two first fingers on the left hand and worked my wrist on the left hand up and down giving the impression of a bucking horse. He said, "Maybe so. You savvy, crazy pony good." Then he told me he had lost the pony he had. That he had been over in Greer County to get him back. I asked him, "pony heap crazy?" [He answered,] "Maybe so you help savvy crazy pony?" I said, "Yes, help savvy." "How much you take." Meaning how much would I take to ride the pony. He had a good blanket on the back of the saddle, so I told him I would break the pony for that blanket. Instead of saying ride him, he would say "light 'um." He said, "I cut heap load of wood while you light 'um." So it was agreed but I had to borrow his saddle as I didn't have a saddle with me. So I had a pretty good job by myself. I got a rope on the pony, got hold of his ear and tried petting him. I was getting pretty hot. So he reared up and hit me between the eyes and raised a big knot and the Indian just laughed. I got the other end of the rope and tied his front feet close together, then I began to work him out. Hit him in the head with the rope, but finally got hold of the bridle and mounted him. He wasn't any trouble. I rode him around about 3 hours and he was broke all right to ride. The Indian was worried about how he was going to get it to camp, it was about 15 miles north. So I told him to untie the one he had tied to a tree and he would follow back to camp. So they took off up the creek in a long lope, the other animal right behind him.

C. S. Webber, White Cowboy in Kiowa Territory
Vol. 11, pp. 299–305

KIOWAS

My husband was out on the line one Monday morning and was riding over on the North Fork of Red River and met an Indian they called Little Bow. The Indians call all of the white men John. Little Bow said, "Hello John," and my husband asked him what he was doing out there and Little Bow said, "White man talk heap Jesus on Sunday, and steal Kiowa's wood on Monday." The Indian would give the dead wood away but the white people were not supposed to get any green wood and Little Bow had caught the missionary who had been preaching to them with a load of green wood.

Manda S. Evans, White Resident of Kiowa Territory
Vol. 79, pp. 480–92

The Government Issues

COMANCHES

The Government issued rations twice a month. We used most of the supplies, except beans, we knew very little about them, not knowing anything about how they were to be cooked. As for rice, I hate to say, but we threw the rice and beans both away. We thought rice was a kind of an insect; bacon, we threw large slabs of bacon away because we liked beef, not pork. Sometimes we burned it. My! But the Indians were wasteful and some are yet.

We got material for women's and girl's clothing; pants and shirts for the men and boys. Shoes and coats for all. Many times men would take their clothing to a trading post down on the river southeast of here called Charlietown, and sell the things for silver money. This little trading post was located across Red River opposite the place where Charlie, Texas now stands.

Emily Riddles, Comanche

Vol. 82, pp. 41–44

CADDOS AND KIOWAS

My grandmother said that when the government first began to issue the Kiowas rations of flour, bacon, soap, and tobacco, they didn't know what to do with them. They didn't like bacon, so they would throw these things away. The Caddos knew that they did, so on the days that the Kiowas would get their rations, the Caddos would follow to where these things were thrown and pick up the cleanest part and take it home and use it. In this way they had plenty of provisions. When tobacco was issued the Kiowas would lay it down and go off and leave it. My grandmother didn't use tobacco, but she would take it home and when anyone wanted some she had it for them. The Caddos were always a more civilized tribe than the Kiowas. They have always raised their own crops and cattle. My grandfather worked with the soldiers, and my grandmother cooked for them; there were two women that did the cooking. They went wherever the soldiers went.

Sadie Bedoka, Caddo-Delaware

Vol. 53, pp. 14–22

KIOWAS

When I was a little boy and lived at Anadarko, the Government furnished rations to the Kiowa Indians and at certain times all would come to receive their allotment of the food and clothing. Herds of longhorned Texas steers would be driven up and turned over to the Indians alive and they would slaughter the beef themselves.

The older men would use bows and arrows, while the younger men would shoot the cattle with guns. This was a great sight and I would climb upon the top of a telegraph pole (for in my time the telegraph had arrived at Anadarko) and there I would sit and watch the slaughter of the beef, out of danger of being run over or killed by the wild longhorned steers that were always fighting mad. One day I was thus watching the kill and Sam's father, who was then a very old man, I think about one-hundred years old, had come out in a wagon to also watch the kill. He got out of the wagon and was standing beside it, when a large longhorned steer saw him and made for him with head down, coming like a race horse toward the old man who was too feeble to climb back into the wagon with haste. I, like everybody else, thought to see the old man gored and trampled to death, but to my amazement when within only a few feet of him the steer fell down dead. On examination it was found that the steer had been shot and death took him just in time to save the life of Sam's father.

Robert Onco, Kiowa

Vol. 107, pp. 284–92

COMANCHES AND KIOWAS

Back in the days when the Indians were still numerous on the reservations in Oklahoma, the U.S. Government, in an effort to civilize them, realized they must feed them. Since the Indians depended on meat mainly for food, the result was that thousands of head of wild cattle were driven into Oklahoma from the Rio Grande country each year. Issuing of this beef was under contract.

Four tribes, Arapahos, Cheyennes, Kiowas, and Comanches occupied the western area with agencies for the first two at Darlington, for the others at Ardmore.[8] Every two weeks beeves were issued by the Indian Department and 'Issue Day' presented a scene characteristic of the time. For several days before, the Indians gathered in anticipation of the event. Excitement ran high and chattering and yelling prevailed. The cattle were turned into a corral, weighed and inspected. With the help of the Indians they were branded I D (Indian Department) and then turned loose to be killed by the Indians in their own fashion. Painted and feathered for the occasion, the hunters displayed their skill, some using bows and arrows, others using guns.

Each Indian family averaged about fifteen members, a beef was allowed to each family. Other rations given out at the agencies consisted of flour, coffee, beans, clothing and firearms. Giving them food only made them more shiftless. . . . Before the use of coffee they had depended on a drink made from the mescal bean, but found they liked coffee better as it did not make them drunk. They squaws made the flour into a sort of pone—flour and water mixed into a stiff dough, formed into cakes about two inches high, bake on hot rock. This was more like hardtack but suited their purpose as it lasted for sometime, and could be easily carried from place to place. The government often gave them dried fruit and salt pork but this was quite promptly thrown away, they were too primitive for foods as artificial as that. They wanted food in the raw stage, as witness their method of eating their meat. In killing the beef the idea was to save the blood, which they promptly drank, then the pièce de résistance was the liver and entrails eaten raw. Then all the meat was stripped from the bones and dried in strips to be eaten that way or cooked.

The government tried to encourage farming—issued seeds for spring planting but did not seem to get farm implements to them in time to prepare the soil, so the process was slow.

The Indian men wore shirts, leggings and moccasins with their blankets draped around them and fastened with a belt, they resented wearing pants— another primitive holdover. The squaws wore a sack-like dress under their blankets. The clothing was furnished by the government, the only articles made by the Indians were their moccasins. They were very particular about their hair—kept shiny and smooth. A favorite practice was to braid strips of hide of the otter or other small animals into the hair, possibly to keep it oiled.

They made their own bows and arrows until they found the government would give them firearms (for hunting); it was safe to do this for in return for food and clothing the Indians were peaceful in behavior. Their commodity of exchange was ponies. As of old an Indians' wealth (and bride) depended on the number of ponies he owned. Raising ponies and hunting was the chief pastime. The only handicraft of the squaws was beadwork—decorating moccasins, headbands, and belts.

W. J. Nicholson, White Government "Beef Issuer"
Vol. 7, pp. 505–12

TONKAWAS

Supplies of food and clothing were furnished to the Indians; these supplies were hauled from Arkansas City, Kansas, about every three months and issued to the Indians in proportion to their respective family needs. These supplies consisted principally of beef, flour, sugar, baking powder, coffee, beans, salt, and were issued twice a week. The coffee was green, not roasted and had to be "parched" or roasted by hand.

It was a custom for such tribes of Indians as were on friendly terms with the Tonkawas to make visits about once every two years at which times they would kill beef cattle to supplement their usual issue of rations and would trade ponies, hold dances and relate their experiences for a period of about one week and would then return to their own reservation. The Tonkawa tribe would in due time return the visits.

Bertha Brewer Plummer, White Daughter of Agent to Tonkawas
Vol. 40, pp. 162–71

CADDOS AND COMANCHES

The Caddos and Comanches drew their rations every two months in the summer and once a month in the winter. They would tie two poles together with rawhide so they would hang on each side of the horse, and make a raw-hide bag to swing from pole to pole under the horse, to carry the children and supplies in. They traveled in large groups and when they camped, it was similar to a tepee town. They did not wear blankets. The government issued white sheets with their rations, and they wore them instead of blankets. The government issued them live beef and the Indians' police usually did the killing. They would run and shoot the cattle until they were killed, some-times shooting a beef a hundred times.

A Mr. Fant, a cowman from Texas, was given a contract by the govern-ment to furnish corn-fed beef to the Indians. Instead he shipped in poor Texas cattle and unloaded them at Comanche. These cattle were so poor and starved the meat was blue. When an investigation was made, Fant lost his contract and the boss, Jim Myers, a half-breed Negro, who had given the con-tract, lost his job.

Henry Beaty, White Resident of Caddo Territory
V. 14, pp. 126–37

WICHITAS AND CADDOS

When I first came among the Wichitas in 1893, I estimate that eighty-five percent of them were living in grass houses, ten percent in tepees, and the remainder in houses of a very cheap type. When I made my first visit up Sugar Creek to the homes of the Wichitas, about a half a mile ahead of me I saw a cluster of grass houses which were nicely located on a twenty or thirty acre mound but the houses impressed me as being a group of hay stacks. When we reached the grass houses my attention was attracted by the men who wore nicely braided long hair and sheets tied around their waists instead of pants. The women wore waists of some kind and sheets instead of dresses. I talked to a number of them through an interpreter but the Indians appeared timid and quite indifferent. They had lately received an issue of supplies from the government, which issue was made regularly each two weeks, and had just completed the task of cutting their beef into long thin strips and hanging it on poles about an inch and a half in diameter and eight or ten feet above the ground. It was necessary to hang the beef high in order to keep the many dogs about the camp from getting it for it was not uncommon for an Indian family to have five or six dogs. When the beef was fully dry, it was usually sacked up in empty flour sacks and stored away in their grass house.

The rations issued to the Indian each two weeks consisted of beef, some bacon, flour, baking powder, salt, coffee, sugar, and some soap. At that time the Indians were divided into bands to receive the beef issue to them and each band was headed by a man called their Beef Chief. The cattle to be issued were turned over to the Beef Chief, who took charge of the slaughtering and of dividing the beef among the Indians composing the band. The Beef Chief and a number of his band would usually drive the cattle to be slaughtered some distance away from the corral before shooting the animal or animals. If a poor shot would injure the animal without killing it, frequently it would result in a real chase before the animal was killed and the chasing of the beef cattle before killing them was somewhat like chasing a wild buffalo. This practice brought about opposition to slaughtering the cattle in this way and led to the issuing the beef from the block in the late '90's.

John A. Buntin, White Teacher at Riverside Indian School
Vol. 89, pp. 319–53

COMANCHES AND KIOWAS

As a young boy I watched the western wild tribes shoot beeves that the government issued to them at the old trading post near Cache and Medicine Creek in the western part of Oklahoma. When the animals were turned loose the Indians would jump on their horses and run after them, shooting them with a rifle or bow and arrow. Then the women would skin the beeves all and devour it raw. They would strip the intestines, then char them over the fire, and eat them with great relish. Little children ate the raw meat like dogs, smearing blood all over their faces.

Albert N. Averyt, Jr., White Minister among the Comanches
Vol. 13, pp. 30–39

Indian Enterprise

CADDOS

We had to cross the Canadian at Caddo Jok's [Jake's] Crossing; some time we would have to wait a day or two for the river to go down. So we could cross, as this is a treacherous stream, quick sand bottom.

I have seen numbers of "Movers" try to cross when the river was up and the swift water would wash their chickens out of the coups down the river and drown their dogs and they had to move fast to save their own lives. Later Caddo Jok (Indian) built a ferry across the Canadian. That is he threw straw and hay across the deep sand until they came to the deep water. Then he had a flat boat to cross over on, and charged 50 cents' fees for crossing.

Mary Forgay Holmes, White Resident of Caddo Territory
Vol. 5, pp. 144–49

CADDOS

I forded Red River in the summer of 1886, and came into Indian Territory. On my way north I saw all kinds of wild turkey, deer, quail and a few mountain lions.

I stopped over night at the Swinging Ring Ranch in the Chickasaw nation, where Chickasha is now. Next day I went over to W. G. Williams's Half Moon Ranch in Caddo country, where I got a job as overseer over his farm.[9]

The corn made forty-five and fifty bushels to the acre, but Mr. Williams never sold any while I worked for him. He furnished my wife and me a house to live in and boarded us and gave me forty dollars a month. We baled lots of hay as Mr. Williams fed about a hundred head of saddle horses all the time. Grass was as high as my head.

We got our supplies from Kansas or Texas. I made three trips to Kansas, after supplies, and always got enough to last the ranch six months. Our nearest post office was Fred, about twenty miles southeast of the ranch. The mail was brought to Fred in a stage. Four horses were driven to the stage, and teams were changed at stage stands about twenty miles apart.

James M. Davis, Pat Pruner, Julius Doss, and Jimmie Jones were some of the most prominent men in the territory when I came. Mrs. W. G. Williams was one half Caddo. She dried lots of beef and it sure was good. Hiram Williams taught school at the ranch during the week, and preached on Sunday. The frontier people were very kind and friendly, and always glad to see "company" coming. I had many Indian friends, and found them to be very honorable. They would ride many miles to get to do a small favor for a friend.

Johnny Maguire, White Worker on Caddo Ranch
Vol. 33, pp. 536–38

CADDOS

I was told by my mother, that her father, James M. Davis, a white man, sawed and put up ice in a dugout in the winter of 1885 and 1886. The ice, which was cut on the Washita River, was about five inches thick. He cut about two tons and packed it in sawdust, that was gotten at the Government sawmill at Anadarko, on the north side of the river.

The dugout had a pitch roof made of poles and covered with straw and dirt. The door was made tight and wasn't opened until July and the ice lasted for about two months.

Before any land was broken the river was clear, and made good ice. . . .

After the Caddo, Kiowa, and Comanches Country was opened, white men made quail hunting trips in the Fall and Winter, taking big traps and nets. The nets were stretched up so that the quail, then gentle, could be driven into the traps. They were caught by the thousands, cleaned and packed in barrels, and shipped East for sale.

Mrs. Cragg Goetting, Caddo
Vol. 105, pp. 405–408

I came to the Indian Territory in 1894 . . . [and] went to work for an Indian named Tar Pony; he was a Comanche and he had three squaws; he lived on Cache Creek, southeast of Fort Sill. I went to work for Tar Pony and another Comanche named Petachee. I was breaking horses to ride and I would get one horse for breaking three. I would work all winter and in the spring I would take my horses that I earned back to Texas, and sell them.

The Indian police were always on the watch out for anyone taking horses out of the Comanche country across Red River, but Tar Pony and Petachee would help me with my part of the horses as far as Red River and then would go back home and I would take my horses on across Red River. My father was dead and I had to make the living for my mother and seven brothers and sisters, all younger than I was.

The second winter I had been working for these two Indians, I had worked hard all winter and had fifty-two horses for my part. I had done a good winter's work, so in the spring I started for Red River with my horses. I had them tied one behind the other, I had one horse's tail tied to the other horse's head. Tar Pony went with me, that was in our agreement that he or Petachee was to help me to Red River with my part of the horses.

On this trip Tar Pony helped me and when we came to a place within about five miles of Red River and I thought I was out of danger of the Indian Police, I told Tar Pony that he could start back as he had a long hard ride ahead of him. He waved good-by to me and left. I rode about three miles on towards the river, leading my horses and as happy as I could be thinking that when I got home, I could cash out for over $1,000.00, but I got fooled. Up rode three Indian police and stopped me, they untied my fifty-two horses and gave them a scare and scattered them. After they were gone, I tried to find some of my horses and out of fifty-two, I got four. I was lucky to find that many; so four horses was all I got home with out of my winter's work, but that was the chance I had to take.

Eugene W. Flippen, White Cowboy in Comanche Territory
Vol. 51, pp. 466–69

Cattle, Grass, and Timber

CADDOS

In the '90s my father, Thad Smith, had one of the biggest ranches in the Caddo country. He controlled forty thousand acres of land, which he had leased from the Caddo Indians through the Department of Interior. He hired lots of cowboys, who slept and ate in a bunk house near our house. One of our best bronc riders was Turner Cochran, a half Chickasaw and half Cherokee Indian. Nearly every Sunday was spent riding broncs.

Mrs. Cragg Goetting, Caddo
Vol. 105, pp. 405–408

CADDOS

I can remember seeing my mother count her money. She used corn to count with. She would take the different colors of corn and each color would represent a certain denomination. When she finished she knew just how much she had. She never forgot how many nickels or dimes, or such as she might have, that she had.

Mrs. Frank Cussins, Caddo
Vol. 21, pp. 376–88

KIOWAS

For fuel, we had to haul wood and as there was so much more and so much better wood on the Indian Territory side of North Fork of Red River which was about ten miles to the north. I hauled our wood from there. . . . One day I had crossed the river near the mouth of Devil's Canyon and gone over on Tepee Creek and was chopping wood. I heard someone say, "Heloo, John." I looked around and there stood an Indian buck in his blanket, paint and feathers. He said, "Maybe so, unload the wood." I told him, "No, I need it." He said, "Maybe so, you give me one dollar." I said, "I do not have any dollar." He said, "Maybe so, you come back tomorrow, bring two dollars." I said all right and went home but I did not go back the next day.

A few days later I went back but to another place trusting that I would not see any Indians but to my dismay the same Indian showed up. It was the Kiowa Chief Komalty. He said, "Maybe so two dollars." I told him that I did not have two dollars but my father had a store at Dot and for him to come there and we would make it right. He said, "No, you heap lie," but he let me take the wood and go home.

James Huling, White Resident of Greer County
Vol. 62, pp. 301–304

COMANCHES

The Indian men used to make wooden saddles and ropes of hide. The pattern of these saddles was taken from the government saddles furnished the soldiers, but the Indians did not have any way of keeping the saddles on. The seat was carved from the hardest of woods, then covered with buffalo hides. Several blanket thicknesses had to be used under the saddle or the wooden saddle would skin the horse's back.

Once a smart white boy thought he was such a cowboy, and put one of the saddles on his horse and tried roping a buffalo calf; he finally roped it, tying the rope to the horn of the saddle. When the calf decided to run away, as the saddle was not tied on the horse in any way, off came the saddle, cowboy and all 'way up in the air. The boy's face was very red and he surely was embarrassed when we reached him.

My first husband was a Comanche Indian. His name was Frank Moetah. . . . Years ago my husband helped drive several hundred head of cattle from here to Kansas City. It took quite a long time to make these trips. I stayed alone most of the time.

My present husband is a white man. I have my allotment which I chose in the early days, here on West Cache Creek.

I like to go to Deyo Mission. Its location is very convenient for most all the Indians in this country. On Thursdays the Indian women have quilting parties.

Emily Riddles, Comanche
Vol. 82, pp. 41–44

CADDOS, COMANCHES, AND KIOWAS

The money paid to the Indians was known as Grazing Money or Grass Money. The money was paid to the Government by the cowmen and divided among the tribes according to the share of each one. When it came time to pay off these Indians, the Chiefs of the various tribes would meet, sit around the table with their interpreters and a Government agent.

The Government agent would call out the amount of Grass Money owing to the tribe and the interpreter would interpret the amount to the meeting. If, for instance, it was for the Comanches, the amount would be called out in the Comanche language. If the amount called out was correct the Comanche Chief would nod his head, either in approval or disapproval. This procedure would go on until all the different tribes were paid. Then these checks were cashed and the money was given to the Indians in silver.

Most of the time this money was given all in dimes as the Indians did not like dollars, and they did not understand gold money. The money was hauled into the pay place in wagons, and at one time in paying the Indians, ten thousand dollars was paid in dime pieces. That was the time I believe that the cowmen had given a draft to pay these Indians, and all the money came in at once. At that time the Indians were not paid by check as they are now. Colonel Randlett was the first Indian Agent to pay grass money by checks.[10] The Indian Police at that time were paid by checks, but they were the only Indians to receive money by check—all the rest were paid in silver.

R. L. Boake, White Merchant in Wichita and Caddo Territory
Vol. 90, pp. 403–10

KIOWAS AND COMANCHES

One of my earliest memories was when the Indians were paid their "Grass Money." This money was paid to Washington by the cattlemen who used the land for pasturing their herds of cattle. Then in turn it was paid to the Indians, for the use of their land. It was hauled to the Agency in hacks, with a military guard, to keep off any raiding party. The Indians at that time couldn't count their money, it always came in silver coins, so a number of the oldest Indians would bring their money to my father to count. Many a time I have seen him sit on the floor or at his desk and count their silver. One time an old man by the name of Red Bird brought his tied in the corner of his blanket and when it was counted he had about sixty or seventy dollars all in dimes.

Lillian Gassaway, White Daughter of J. J. Methvin, Missionary to the Kiowas and
    Comanches
Vol. 25, pp. 407–14

The supplies which I hauled were issued to the Indians (Comanches, Kiowas, and Apaches) once a month. Twice a year they made payments, which was the rent or permit money received from cattlemen for the western plains country for grazing purposes. They always paid money. The Indians would not accept checks. They were paid in gold or silver or currency. When these payments were being made there were numerous tepees covering two sections of land or more near the agencies at Fort Sill and Anadarko. The Indians usually camped a week or two before and after the payment was made. This was a gala time for them. They spent their money freely. There was much gambling among them.

Frank Kuehn, White Supplier of Goods to the Anadarko Agency
Vol. 32, pp. 446–50

COMANCHES AND KIOWAS

This land was leased to big cowmen, sometimes at prices as low as 6 and 8 cents an acre. Very few white people were here. The Indians first learned of the white people through the soldiers who were stationed at Fort Sill. They were not very much surprised to learn that this country was to be opened for white people because the government had told them already.

Each Indian was paid the same amount, I was told, until the year 1895. They were paid in cash. The money was hauled from Anadarko by an army wagon and guarded by soldiers from Fort Sill. Then a General or retired officer took the money that was to go to the three sub-agencies in an ambulance with a Negro driving it and paid the Indians. The three agencies were at Red Store, Cache, and Rainy Mountain. The agency at Cache was run by two men named Mac Harris and James and the one at Rainy Mountain by a man named Boake. Rice and Quinnette ran the post trading store.

E. W. Livingston, White Store Employee in Comanche and Kiowa Territory
Vol. 33, pp. 331–33

COMANCHES, KIOWAS, AND APACHES

The reservation consisted of several thousand acres which had been bought by the Government from the Chickasaws for the Apaches, Comanches, and

Kiowas. The Kiowas were always known as one large band of Indians. The Comanches consisted of five bands, each having its own leader.

There was a dividing line for the Indians on the reservation. The Comanches and Apaches agree among themselves at a council meeting, that the Comanches should occupy the south half of the reservation and the Kiowas and Apaches should occupy the north half.

After the Cheyennes released the land to cattlemen for grazing purposes at 6 cents per acre, the Kiowas and Comanches decided they would like to lease their grassland but after a council meeting the Indians did not agree. The Kiowas were opposed to the leasing but the Comanches were in favor of it. So the Comanches agreed to lease immediately. After the lease had been made the agreement read "pay in cash semiannually." The first payment was made about twenty miles southwest of Fort Sill on Cache Creek. The white men met the Indians there and paid each Indian a $10.00 gold piece. Thereafter the payments were made at headquarters by the Indian Agent. During the time of the lease for about fifteen years the payments every six months ran from about $15.00 to $20.00

Blanche Hammond Quinnette, White Daughter of Fort Sill Chaplin

Vol. 113, pp. 49–51

Relations with Other Peoples

WICHITAS

My father cleared about four acres of bottom land and planted corn, and when the corn was old enough to eat, a herd of Indian ponies, with a little sorrel pony as the leader, entered the field. My father caught the leader and put a cow bell on his neck so we could hear the bell and know when they headed for the corn field.

One morning four tall Wichita blanket Indians came up to my father's house with guns and pointed and made motions with their guns that they were going to shoot at sun down. My father thought they intended to shoot him, but he heard the bell on the horse, the leader of herd, coming to the corn field, and in a few minutes we heard a shot fired and it wasn't long until the four blanket Indians came marching up to the house and then handed him the bell and made motions that the pony would not bother the corn any more. A few days later the Indians had their annual green corn or Busk Dance and when everything was ready and the cooking started the Indians came to my father's corn field and carried sacks of corn each day until the field was stripped of corn. My father didn't dare refuse their getting all the corn they wanted.

About a month later, the Government brought the Wichita Indians their rations which were groceries, meat, blankets, and clothing, and the Indians well paid my father for the corn for they came to the house with groceries, blankets, and meats of all kinds.

Robert Butler, Cherokee Resident of Wichita Territory
Vol. 89, pp. 427–29

COMANCHES

My nearest neighbor was a full blood Comanche Indian, whom I learned to like very much. In the spring, I had to go back to the Chickasaw Nation after some cows, and I asked him if he would haul a barrel of water for my wife while I was gone. He consented. She was afraid of the Comanches, but when she needed the water she sent him word. He came with this wagon and team, but refused to go to the spring unless she went with him. She was frightened, but she had to have water, so she climbed into the wagon. There lay an ax covered with blood. Brave but sure she would be murdered she went along with him.

When they got to the spring he motioned to her to get out and dip the water. She finally got him to fill the barrel. Then she was greatly amused at the whole affair. It was the custom of these Indians to have their women do the work. When they went for a load of wood or a barrel of water the squaw rode on a pony behind the wagon and she dipped up the water, or loaded the wood on the wagon. This being their custom, he expected my wife to go along with him and do the work. He was willing to haul the water, but she must fill the barrel as his own squaw would do.

L. A. Davidson, White Resident of Comanche Territory
Vol. 21, pp. 486–97

COMANCHES

The Comanche Indians used to go to Pecan Grove, Texas, to pick pecans. The white people would fight with them, killing many. One night we heard someone moaning and groaning pitifully in the brush near our home. Upon investigation we found an old white-haired Indian woman who could not speak a word of English, lying there badly cut and slashed. We took her into our home, and kept her for a month, at the end of which time her wounds were healed. We found out that she had been in Pecan Grove when one of these fights occurred and had barely escaped with her life by hiding and creeping cautiously through the brush. She slept on a buffalo rug in the corner of the room and each night some of her tribesmen came and peeked through the cracks in the door to see that she was safe. My stepfather wanted to kill her but Mother begged him to spare her life. The Indians would probably have burned our home and killed all of us, had the old woman been killed. Mother fed and cared for her during the month. One night we saw her go out and look at the stars. She stood there for a long time making peculiar gestures. Then she came in and went to bed on her buffalo robe. The next night she crept stealthily away while we slept, and we never saw her again.

Margaret Russell, White-Chickasaw Resident of Chickasaw Territory

Vol. 43, pp. 167–74

COMANCHES

When I was 15 years old I went west to the Kiowa and Comanche country on an adventure among the Comanche Indians. These Indians were very different from the Chickasaw and Choctaw tribes. They were of a rather hostile nature and lived altogether in tents or tepees. They wore nothing at all in the way of clothing except a breech clout and blankets. The Government was building houses for the Indians although they wouldn't live in them. They would put their horses in the houses and continue to live in their tents. The bucks or men would not work at all; all the work that was done, which was very little, was done by the squaws or a white man that would be hired by the buck. Once a Comanche Indian hired me to change a lock on one of the doors of a house, which required only about two hours and for pay the Indian gave me four head of horses. A white man could never get money from them for work, but always got good pay in the way of horses or cattle.

S. R. McGuire, White Resident of Comanche Territory

Vol. 78, pp. 465–68

We followed the trail that was known as the Western Trail, going by way of the Wichita Mountains and the North Fork River. The drive started two hundred miles south of San Antonio. We went across the corner of the Comanche Reservation, stopping for dinner while crossing the Reservation. While we were eating dinner, the old Comanche Chief, Quanah Parker, and two bucks came to our camp. We thought they were going to cause us trouble but everything went along fine. When they left our camp, the foreman gave the Chief a fat two-year-old steer. Chief Parker could speak a little English. His mother was a white woman named Cynthia Ann Parker. Mrs. Parker was stolen by the tribe when only a child. When she was old enough she married Peta Nocoma, a Comanche buck. She had three or four children, one being the great Chief, Quanah Parker—the one who came to our camp. Cynthia was later forced by the tribe to go back to her people where she died of grief for her Indian husband and children.[11]

J. O. Mawlow, White Cowboy Passing Through Comanche Territory
Vol. 6, pp. 442–50

COMANCHES AND KIOWAS

The wild Indians were fond of dog meat and many dogs that were following their masters through the Territory behind the wagons disappeared. I remember when I was a boy nine years old, my older brother and I were in the woods gathering pecans. We were up in the tree when a big Indian rode under us with a very angry look on his face. He made signs for us to come down but we began to climb higher up the tree. When brother noticed the Indian preparing to shoot an arrow in our direction, he cried out: "Don't shoot, we the Jesus man papoose." With a smile the Indian made friendly signs to us, and when we came down from the tree, he helped us gather pecans and invited us to his tepee to eat. The "Jesus man" was the name the wild Indians gave my father. During the meal meat was passed to me and brother nudged me not to take any. Later he told me that it was dog meat. I wish brother had let me eat it, so I could say now that I had eaten dog meat.

Albert N. Averyt, Jr., White Minister among the Comanches
Vol. 13, pp. 30–39

The first case I had of any prominence was for Lone Wolf's young men. An Indian loves races more than almost anything and a horse that can win about every race is almost deified by the Indians. These braves of Lone Wolf had an old paint horse that was pretty well known among all the Indians for he could outrun about anything on four legs.

Sometime in the fall before the Fair of 1900, this horse disappeared. Search as they would no trace of the horse could be found. As the Indians gathered for the Fair in Hobart, the horse was found on the streets of Hobart hitched to a delivery wagon. The Indians recognized him at once and laid claim to him but as he was claimed to be owned by a white man there was nothing doing. Old Lone Wolf got an interpreter and came and laid the case before me. He have a perfect description of the horse all right but there seemed no mark or brand on the horse that he could prove identification by.

I said how come no brand. The Indian explained, "Horse jump when hot iron touch and brand slight—only show when grass short in the spring. H in an O on right hip. Horse cut one time on wire. Little long scar where neck joins body—slight worm scar on left leg." I made out papers and summoned them all to appear in court on a certain day. The white man and Indians were all there. The white men swore there was not a mark or brand of any name or nature on the horse, that he was a white man horse—raised by white men. The horse was more white than any other color and "White Man" happened to be what the Indians called the horse, so when the white men called the horse "White Man" I could not make the Indians understand. I asked that the horse be brought to the court for evidence and the judge and jurors all came down onto the courthouse steps to look at the horse. The white men claimed no marks or brands at all and the Indians claimed a brand and two scars that showed in short grass time. When the horse was brought I sent for a barber and told the Indian to put his finger where the brand should be. Without hesitating, the Indians stepped out and placed his finger on three separate places on the horse.

I ordered the barber to take the clippers and clip the hair but nothing showed so I told the barber to shave the place the Indian had indicated. When the spots were shaved, there were the brand and scars as plain as could be, just as the Indian said. We gave the horse to the Indians and they cleaned up every race during the fair.

P. K. Morrill, White Attorney and Judge in Kiowa County
Vol. 107, pp. 116–22

COMANCHES, KIOWAS, AND APACHES

The Kiowas mounted their horses on the run. They ran along by the side of the horse as he ran and leaped onto his back from the ground. The Comanches, Kiowas, and Apaches hauled their own freight from Caddo to Fort Sill and Reno, having a white man for their boss. They often camped on Boggy [Creek] when freighting and we enjoyed going to their camp. Sometimes we killed a beef and took it to them, asking if they would have a War Dance that night. They built a fire and dance around it. The beef was eaten in a raw state. They enjoyed having a white boy dance with them. They called him "Heap Good Warrior." When the dance was over they would say, "Tobo, Go Home" and it was time to move. They meant what they said and we would depart hurriedly to our house. Their bread was made of cornmeal and water, patted into cakes and fried in a skillet. They were turned with a long stick. If one went to see these Indians and they went into their tepees and closed their doorways they meant you were not wanted there and it was time to get away from the camp. They were very temperamental. Sometimes visitors were welcome and sometimes they were not.

W. S. Peterson, White Resident of the Chickasaw Nation
Vol. 107, pp. 348–54

KIOWAS

It was against the law to trade with the Kiowa Indians who were yet on the Kiowa Reservation, in what is now Kiowa County. We had numbers of friends among them who did not appreciate the value of the clothing which the Government issued to them; in fact, they would not wear them; they wore their blankets. We traded corn and watermelons to them for their cloth and clothing; one Indian gave my father a complete suit of clothes for my younger brother for one watermelon.

James Allen Stubbs, White Resident of Kiowa Territory
Vol. 87. pp. 434–44

Navajo was an Indian trading post and I have seen as many as eight hundred Indians there at one time. The Indians drew money quarterly from the Government. They spent it quite freely. The men played poker and monte, a game which I have never understood. It was played with cards having pictures of trees, etc., on them.

One day in 1899, a big crowd of Indians and white men were gambling. The Indian Chief was called "Chicken." A cowboy who said his camp was at Lone Wolf joined them in the game. "Chicken" and the cowboy began winning all the money. "Chicken" became suddenly ill about midnight and died. It was apparent that the whiskey he was drinking had been poisoned. The Indians left wailing and crying, every one in town was afraid there would be trouble, for no doubt the Indians knew there had been foul play, but no further trouble developed.

V. G. Estes, White Resident of Comanche Territory
Vol. 64, pp. 44–48.

KIOWAS

On one of these hunting trips my father told of coming upon a band of Crow Indian Scouts that had stopped on the Little Wichita River on the Texas side.[12] The river was low and the shallow holes were full of fish. These Indians had caught the fish with their hands and had roasted a great number of them. Father watched them until all was ready to eat, and then he took aim with his big buffalo gun away above their heads, for he did not want to hit them. He then fired the gun. The Indians did not wait to see what had happened but dashed away. Father let them get well gone, then he went down and ate their fish. The Indians left the country.

Jess Lynn, White Resident of Comanche Territory
Vol. 61, pp. 493–503

KIOWAS AND COMANCHES

When we first came into this Indian country and would prepare a meal where an Indian could see or could find out that we were eating, the Indian would walk up and sit down without saying a word and would begin to reach for the food and eat. Once we had just been here a few days and we got dinner ready and began to eat and some Indians came along and saw us eating and they came in and began to eat, too, and the women ran away screaming, "Robbers! Robbers! Hijackers!" I noticed the Indians were just as unconcerned and were jabbering and talking and laughing. I soon learned that this was their custom and finally when I caught the Indians eating, I would run in and try to get all the food I could carry off and eat.

John Gomer, White Resident of Comanche and Kiowa Territory
Vol. 26, pp. 139–46

KIOWAS

I was working near North Fork of the [Red] River, and had these horses on pasture next to the river. The [Kiowa] Indian reservation was just across the river. I had reason to believe that the Indians had taken my horse, but I did not want to have any trouble with them, so I said nothing. One day I was on the Indians' territory when suddenly I rode up on Lone Wolf, Chief of the Kiowas. We stopped and talked a while. We had always been friendly when we met. When I started to leave, I said, "Lone Wolf, come go back with me and take supper with me." Lone Wolf looked at me a moment and said, "Maybe so I go." And without further ado turned and rode home with me.

I had a big pot of beans cooked, plenty of fresh beef killed and managed to prepare Lone Wolf a real good substantial supper which he ate with evident relish. We had a nice visit and it was quite late when he departed. I asked him to return the next day and bring his family for dinner. He smiled broadly and replied, "Maybe so I come."

The next day Lone Wolf returned with his family and spent the day. They seemed to enjoy every minute of the time. When they started to leave, Lone Wolf's wife asked me for some soda. I gave it to her. Then she asked for some flour and she got that.

Well, I felt sure that I had their entire confidence and friendship. I commanded their respect by kindness. Next day, sometime, I looked out and saw my stolen horse grazing in the pasture with the rest of the horses.

W. Fox Chambers, White Cowboy near Kiowa Country
Vol. 54, pp. 454–61

KIOWAS

The Kiowa Indians came to our place very often and would beg for things. They did not try to harm us but if we had anything they wanted, they kept on begging until we had to divide with them. One thing, especially, that they liked was syrup. We usually kept our syrup in a jug and sometimes we would avoid giving them any. One time we had about half a gallon of syrup in the jug and had it setting on a shelf in the dugout. We told them we did not have any syrup. One of the squaws pointed to the jug on the shelf and said, "Heap syrup, heap syrup." We then had to divide it with them.

Old Chief Komalty was very friendly with us. Often times he invited us to his home. He had a nice house and it was furnished similarly to the way we furnished our homes, but the chief and his family did not live in it. They lived in their tepees.

Clara Tuton, White Resident of Greer County
Vol. 68, pp. 335–39

KIOWAS

We came to what was then known as H County, now Washita County, bringing with us twenty-five hundred head of cattle, seventy-five head of horses, one chuck wagon and six men besides [my brothers] to help drive the stock. We came up what is called the Chisholm Trail and forded Red River at Doane's Store and came across the country and hit the Kiowa country. The Kiowas would be camped upon the ridges and when they would see the cattle down in the valleys they would paint their faces, rough up their hair, put on their garb, get their guns, and get on their spotted Indian ponies and come running and waving and tell us to go back.

When they saw that we were not scared and we told them that we were not going back they asked, "Where is the wa-ha chief?" Then they held up their hands and said, "Just give us one wa-ha and all of the grass and water is yours." We cut one out and ran it up to their camp and an Indian man came out of a tepee and knocked it in the head with an ax. The Indian women and children then came out and skinned it; in this way we never had any trouble with the Indians.

Wiley Gunter, White Cowboy in Kiowa Country
Vol. 84, pp. 501–508

I thought the [stampeded] cattle had gone that way as the tall grass was all trodden down, so I started down that way and I saw a tepee over in the tall grass and all at once the Indians began to spring up out of the grass in every direction around me. The old chief started to motion to me to come on but I stopped and he came on to me and held up his hand and helped me off my horse, and had the horse watered and fed and then went with me into the tepee and offered me something to eat, but I could not even think about eating because I was scared most to death; I just knew that I was going to be killed. They all sat around on the ground on their blankets and about midnight the old chief got up and lit his big old pipe and took two draws of smoke and passed it around and the rest of them took one draw; it seemed to me like it was thirty minutes before they ever would blow the smoke out of their mouths.

They never said one word to each other, after they did get through smoking they put their blankets down and spread a buffalo robe down for me to sleep on and gave me another to cover with. Then they all jumped up and began their war dance all around me after which they all sat down on their blankets again until about four o'clock when they all jumped up again and started their dancing around me again. The old chief came over to me and asked me if I was afraid of them and I said, "No, why should I be afraid of you people?" (I was scared most to death, but would not tell him so. I had not closed my eyes all night or hardly moved.) The old chief patted me on the head and they all then lay down and went to sleep and I guess I slept about one hour for when I woke up it was daylight. The old chief asked me if I wanted to go and I said, "Yes." He told me then I could go if I wanted to, so I left and took my leisure time getting off out of sight of the Indians, but how I did ride when I got to where they could not see me and I was burning the breeze. About eight miles over the hills when I met the soldiers coming, they were after these Indians. They were Kiowas and I know the only reason that I escaped alive was that I made them believe I was not afraid of them.

Frank Gill, White Cowboy in Western Oklahoma

Vol. 84, pp. 151–60

The Opening of the Reservations

COMANCHES

When the country was first to be opened for the white people's homes, white men came here surveying it. The Indians would go where the surveyors were working and talk with them. We couldn't understand much they said only that on our land was to be white people's homes. We didn't care too much for this, but when we were told to pick the land for our homes, it seemed much better. As I had herded my father's stock up and down this creek now known as West Cache Creek, I knew where springs were located so I chose this farm I am now living on.

Andrew Perdasophy, Comanche
Vol. 39, pp. 437–39

COMANCHES

The opening of the Kiowa-Comanche Indian land had a most demoralizing effect upon the Indians, for with the opening came hundreds of saloons and the white man would sell whisky to the Indians for a "big price." These persons were akin to the human leeches who hung around the camps at payment time ready to get the Indians into gambling games and fleece them. The Indians love to gamble and "monty" is the one game they like best.

Mrs. H. Ridgley, White Resident of Comanche Territory
Vol. 70, pp. 486–89

Chapter Six

◆ ◆ ◆ ◆ ◆ ◆ ◆ ◆ ◆ ◆ ◆ ◆ ◆ ◆ ◆

Old Ways, New Ways

◆ ◆ ◆ ◆ ◆ ◆ ◆ ◆ ◆ ◆ ◆ ◆ ◆ ◆

The period after the end of the Red River War in 1875 to the 1930s was a time of drastic change for the traditional Indians of Texas. Many Comanches, Kiowas, Caddos, and Wichitas wistfully recalled the old days. They also commented upon the great changes sweeping through their world, and how difficult it could be to walk two roads, that of their traditional culture and that of the white man. Also, white settlers, cowboys, and businessmen recalled their experiences with these peoples and their lives on the reservation.

KIOWAS

When I could first remember, my people used to live in the western section of this country and passed through the valley in which Lone Wolf is situated on their trips from the northern part of the Territory to Fort Sill. We seldom crossed the North Fork of Red River because that was the white man's country. The grass was very high and thick all over the country but my people thought that the very best part was in the Elk Creek valleys. Here the grass grew wonderfully well and our ponies were always driven there for the winter. Our food was mostly fresh meat and then there were many buffalo, deer, antelope, wild turkeys, prairie chickens and many smaller birds. My people were great hunters and the Government also gave us some food. The Government gave us some blankets and we had buffalo robes and hides of many kinds. The Government gave us cloth like linen, which we used some for clothing.

I grew up like all the Indians boys of those days, riding, hunting and fishing, mostly on the Washita River. Early in life I professed Christianity and united with the Baptist Church. I count this the biggest thing in my life. I have continued to live in the Church and to take an active part. At present, I am a deacon in the church and attend regularly. I own a farm between Saddle Mountain and the town of Sedan and we make our living there. Many of my people live about there and we are citizens of Oklahoma, ride in automobiles and live like other people. I sell pecans and produce off my farm.

Stephen Kotay, Kiowa
Vol. 32, pp. 435–37

WICHITAS

I was born on Sugar Creek, about five miles north of Anadarko in about 1876. I don't know the exact date. . . . I don't know where my mother and father were born, probably in the Wichita Mountains. My uncle, Tawacony Jim, (former chief of Wichitas, and now deceased) said that God put man on the Wichita Mountains more than four hundred years ago, and he was a Wichita Indian. And I guess that is where my folks come from.

I don't know where they are buried. For then we buried people where they died, and didn't have any grave yards like now. Maybe buried down in Wichita Mountains; maybe out north of town; maybe down by Rush Springs, I don't know. I was in school when they died.

The reason my uncle Tawacony Jim was made Chief of the Wichitas was because he talked good English. I don't know where he learned English as he never went to school. He was smart man. He was the only Indian who talked good English. In 1884 I went to school just north of town [Anadarko]. In 1886 I went to school at Chilocco.

Government offered Wichitas land either north or south of town [Anadarko], and my people chose land north of town. Also Caddo took land north of town. We have always been friends of the Caddos.

Our language is not like Caddos, but we have always been friends.[1] We don't use old words like we used to long time ago. We have forgot our old languages. We talk Wichita but not like our fathers and mothers used to. We pronounce our words different. There are several different bands of Wichitas called different names but we are all Wichitas.

Jay Johnson, Wichita
Vol. 31, pp. 243–51

I was born in the Indian Territory about 1888. I do not know the exact month, day or year, but that is close to it. I was born west of the Washita at the Comanche camp on Deep Creek. My parents came from the Comanche band from Old Mexico. They moved into Texas during the time the Spanish owned Texas. They lived in Texas during the time that Texas won her independence from Mexico and also when the United States annexed Texas and made her one of the Union. But when the Civil War broke out they moved into Indian Territory. They settled near the town site of Verden, then called Cottonwood Grove.

When our tribes were moved to the Indian Territory the Government made a treaty giving a scope of territory to the Indians for hunting grounds. The part was called the Medicine Lodge Treaty. This land ran up the Arkansas River to the Kansas line, then south and west to a point where it meets the east New Mexico line, then northeast to a point where it meets the east fork of Red River, and then down the river.

The Buffalo Dance is a dance originated by the Comanches and is used by the Comanches only. The costumes are made to imitate a buffalo. I can't tell much about the dances and tribal customs because I was not old enough to remember.

I went to school to a Reverend Methvin at the Methodist Indian Mission in Anadarko. In 1900, I went with Reverend Methvin and others, ten to be exact, to Carlisle, Pennsylvania, to an Indian school. This was located eighteen miles west of Harrisburg, Pennsylvania, the capital. I graduated from this school in 1906 and returned home. In 1907, I was elected committeeman for the Comanche tribe and I still serve in that capacity.

There were several different tribes of the Comanches. There was one band out on the Staked Plains that was more warlike than any of the others. These were always warring with other tribes until the United States Government settled them. Our tribe was one of the first to make treaties with the Government.[2] There were lots of Comanche Scouts who worked for the government. The Government gathered all Comanche tribes and made one from it.

Wilbur Pewo, Comanche

Vol. 93, pp. 280–81

COMANCHES

I have lived in Comanche County all my life. I was born near Indiahoma and have lived near Faxon about twenty years. I cannot remember anything of my parents. They died when I was very small. I lived with aunts and uncles.

A great thing that has helped me all through my life was that I learned to work when I was a boy. The older relatives would ask us to do little errands. My cousins would not do the tasks but would make me do it. When but a very young boy I worked at hay balers for 10 cents a day.

The older Indians taught the younger ones to live a true life. Be true to the Great Spirit, which was the man above the sun. I was taught to always be kind to those that aid you and never take anything that doesn't belong to you. If a task is done, we owe it to the Great Spirit for enabling us to do the task. Always be kind to father and mother. Another thing, never make fun of any older person, for we some day may be old and make the same mistakes as they make. Never gossip about our friends, always be peaceful and agreeable, never fight someone else's child; if he fights, get away, some older folks will protect you. This is the truth, and the way the Great Spirit meant for us to live. We must love our God.

The great warrior takes his bow and works with it for hours and hours, never calling it completed until it had a perfect spring. The bow and arrow has always been praised very highly, for with it the Indians have supplied their tables a long time. The bow is kept as a white man keeps his weapon. A bow is oiled with a fine grease and tested often. Many are kept handy at all times so if one failed others are ready.

The Indians are always taught to always take pride in whatever undertaking they might do, whether they liked it or not. If the task is started, stay with it until finished, then you will get full benefit; if you choose to be sportsman, be a good one. Thinking things over, before jumping in, is the best policy. Smile big and walk away.

Up to this time, comes the white settlements. The Indians are used to outdoor life. We have four generations living among the Indians of today.

John Wa-Ka-Quah, Comanche

Vol. 75, pp. 8–10

My name is Margaret Totite. I am a Comanche Indian, 37 years old. My husband's name is Lemuel Noddayaka, he is 35 years old. We have had fourteen children, ten of whom are now living. I was born at Turkey Pond in the Oklahoma Territory where Greer County now is, near where the town of El Dorado, Oklahoma, is located.

My husband, Lemuel Noddayaka, [is] a World War veteran and he is a good worker in the church and a good farmer. We live on the farm adjoining Cache and we try to imitate the white race in every way. My father could not speak English nor my mother, but I try to be educated and try to educate my children.

Margaret Totite, Comanche
Vol. 47, pp. 248

My father made a get away from the Comanches—[he was] accidentally killed in the olden times. My people came to Oklahoma from the Black Hills, South Dakota. We traveled on horses with tepee poles tied on horses. That was our only way of traveling in those days—before the white man came.

My first husband was in the U.S. Army at Ft. Sill, OK, Indian Territory. I was assistant girls matron at the old Kiowa Indian School, near Anadarko, OK, Ft. Sill Indian School.[3]

My own father was accidentally killed after the war party arrived at the village, when I was 1 year old. His brother married my mother. On my father's side, my grandfather had 10 wives in the olden times. That's where our ancestors originated from. We have a large relatives in the tribe.

I divorced the first husband. My second husband was taken prisoner of war to St. Augustine, Fla.—Ft. Marion Barracks to Hampton, Va. Then to the Hessian Barracks at Carlisle, Pa.[4]

Mary Buffalo, Kiowa
Vol. 77, pp. 333–34

When I was born the Kiowa Indians did not reckon time after the manner of the white man, therefore the date of my birth is not so clearly established as that of younger members of our people. Sam, who is among the oldest and holds a place of honor among the Kiowa Indians, is my uncle and tells me that I was born in February of 1884, the day I do not know.

My people came with the Kiowa Indian tribe from the Black Hills of South Dakota to Kansas and later to the Panhandle of Texas where my father, Onco, from whom we take our present family name, was born. My mother's name was Bopiae, I cannot translate it into English and I am not positive at this time where she was born, for among the Kiowa Indians of that time women had no standing at all and the custom prevailed that a man never spoke to his mother-in-law after he married her daughter.

I was born at Anadarko on the Kiowa Indian Reservation and attended school there until I finished the eighth grade, after which I have studied correspondence courses and in every way I knew how have made an effort to inform and to educate myself. I have received little instruction other than what I could learn from reading and study.

I reverence and respect the traditions, customs and faith in God which my people have preserved through all the past generations, but I, as do many of my people, understand that time brings changes and the Kiowa Indians must accept that which is for the good in the change.

I am a member of the Baptist Church and am rearing my family just like any other American citizen, sending them to school and taking part in social activities. I would like for all of my children to learn and be able to speak the Kiowa language, but some of them are not doing this, I regret to say.

The Kiowa people are intermarrying with the whites until it is my opinion that many of their customs and traditions will disappear and be lost completely if not preserved at once. . . . I expect to assist my people in every way I can for they are like children and do not understand many things which will rob them of their living and what the Government is endeavoring to do for them. I also expect to maintain my place as an American citizen to the best of my knowledge.

Robert Onco, Kiowa
Vol. 107, pp. 284–92

COMANCHES, KIOWAS AND APACHES

We came to Indian Territory, July, 1885, in three covered wagons pulled by oxen. We hauled feed, oats and corn for the Government to Fort Sill, Oklahoma. We had to chain wagons together to ford Red River. I rode in the skiff. . . . [I] saw Indians breaking wild horses in Cache Creek west of Fort Sill, Oklahoma. While the Indian men were breaking the wild horses in the creek, the squaws would be up the creek about one hundred yards ducking their little papooses in the creek to learn them to swim.

Quannah Parker was leader of the Comanche Indians. I saw [an] old Indian squaw take a knife and cut her ear and slash her arms. She said the Old Chief would give more ponies to the ones who cut themselves most. We were there and saw them when their chief died. They built a big fire with all his possessions, it burned all night. They danced and sang war songs, and the next day at sundown they wrapped the chief in a blanket and tied him on a pinto pony and two squaws took him and went west.

Mr. Farmer and Mr. Lee Dwyer went over to watch them but the Indians made them leave; we watched them from where we were camped. These were the Kiowas Indians, I believe. The Indians came and sat on their ponies all day and watched us. They wanted to know what Mr. Farmer was doing; they were afraid he was taking their ponies. I made them understand he wasn't taking their ponies. I made them understand he was hauling cord wood for the Government at Fort Sill, Oklahoma, and drove oxen.

We were in Apache, Oklahoma, and there the Apache Indians ran off our oxen. Mr. Farmer trailed them and in over a week we had them back. So we left there as they were not friendly .

Alice Smith Farmer, White Resident in Comanche Territory
Vol. 3, pp. 427–29

CADDOS

My mother was the last surviving Caddo woman that came from Louisiana. She told me everything but I never wrote it down and now I can't remember very much. The Caddo Indians were always a peace-loving tribe, but when they were moved to Texas, the Texans had suffered so much from the Plains Indians who would come to Texas on their raids, that they were afraid of all Indians. So the Texans took no chances and at every excuse would kill them. The Caddos were losing so many of their members that they made an agreement with the Wichitas and became affiliated with them. Not all of the Caddos came to Oklahoma, some of them went west. All trace was lost of them as far as I know. Several years ago my brother was in Oregon, and one day while down on the coast he saw two Indians who had just come in from fishing. He overheard them talking, and was somewhat surprised to recognize his own language. When he came home he was telling my mother about them and she asked how they were dressed. He told her that they did not dress like the Caddos here, then described their clothes. She said that they dressed like they used to in Louisiana. He never tried to talk to them because he couldn't talk very well. He had been among the white people more than with his own people.

I don't know anything about my father's people. When the Caddos came to Texas, my grandmother married a white man. When they were removed to Oklahoma, my grandfather begged my grandmother to stay there with him. She stayed there for a few weeks but got so lonesome for her people that she put my father, who was a small baby, on her back and started out to follow her people. My grandfather, who was away when she left, followed her. When he found her he told her that if she wanted to go with her people that it was all right, and he would let her keep the baby until it was old enough to go to school then he would take it and educate it. This she agreed to. He went back to Texas then. Sometime later he came to see the boy and told my grandmother that he would come again to get him when he was old enough to go to school. That was all right with her. He left and was never heard of again. It was never learned whether he was killed or what happened to him. I don't even know what my father's real name was. The Indians called him Inkanish, meaning "White Man." The white people called him John, so he was always known as John Inkanish. The only man who knew anything at all about my father was a man called Caddo Jake who lived on the Canadian [River] north of here. He could have told us my father's real name and who his people were, but as so often is the case none of us went to see him and now he is dead and no chance of learning about my father remains.

My father was killed in an encounter with the Dalton Brothers in 1894.

Mrs. Frank Cussins, Caddo
Vol. 21, pp. 376–88

COMANCHES

I moved here with my parents in 1896, to what is now McQueen, from Quanah, Texas, in a covered wagon, bringing everything we had. There were eight children, five boys and three girls. It was a distance of about 30 miles from

Quanah, Texas, to Gould, and we passed one house on the trip. Our home was a 30 mile square ranch. I lived around Gould, Oklahoma, for over 40 years.

Its population now is one family to every 1/4 section. Its good churches, good schools are making Oklahoma prosperous. We now have several oil wells in progress here in Harman Co., when we came here Harman was Greer Co. . . . I have seen quite a few of the Comanche Indians at Quanah, Texas when we lived there. Have seen the Chief of the Comanche tribe, Quanah Parker, many times. He was a friend of my father, S. A. Neeley.

The customs of the Comanche Indians, of which is the only tribe I know much about, was all rode horseback, the men wore long hair, with a hat of feathers, also lots of beads. The men carried bow and arrows. The women wore blankets and carried their babies strapped on their back. They ate raw meat, when they came to the fair at Quanah. They would kill a beef, hang it on a line, and at night they would have a War dance. One of their fords on the Red River was between Eldorado, Okla. and Quanah, Texas.

Ida Neeley Shelton, Comanche-White
Vol. 74, pp. 5–7

COMANCHES

Years and years ago, my mother told me that there was an Indian camp where Lake Lawtonka is now.[5] We lived there. The only schooling was taught us at home. There were no churches close.

The name of the Wichita Mountains originated from a settlement of Wichita Indians. A great sport among the Indians was to kill buffalo and deer. The buffalo hides were used as covers on beds and also used for trading.

Many times the soldiers have driven our horses away, but the Arapahos were worse than the soldiers. Indians used to go to the mountains for burial; then a cemetery was located where the Fort Sill Airport is now located. The remains were placed in the little Mission Cemetery north of Lawton.

Many years ago the Indians just had one name. The father and mother carried separate names. The children could use either name they preferred. When the Government started paying the Indians, they were given names such as (John, James, Eunice, Ruby and Edith) but the Indian could carry either the father's or the mother's name. Sometime the name is shortened, as, Tippiconnic, John Tipp.

One time an Indian went down into Texas. He bought himself a gun.

Not knowing anything of guns, he accidentally shot his hand. Soon he came home and as the Indians always felt toward Mr. Deyo (our first minister in this country) as our God and doctor, this Indian man went to Mr. Deyo to dress his hand, staying around the church for a few days until his hand was better. As his hand was being dressed, Mr. Deyo said, "I think you need a haircut," and he cut the Indian's hair off. The Indians took the haircut joke good-naturedly, but soon let his hair grow long, and today it is still worn long.

Ella Wer-Que-Wa, Comanche
Vol. 49, pp. 178–80

COMANCHES

I was born on July 4, 1881. Years ago the Indians didn't have any calendars. They went by the seasons and different changes of the moon. The reason why my mother remembered the exact date of my birth was, years and years ago when Fort Sill was just a young fort, the soldiers always celebrated on July 4. Of course many Indians attended this celebration from miles away. Some few Indians took a little part in this performance. My father was away at one of the celebrations the day I was born.

Before the opening days here, the Indians used to go to New Mexico on war parties and to trade with the Arapaho and Pueblo Indians. We traded them cattle, ponies, buffalo and furs for different kinds of garden seed and herbs, but especially liked by all were pumpkin seeds.

Emily Riddles, Comanche
Vol. 82, pp. 41–44

COMANCHES

A few miles north and west of Fort Sill, on Medicine Creek, there is a high limestone bluff, named Medicine Bluff because of the fate, according to legend, of two young Medicine Men who were both in love with the same beautiful Indian maiden, a chieftain's daughter. The story goes that to settle their rivalry they decided that they would both ride off the bluffs on horse-back, and the surviving one should have the heart and hand of the maiden, so a day was set and a great crowd of Indians, friends of the three, gathered at the bluffs. At a given signal from the chieftain the run was started and both boys went over the cliff, falling to death, two hundred feet below, in the waters of the creek. The maiden, above, watched for the one she loved to emerge from the creek triumphant, but to her horror, he did not appear so in a few moments she joined her lover in death, leaping over the ledge before anyone knew what she was doing. Thus ever after the bluffs, and the creek below, have been called Medicine Bluff, Medicine Creek and Little Medicine. In later years some Indians and a few white people actually have gone to death over these same bluffs.

Johnson Poahway, Comanche
Vol. 81, pp. 380–82

COMANCHES

I am a full blood Comanche Indian and live at Indiahoma. I am sixty years old, am married and have three children. My wife, Bessie, is a daughter of Quanah Parker. I am the interpreter for the Government at Indiahoma, where the Comanche Indian Agency is located and where the government issues out checks and pays the Comanches their annuity money.[6] The Agency formerly was at Red Store, then was moved to Cache, and in 1933 it was moved to Indiahoma. It is a branch of the Kiowa Indian Agency at Anadarko. The Comanches live all over Comanche County but a great many settled around Cache and Indiahoma on Post Oak Creek, Cache Creek, Beaver Creek and Pecan Creek because it was close to the Agency and trading store of G. M. Harris, established in 1889 by Harris and James and operated until 1908. I was the police and Government interpreter, am a graduate of Carlisle.

Herman Asanap, Comanche
Vol. 99, pp. 233–37

COMANCHES

The Indians are generally known to move very often. The Indian camps were several families always located near creeks or springs, where there was a good supply of wood and water. In the warmer weather we moved our tepee up on the hills; in the colder weather, we would move into low places and near timber, using the timber as wind breaks. . . . At Christmas time even yet some of the Indians attend the Indian encampments in this country south of Lawton about eight miles. Sometimes the encampment will last as long as ten days. Here the Indians have dancing, games and hold Medicine meetings while other Indians attend the Christmas services that are held at all our churches.

Andrew Perdasophy, Comanche
Vol. 39, pp. 437–39

CADDOS

All this was before my time, but my grandmother has told me all about it. Usually it was when we were out in the timber that she told me.

When the Caddos went back to Texas[7] they had all kinds of brass kettles and pots and heavy dishes, like they use in eating houses now, and they were too heavy to pack and carry so the Indians decided to bury them. This they did. They dug a deep hole and lined it with cowhides and put these pots and kettles in it and covered it with cowhides, then they put poles over that and more cowhides over that and covered the whole thing with dirt and brush. They did their work so well no one could tell it was there. They marked trees and other landmarks to tell where they could find them but only the workers knew what the marks meant. When the Indians returned some of the men who had done the work had died and so the exact location was lost. And these things have never been found. One of the places is near where the Riverside School is now, about two hundred yards southwest of the new lake.

Sadie Bedoka, Caddo-Delaware
Vol. 53, pp. 14–22

COMANCHES

In 1892, Quanah Parker had five wives. They had been married by the Indian custom and he had by these wives, fifteen children. His first, and oldest wife, We-Ke-Ah, had charge of all his personal papers. His second wife, Wh-We-Tah-Quah, fed and curried his horses, took care of all the harness and saddle horses and also helped harness or saddle his horse whenever he wanted to ride or drive anywhere. His third wife, Su-Ta-Quah, did all his laundry, took care of his fancy clothes and saw that every garment he owned was always mended and ready at all times for him to wear. His fourth wife, Nan-Noo-

Ky, did all the cooking and preparing of the meals. His fifth wife, Pop-Pye-Ah-Wan-Nah, carried all the water, chopped the wood, swept and cleaned the yards.

About nine miles down the creek from Quanah lived an Indian girl, who when she was very young, had been sold for so much bounty by her mother to an "old" Indian man, whom she hated and loathed, because he was so mean to her. This girl in her youth was very beautiful and had been in love with Quanah for many years. They often had clandestine meetings, as Quanah loved her too. Each time they met he told her it would be impossible to take her home with him as either his wives or her husband would kill her.

On a certain day this girl's husband tried to make her do something she disliked, so that night she waited until he was asleep then slipped out of the house. Never thinking of the danger from wild animals in the forest, she made her way that dark night, afoot, to Quanah's home, reaching it just before daylight. Quanah had a room on the ground floor all to himself. This room was furnished beautifully with pretty and expensive Indian articles, also other beautiful presents that had been given him by his many white friends. Quanah owned horses and cattle by the hundreds, he did not know really how many he owned. He had any number of beautiful buckskin suits and headdresses together with several civilian suits. He was a handsome Indian in his younger days and always wore midnight blue suits.

On the night that this beautiful Indian girl, Too-Ni-Ce, left her husband and reached Quanah's home she made her presence known by tapping on his window. There were no screens on the window so he opened it, and let her into his room.

She told him why she had come and they talked of what to do. He told her again it would be impossible to keep her in his home as his wives would kill her. Finally he told her to go about one-half mile to the home of a white man by the name of Granthum to keep her hid, cautioning his family not to dare reveal her presence; and for her to stay there until he came for her. This she did, and the white man hid her in his home.

Sometime during the next day, Quanah had his buggy greased, his best team harnessed and hitched to the buggy. He drove off without saying a word or telling anyone where he was going. He drove straight to Granthum's, picked up Too-Ni-Ce, and they drove to North Fork to the Herring and Stimson Ranch where Quanah had friends and stayed part of that night. Just before daylight they started for Vernon, Texas, and stayed that night with some people by the name of Shrapshire, whom Quanah had known in an early day. This man had a daughter who had taught school in old Greer County. Through this young lady, Quanah purchased clothes for his new love, telling the white girl to buy his young love all the new and beautiful clothes she desired for he wanted her to be dressed like "white woman." So he spend hundreds of dollars to dress up Too-Ni-Ce.

From there they went to Old Mexico, stopping on the way with friends of Quanah who gave him all the money he wanted. They lived in Old Mexico for three months and no one ever heard from them during this time.

When Quanah's disappearance became known at home, it was reported to the Indian Department at Anadarko. A search was started as his people didn't know what had become of him. They thought maybe he had been murdered or some other misfortune had overtaken him. When the husband of Too-Ni-Ce reported "her" missing, suspicions were aroused.

The Indian Department sent out a scout to hunt for Quanah and soon had a trace of them through the friends they had stayed with in their flight. They were finally found through the efforts of the Mexican and United States Governments and brought back. Too-Ni-Ce was taken to Anadarko where Quanah left her and she was guarded for fear of her life.

Quanah went home and his wives asked him if all this story they heard was true. He told them it was. Wife Number One packed her clothes, picked up her kids and left. Wife Number Two made a fuss and he kicked her, telling her to get out. Wives, Number Three and Four said nothing. Wife Number Five got smart, raised a fuss and he also kicked her out and sent her and her kids away.

An Indian police was sent out to make some kind of agreement between the wives who left and Quanah, after Too-Ni-Ce said she would die before she would go back to her husband. An agreement was reached and Too-Ni-Ce became Quanah's favorite wife and reigned supreme in his home until his death. She still lives today not far from Quanah's homes. It cost Quanah the greater part of his horses, cattle, and most of his beautiful personal belongings to make peace with all concerned and took six months to settle. He afterwards made Too-Ni-Ce his legal wife.

Mrs. Lena R. Banks, White Resident of Comanche Territory
Vol. 99, pp. 485–90

[I] was employed by Waggoner brothers, cattlemen who had thousands of acres of Indian land under lease. [I] was designated by [my] employers to stay with Chief Yellow Bear and Quanah Parker, to provide them with entertainment and to keep them in a good humor. [I] accompanied the two leaders to Fort Worth in 1885.

The Comanche leaders were sleeping in the same room; Quanah Parker retired early, while Yellow Bear was out seeing the sights. When Yellow Bear went to the hotel, he undressed and prepared to retire. He turned out the gas lights, then turned the gas on again immediately and was asphyxiated.

[I] was sleeping in a nearby room but did not learn of the tragedy until the next morning; [I] arose early the next morning and went to visit an artesian well, returning to the hotel about eleven a.m.

When [I] returned to the hotel, some of the hotel officials asked if [I] had seen Chief Yellow Bear and Quanah Parker. Learning that they had not appeared that morning, [I] went to their room and broke down the door.

Chief Yellow Bear was dead. Quanah Parker had rolled off the bed and had fallen in such a way that his nose was immediately in front of the crack under the door only six inches away. He had breathed enough pure air to escape death.

Quanah Parker was unconscious for two days and little hope was held for his recovery, but he did recover to become the great leader of his tribe and the friend of President Theodore Roosevelt. [I] remained constantly at Quanah Parker's bedside until he began to show marked improvement. [I] then asked Buck Inglelow, Greer County cowboy, who was visiting in Fort Worth to stay with the Indian while he slept for a few hours.

Quanah Parker had asked [me] numerous times: "Where is Yellow Bear?" Each time [I] would reply that Yellow Bear was in another room, adding "he is sick like you, Quanah."

When Inglelow arrived at the room, the Indian asked: "Buck, where is Yellow Bear?"

"Yellow Bear is dead'rn hell," replied the cowboy.

"Uh," grunted Quanah, turning to me, "George, you lie."

Quanah Parker was a man of remarkable intelligence. As soon as he was able to be up, he called a lawyer and secured as many affidavits as possible, giving the exact details of the death of Yellow Bear. He wanted to be elected

Chief of the Comanches and wanted to show the Indians just how Yellow Bear died so that they would not suspect him of having caused the death of the Chief.

When the Indian was able to travel and had secured the affidavits, he and [I] started back to the Comanche Reservation. [We] were met at Harrold, Texas, by a band of approximately five thousand Comanches.

Quanah Parker was elected Chief of his tribesmen.

[I] was associated constantly with Quanah Parker for two years. The Waggoner brothers wanted to keep on good terms with the Comanches so that they could use their land at a very low rental.

They gave many presents to Quanah Parker, including a carriage costing $1,000.00; a suit of fine clothes and many other expensive presents.

On one trip to Fort Worth, Chief Yellow Bear and Quanah Parker were dressed in tuxedos given them by the Waggoner brothers.

When [I] first began associating with Quanah Parker, the Indian could speak only a few words of English. [I] taught him to speak excellent English. [I] told him much about the ways of the white man.

Quanah Parker liked beer, but always refused to drink whiskey.

During one visit to Fort Worth, [I] and Quanah Parker went into the White Elephant saloon to drink beer. It was a large and beautiful saloon with several plaster elephants twenty feet in height placed in the corners.

As [we] stepped up to the bar, [I] noticed a friend, Colonel John Simpson of Dallas, sitting in a far corner.

Speaking rather loudly and waving [my] hand, [I] said: "Colonel, come up and drink with me."

[I] introduced Quanah Parker to Mr. Simpson and they talked pleasantly for a while.

Later in the day, while I was reading in the hotel lobby, Quanah Parker returned to the saloon. That night he told [me] what happened.

"I went back to drink beer," Quanah Parker said. "When I walked up to the bar, I looked and saw Colonel Simpson and waved at him and said, 'Colonel, I'm going to take another drink, come up and drink with me.' Forty men got up and came. Too damn many colonels in White Elephant."

George W. Briggs, White Business Associate of Quanah Parker
Vol. 16, pp. 297–309

Eighty different tribes of Indians have lived in Oklahoma. Kicking Bird and Stumbling Bear, both famous Kiowa warriors, are buried at Mt. Scott; Stumbling Bear had been a noted scout and was the proud possessor of a Jeffersonian medal, given as a reward for bravery. Satanta, Satank, and Lone Wolf were also noted warriors of the Kiowa tribe, who terrorized the whites and were the cause of Fort Sill being established.

Per-mum-ske was a noted Comanche scout. He was born in a tepee on the banks of the Canadian River, near the Antelope Mountains, in 1851. When he was about ten years old his parents moved to the Wichita Mountains, where Per-mum-ske lived the rest of his life, and where he died. At the age of nineteen, Per-mum-ske, who name means, "The Hairy One," took to the warpath against the white man, but one year later he realized it was hopeless for the Indians to fight against the advance of the white men, so he cut off his braids, cast aside his blankets and on December 1, 1874, enlisted for two months' service with the Indian Scout Detachment and was discharged with his character "good," in February, 1875, by Lt. R. R. Pratt.[8] He immediately re-enlisted as head of the Scout Detachment, taking part in the Kiowa-Comanche-Cheyenne campaign of 1875. He returned to his people and was chief for thirteen years.

Quanah Parker, who was chosen chief after Per-mum-ske, was chief at the opening of the Kiowa-Comanche country in 1901. Both he and his mother are buried in the Post Oak Cemetery near Cache.

I-O-See, a noted Kiowa Scout, served under Hugh L. Scott, who was commanding officer at Fort Sill in 1889. During the winter of 1890, while the Ghost Dance was going on, the battle of Wounded Knee was fought and Old Sitting Bull was killed. The Indians believed that Jesus would push all the whites into the sea. The whites were clamoring to have all the Indians placed under guard of soldiers but Scott, knowing that would only start trouble, went to the Indian Agent and asked to be allowed to handle the matter. During this time, I-O-See came and offered his services, and although he could not speak English, he was Scott's greatest standby. The Ghost Dance finally died out, and with the wonderful help of I-O-See, Scott was able to arrange peace with seven tribes, and bring about the signing of the Medicine Lodge Treaty.[9]

Houn-goon, the tribal artist, worked with the late James Mooney of the Bureau of Ethnology, Washington D.C.; he made the designs on the tepees shown by Mooney at the St. Louis World's Fair.[10] The work was done in the old Government House that stood at the junction of Ararantha Creek and Medicine Creek in the shadow of Mount Scott.

Other Kiowas of note were Hunting Horse, Hanneh-me-tah (Not Afraid of the Devil), Erudato, Quetone, Haw-vat, Kicking Bird (a preacher), San-Ka-Do-Tah and Old Man Horse. Noted Comanches were Ner-mo-rake, Pas-sah, Wes-ap-peah-py, and Poxicut and among the younger Indians were Howard White Wolf, a Carlisle graduate, a Comanche, and Guy Quetone, a Kiowa. Noted artists among the younger Kiowas are Howard Hunting Horse, Steve Mopope, and Jack Ho-keah; their work is shown both in America and Europe and they are also famous as tribal dancers, keeping alive the "old" Indian dances.[11]

Ed Barnes, White Cowboy in Kiowa Country
Vol. 90, pp. 18–21

Epilogue

◆ ◆ ◆ ◆ ◆ ◆ ◆ ◆ ◆ ◆ ◆ ◆ ◆

At the end of the nineteenth century, these Indian peoples who once called Texas home entered a period that would hold just as many events and be as momentous as those they had experienced in the previous two hundred years. Militarily defeated and removed from their homelands, they were virtual prisoners on the reservations. Though these reservations may have been much smaller and pale imitations of the huge territories they had once claimed as their own, at least the land still belonged to their nations, and all Indian nations held their reservation land in common as a separate people. Here, most of these traditional Indians of Texas merely wanted the government to uphold its treaty obligations and then leave them in peace. Since the Kiowas and Comanches could not hunt buffalo anymore, they became ranchers, raising large herds of cattle and horses.

They earned extra money by leasing pastureland to Texas ranchers. The Wichitas and Caddos, always a farming people, continued farming their small plots of corn, beans, squash, and pumpkins, supplementing this by raising smaller herds of horses, hogs, and cattle. For humanitarians and government officials, this activity was not good enough, and they felt that the Indians must give up every aspect of their Indianness and become the red equivalent of Anglo-Americans. Missionaries, teachers, model farmers, home agents, and government officials with the power forcibly to stop the Indians from doing anything they did not like descended like locusts on the Comanches, Kiowas, Caddos, Wichitas, Tonkawas, and Apaches.

It never occurred to these humanitarians that the Indians did not want to change their culture. Surely, they imagined, all they had to do was show the Indians the American way and they would all clamor for it. This did not happen. So when the Indians did not change fast enough or express appreciation for the attempted destruction of their culture, the humanitarians and government officials decided more direct action was needed, if only for the Indians' own good.

As Merrill Gates, a "friend of the Indian," said in 1896:

> To bring [the Indian] out of savagery into citizenship we must make the Indian more intelligently selfish before we can make him unselfishly intelligent. We need to awaken in him wants. In his dull savagery he must be touched by the wings of the divine angel of discontent. Then he begins to look forward, to reach out. The desire for property of his own may become an intense educating force. The wish for a home of his own awakens him to new efforts. Discontent with the teepee and the starving rations of the Indian camp in winter is needed to get the Indian out of the blanket and into trousers,—and trousers with a pocket in them, and with a pocket that aches to be filled with dollars! [italics are author's].[1]

It was this thinking that brought on the Dawes Act that broke up the reservations and gave each Indian or Indian family a small parcel of land. The allotment of Indian lands became what Merrill Gates described as "a mighty pulverizing engine for breaking up the tribal mass."[2]

Almost every Indian protested the government's decision to allot tribal lands. Chief Lone Wolf of the Kiowas even filed suit in federal court to stop this "theft" of their reservation lands. In January 1903, the Supreme Court ruled in *Lone Wolf v. Hitchcock* that Congress exercised absolute authority when it came to Indian relations and could ignore, or break, the stipulations agreed to in past treaties made between the Indians and the United States government whenever it wanted. Essentially, the past treaties were now not worth the paper they were written on, and Congress could force the Indians to give up their reservation land. So began the allotment process where Indian families were allotted about one hundred and sixty acres. In 1901, the Wichita and Caddo reservation and the Kiowa and Comanche reservations ceased to exist as the surplus lands were opened to white settlement. It also condemned them to lives of poverty for much of the twentieth century.

It was one thing to receive 160 acres and another thing to hold onto it. Due to the dry climate of southwestern Oklahoma, it was hard to turn a profit by farming a meager 160 acres. Also, 160 acres was not enough to raise large herds of cattle or horses. To make matters worse, judges deemed some Indians as "incompetent" and appointed white guardians for them, who of ten cheated them out of their land. What the humanitarians had seen as poverty on the reservations and had made them agitate for land allotment now became a reality during the early part of the twentieth century due to the very same allotment process that was supposed to cure it all.

The Cherokees, Choctaws, Creeks, Chickasaws, and Seminoles, suffering the same fate, hoped to create an Indian state inside of the United States—the State of Sequoyah—which would include all the eastern part of Indian Territory. Congress ignored their efforts and instead divided Indian Territory. In 1900, the eastern part where the Cherokees, Choctaws, Creeks, Chickasaws, Seminoles, and many other smaller eastern tribes lived would remain Indian Territory, but the parts west of this now became Oklahoma Territory. Then in 1907, Oklahoma became a state in the Union.

Despite all these problems, the traditional Indians of Texas survived. The Comanches, Kiowas, Caddos, Wichitas, Tonkawas, and Apaches are still there. While their culture is much changed, they still celebrate a distinct Indianness. Here in the late twentieth century, in and around Anadarko on any given Saturday night in the summer, one may still find a pow-wow or a tribal dance going on. The Caddos still dance the Turkey Dance; the Kiowas still do the Gourd Dance; and Wichitas still make drums. The Native American Church thrives. Old stories are still being told by elders. New oral history is being made and told by each new generation. Indian culture and Indian history continues.

Notes

◆ ◆ ◆ ◆ ◆ ◆ ◆ ◆ ◆ ◆ ◆ ◆ ◆

Introduction

1. W. W. Newcomb, Jr., *The Indians of Texas*, pp. 104, 133–36, 157, 247–48; Ernest Wallace and E. Adamson Hoebel, *The Comanches: Lords of the Southern Plains*, pp. 6–9; James Mooney, *Calendar History of the Kiowa Indians*, pp. 152–62; Mildred P. Mayhall, *The Kiowas*, pp. 6–8; Vynola Beaver Newkumet and Howard L. Meredith, *The Hasinai: A Traditional History of the Caddo Confederacy*, pp. 4–7; Deposition of Kiowa, Wichita Chief, September 24, 1927, Indian-Pioneer Histories, Oklahoma Historical Society Archives, Oklahoma City, Okla., Vol. 109, pp. 7–35.

2. Francis Jennings, *The Founders of America: From the Earliest Migrations to the Present*, pp. 25–31; Newcomb, *The Indians of Texas*, pp. 9–14.

3. Newcomb, *The Indians of Texas*, pp. 14–17; Jules H. Billard, ed., *The World of the American Indian*, pp. 43–51; Marshall Sahlins, "Notes on the Original Affluent Society," in *Man the Hunter*, ed. Richard B. Lee and Irven DeVore, pp. 85–89.

4. J. Daniel Rogers, "Patterns of Change on the Western Margin of the Southeast, A.D. 600–900" in *Stability, Transformation, and Variation: The Late Woodland Southeast*, ed. Michael S. Nassaney and Charles R. Cobb, pp. 221, 224, 237; Timothy K. Perttula, *The Caddo Nation: Archaeological and Ethnohistoric Perspectives*, p. 13.

5. Philip Phillips and James A. Brown, *Pre-Columbian Shell Engravings from the Craig Mound at Spiro, Oklahoma*, 2 vols., I, pp. 9, 16; Rogers, "Patterns of Change," pp. 232–33.

6. Dennis A. Peterson, "A History of Excavations and Interpretations of Artifacts from the Spiro Mounds Site," in *The Southeastern Ceremonial Complex: Artifacts and Analysis, The Cottonlandia Conference*, ed. Patricia Galloway, p. 119; F. Todd Smith, *The Caddo Indians: Tribes at the Convergence of Empires, 1542–1854*, pp. 8–9; Susan C. Vehik, "Cultural Continuity and Discontinuity in the Southern Prairies and Cross Timbers," in *Plains Indians, A.D. 500–1500*, ed. Karl H. Schlesier, pp. 248–49, 260–61; Herbert E. Bolton, *The Hasinai: Southern Caddoans as Seen by the Earliest Europeans*, pp. 31, 63–64; Perttula, *The Caddo Nation*, pp. 16–17.

7. Timothy G. Baugh, "Ecology and Exchange: The Dynamics of Plains-Pueblo Interactions," *Farmers, Hunters, and Colonists: Interaction between the Southwest and the Southern Plains*, ed. Katherine A. Spielmann, pp. 107, 121; Vehik, "Cultural Continuity and Discontinuity in the Southern Prairies and Cross Timbers," pp. 260–61; Alex D. Krieger,

Culture Complexes and Chronology in Northern Texas, p. 73; Newcomb, *The Indians of Texas*, pp. 247–56.

8. Karl H. Schlesier, "Commentary: A History of Ethnic Groups in the Great Plains, A.D. 150–1550" in *Plains Indians, A.D. 500–1500: The Archaeological Past of Historic Groups*, ed. Karl H. Schlesier, pp. 355; Newcomb, *The Indians of Texas*, pp. 133–36; Frederick W. Hodge, *Handbook of American Indians*, II, pp. 778–83.

9. Baugh, "Ecology and Exchange," pp. 121, 125; David R. Wilcox, "Changing Contexts of Pueblo Adaptations, A.D. 1250–1600," in *Farmers, Hunters, and Colonists: Interaction between the Southwest and the Southern Plains*, ed. Katherine A. Spielmann, pp. 131–32, 144–47, 152–53; Christopher Lintz, "Texas Panhandle-Pueblo Interactions from the Thirteenth Through the Sixteenth Century," in *Farmers, Hunters, and Colonists: Interaction between the Southwest and the Southern Plains*, ed. Katherine A. Spielmann, pp. 104–5; Krieger, *Cultural Complexes*, pp. 193, 205; Vehik, "Cultural Continuity and Discontinuity in the Southern Prairies and Cross Timbers," p. 261.

10. J. Charles Kelley, "Juan Sabeata and Diffusion in Aboriginal Texas," *American Anthropologists* 57 (October, 1955): 982, 991–92. See Newcomb, *The Indians of Texas*, for a complete description of the early Indians of Texas.

11. Marvin Harris, *Cultural Materialism: The Struggle for a Science of Culture*, pp. 90–92; Patricia C. Albers, "Symbiosis, Merger, and War: Contrasting Forms of Intertribal Relationship Among Historic Plains Indians," in *The Political Economy of North American Indians*, ed. John H. Moore, pp. 106–10; David La Vere, "Friendly Persuasions: Gifts and Reciprocity in Comanche-Euroamerican Relations," *Chronicles of Oklahoma* 71 (Fall, 1993): 322–37. Though it mainly deals with the Cherokees, an excellent discussion of the obligations of blood revenge can be found in John Phillip Reid, *A Law of Blood: The Primitive Law of the Cherokee Nation*.

12. James A. Robertson, ed. and trans. "The True Relation of the Hardships Suffered by Governor Hernando de Soto by a Gentleman of Elvas," in *The De Soto Chronicles: The Expedition of Hernando De Soto to North America in 1539–1543*, ed. Lawrence A. Clayton, Vernon James Knight, Jr., Edward C. Moore, 2 vols., I, pp. 143, 140–47; Charles Hudson, "The Hernando de Soto Expedition, 1539–1543," in *The Forgotten Centuries: Indians and Europeans in the American South, 1521–1704*, pp. 95–97.

13. Elizabeth A. H. John, *Storms Brewed in Other Men's Worlds: The Confrontation of Indians, Spanish, and French in the Southwest, 1540–1795*, pp. 13–23.

14. Marvin T. Smith, *Archaeology of Aboriginal Culture Change in the Interior Southeast: Depopulation During the Early Historic Period*, p. 59; Charles Hudson, *The Southeastern Indians*, pp. 41, 97–119; Perttula, *The Caddo Nation*, pp. 85–87; John R. Swanton, *Source Material on the History and Ethnology of the Caddo Indians*, Fig. 1, pp. 12–13; John C. Ewers, "The Influence of Epidemics on the Indian Populations and Cultures of Texas," *Plains Anthropologist* 18 (May, 1973): 104–15. For a fine discussion of disease and cultural reorganization, see James Merrell, *The Indians' New World: Catawbas and their Neighbors from European Contact through the Era of Removal*, pp. 18–27, as well as Alfred W. Crosby, "Virgin Soil Epidemics as a Factor in the Aboriginal Depopulation in America," *William and Mary Quarterly*, 3 ser. 33 (April, 1976): 289–99.

15. Preston Holder, *The Hoe and the Horse on the Plains: A Study of Cultural Development among*

North American Indians, pp. 110–12; Jack Jackson, *Los Mesteños: Spanish Ranching in Texas, 1721–1821*, pp. 9–11; Nancy Hickerson, *The Jumanos: Hunters and Traders of the South Plains*, pp. 137, 166, 219; Robert Silverberg, *The Pueblo Revolt*, p. 132.

16. Alan M. Klein, "Political Economy of the Buffalo Hide Trade: Race and Class on the Plains," in *The Political Economy of North American Indians*, ed. John H. Moore, pp. 141–43; Frank Raymond Secoy, *Changing Military Patterns of the Great Plains Indians*, pp. 20–32; Wallace and Hoebel, *The Comanches*, p. 241; John, *Storms Brewed in Other Men's Worlds*, p. 59; Holder, *The Hoe and the Horse*, pp. 52–56.

17. Morris W. Foster, *Being Comanche: A Social History of an American Indian Community*, pp. 31–35; Wallace and Hoebel, *The Comanches*, pp. 5–11, 34–36; Thomas Kavanagh, *Comanche Political History*, pp. 57–62.

18. Henri Joutel, "Joutel's Historical Journal of Monsieur de la Salle's Last Voyage to Discover the River Mississippi," in *Historical Collections of Louisiana, Embracing Many Rare and Valuable Documents Relating to the Natural, Civil and Political History of that State*, ed. B. F. French, I, pp. 146–47, 160–63, 169–70; Robert S. Weddle, *The French Thorn: Rival Explorers in the Spanish Sea, 1682–1762*, pp. 33–39.

19. James E. Corbin. "Spanish-Indian Interaction on the Eastern Frontier of Texas," in *Columbian Consequences: Archaeological and Historical Perspectives on the Spanish Borderlands West*, ed. David Hurst Thomas, pp. 269–79; John, *Storms Brewed in Other Men's Worlds*, pp. 187–92.

20. Corbin, "Spanish-Indian Interaction on the Eastern Frontier of Texas," pp. 269–279; Perttula, *The Caddo Nation*, p. 169; Smith, *The Caddo Indians*, pp. 40–43, 52–54.

21. Smith, *The Caddo Indians*, pp. 39–41. For a detailed look at the Indian trade from primary sources, see Herbert E. Bolton, trans. and ed., *Athanase De Mézières and the Louisiana-Texas Frontier, 1768–1780*, hereafter cited as *ADM*. Indian-French marriages can be seen in Elizabeth Shown Mills, *Natchitoches: Abstracts of the Catholic Church Registers of the French and Spanish Post of St. Jean Baptiste des Natchitoches in Louisiana: 1729–1803*. For excellent explanations on the role kinship played in creating commodities, see Eric R. Wolf, *Europe and the People Without History*, pp. 88–100 and Albers, "Symbiosis, Merger, and War," pp. 94–132.

22. Corbin, "Spanish-Indian Interaction on the Eastern Frontier of Texas," pp. 269–79.

23. John, *Storms Brewed in Other Men's Worlds*, pp. 114–15, 154, 226–31.

24. Wallace and Hoebel, *The Comanches*, pp. 25–31, 39; John, *Storms Brewed in Other Men's Worlds*, pp. 231, 243–57; Foster, *Being Comanche*, 37–40; Newcomb, *The Indians of Texas*, pp. 156–58; Kavanagh, *Comanche Political History*, pp. 1–15, 87.

25. De Mézières to Unzaga, February 16, 1776, *ADM*, II, pp. 120–21; Cabello to the Governor of Louisiana, December 15, 1783, in Lawrence Kinnaird, ed. *Annual Report of the American Historical Association for the Year 1945*, 3 vols.; *Spain in the Mississippi Valley, 1765–1794: Post War Decade, 1782–1792*, II, p. 94, hereafter cited as *SMV*; Juan Cortes to Baron Hector de Carondelet, March 22, 1792, *SMV*, III, pp. 18–9; Albers, "Symbiosis, Merger, and War," pp. 100–5; Holder, *The Hoe and the Horse on the Plains*, pp. 79–84.

26. Report of Joachín de Orobio Bazterra, October 1, 1745, Reel 8, Béxar Archives, hereafter cited as *BA*; Deposition of Tejas Chiefs Sanches and Canos taken by Fr. Joseph Calahorra, July 30, 1765, Reel 10, *BA*; Antonio Bucareli to Baron de Ripperda, Octo-

ber 7, 1772, Reel 11, *BA;* Guadiana to Muñoz, March 26, 1797, Reel 27, *BA;* Albers, "Symbiosis, Merger, and War," pp. 108–10; Foster, *Being Comanche,* pp. 41–44.

27. List of the effects which should be given to the three Indian nations of the Post of Natchitoches, O'Reilly to De Mézières, January 22, 1770, *ADM,* I, pp. 132–34; Secoy, *Changing Military Patterns of the Great Plains Indians,* p. 26; Thomas Frank Schilz and Donald E. Worcester, "The Spread of Firearms among the Indians Tribes on the Northern Frontier of New Spain," *American Indian Quarterly* II (Winter, 1987): 1–2; Tom Wintringham, *The Story of Weapons and Tactics from Troy to Stalingrad,* pp. 107–16; Martin van Creveld, *Technology and War: From 2000 BC to the Present,* pp. 92–96.

28. Daniel E. Fox, *Traces of Texas History: Archeological Evidence of the Past 450 Years,* pp. 39–40, 78–79; Perttula, *The Caddo Nation,* pp. 198–207, 217; Smith, *The Caddo Indians,* pp.52–54; Foster, *Being Comanche,* pp. 39–40. A good discussion of how Indians understood the details of the trade can be found in James Axtell, "The First Consumer Revolution," *Beyond 1492,* pp. 125–51 and in Arthur Ray, "The Fur Trade as an Aspect of Native American History," in *Major Problems in American Indian History,* pp. 147–56.

29. Report by De Mézières of the Expedition to the Cadodachos, October 29, 1770, *ADM,* I, p. 210; Fred Kniffen, Hiram F. Gregory and George A. Stokes, *The Historic Indian Tribes of Louisiana from 1542 to the Present,* pp. 64–65; Albers, "Sybiosis, Merger, and War," p. 128; John, *Storms Brewed in Other Men's Worlds,* p. 317.

30. Klein, "Political Economy of the Buffalo Hide Trade," pp. 141–44; Wallace and Hoebel, *The Comanches,* pp. 138–41, 241–42.

31. Ewers, "The Influence of Epidemics on the Indian Populations and Cultures of Texas," pp. 104–15.

32. Joachín de Orobio Bazterra, October 1, 1745, Reel 8, *BA;* De Mézières to Unzaga y Amezaga, May 20, 1770, *ADM,* I, pp. 166–168; Fray Miguel Santa María y Silva to the Viceroy, July 21, 1774, II, pp. 74–76; De Mézières to the viceroy, February 20, 1778, II, p. 176.

33. Corbin, "Spanish-Indian Interaction on the Eastern Frontier of Texas," p. 272; David J. Weber, *The Spanish Frontier in North America,* pp. 154–55, 191, 210–11; Donald E. Chipman, *Spanish Texas, 1519–1821,* pp. 138–46, 201–2.

34. Deposition of Tejas Chiefs Sanches and Canos taken by Fr. Joseph Calahorra, July 30, 1765, Reel 10, *BA;* Chipman, *Spanish Texas,* pp. 159–63; John, *Storms Brewed in Other Men's Worlds,* pp. 296–98, 348–52.

35. Willard H. Rollings, *The Osage: An Ethnohistorical Study of Hegemony on the Prairie-Plains,* pp. 6–7; De Mézières to Unzaga y Amezaga, May 20, 1770, *ADM,* I, pp. 167–68.

36. Chipman, *Spanish Texas,* pp. 181–84.

37. Weber, *The Spanish Frontier in North America,* pp. 223–24; Thomas D. Hall, *Social Change in the Southwest, 1350–1880,* pp. 112–21; John, *Storms Brewed in Other Men's Worlds,* pp. 666–75; Bolton, ed., *ADM,* I, pp. 92–120.

38. John, *Storms Brewed in Other Men's Worlds,* pp. 711–60; Foster, *Being Comanche,* pp. 58–59; Kavanagh, *Comanche Political History,* pp. 148–54.

39. Vaugine to Piernas, May 20, 1781, Legajo 194, Doc. 665, Papeles de Cuba, Archivo General de Indias, Seville, Spain, hereafter cited as *PPC;* Deposition of Louis Fortin, February 18, 1783, Legajo 196, No Doc. Number, *PPC;* David La Vere and Katia Campbell, "An Expedition to the Kichai: The Journal of François Grappe, Septem-

ber 24, 1783," *The Southwestern Historical Quarterly* 98 (July, 1994): 59–78; Journal of an Expedition up the Red River, 1773–1774, by J. Gaignard, *ADM*, II, pp. 83–100.

40. Mooney, *Calendar History of the Kiowa Indians*, pp. 162–65, 228–30; Mayhall, *The Kiowas*, pp. 1–15, 135–36. For the sake of clarity, the term "Apache," in almost all instances in this book, will refer to the "Lipan Apaches" or "Plains Apaches." Usually these will be designated as such. As for the "Kiowa-Apaches," despite keeping a distinctiveness from the Kiowa as a whole, they were still very closely associated with the Kiowas, and so the term "Kiowa" will apply to the Kiowa *and* Kiowa-Apache groups.

41. Information as to Indian Nations of the Province of Texas, Samuel Davenport to Manuel de Salcedo, 1808, Reel 39, *BA*; De Blanc to Miró, September 30, 1789, *SMV*, II, p. 289; De Blanc to Miró, September 2, 1790, *SMV*, II, p. 316; De Blanc to Carondelet, February 18, 1792, *SMV*, III, pp. 9–11; Gilbert C. Din and Abraham P. Nasatir, *The Imperial Osages: Spanish-Indian Diplomacy in the Mississippi Valley*, p. 192; Rollings, *The Osage*, pp. 142–43; Kniffen, Gregory, and Stokes, *Historic Indian Tribes of Louisiana*, p. 91.

42. Location of Indians around Natchitoches, Estevan Miró, December 12, 1785, *SMV*, II, p. 160; De Blanc to Carondelet, April 16, 1792, *SMV*, III, pp. 25–27; Layssard to Miró, June 1, 1787, Legajo 118, No Doc. Number, *PPC*; Sotechaux to Bernardo Fernández, August 25, 1796, Reel 26, *BA*; Fernández to Muñoz, September 25, 1796, Reel 26, *BA*; Fernández to Muñoz, October 23, 1796, Reel 26, *BA*; José Guadiana to Muñoz, November 25, 1796, Reel 26, *BA*; Mary A. O'Callaghan, "An Indian Removal Policy in Spanish Louisiana," in *Greater America: Essays in Honor of Eugene Herbert Bolton*, p. 281; Chipman, *Spanish Texas*, p. 210.

43. Chipman, *Spanish Texas*, p. 237.

44. Dianna Everett, *The Texas Cherokees: A People Between Two Fires, 1819–1840*, pp. 11, 19–23, 25; H. Allen Anderson, "The Delaware and Shawnee Indians and the Republic of Texas, 1820–1845," *Southwestern Historical Quarterly* 94 (October, 1990): 233–34; D. W. Meinig, *Imperial Texas: An Interpretive Essay in Cultural Geography*, pp. 28–30.

45. Stanley Noyes, *Los Comanches: The Horse People, 1751–1845*, p. 205; Hall, *Social Change in the Southwest*, pp. 148–50, 160–63.

46. Sahlins, *Stone Age Economics*, pp. 193–98; Alan Barnard and Anthony Good, *Research Practices in the Study of Kinship*, pp. 150–54; Albers, "Symbiosis, Merger, and War," p. 98; Katherine A. Spielmann, "Interaction Among Nonhierarchical Societies," in *Farmers, Hunters, and Colonists*, pp. 4–5; David La Vere, "Friendly Persuasions: Gifts and Reciprocity in Comanche-Euroamerican Relations," *Chronicles of Oklahoma* 71 (Fall, 1993): 322–37.

47. Kavanagh, *Comanche Political History*, pp. 210–21; Noyes, *Los Comanches*, pp. 205–13; Foster, *Being Comanche*, pp. 61–62; Hall, *Social Change in the Southwest*, pp. 160–61.

48. Everett, *The Texas Cherokees*, p. 66; Anderson, "Delaware and Shawnee Indians," pp. 233–238; Newcomb, *The Indians of Texas*, pp. 343–48. Though it mainly deals with the Cherokees, an excellent examination about how Indian peoples initially viewed such domestic stock as cattle, pigs, and sheep, is Theda Perdue, "Women, Men and American Indian Policy: The Cherokee Response to 'Civilization'," *Negotiators of Change: Historical Perspectives on Native American Women*, pp. 90–114.

49. Stephen F. Austin to Josiah H. Bell, August 6, 1823, in Eugene C. Barker, "The Austin Papers," in *Annual Report of the American Historical Association for the Year 1919*. 2 vols.,

2 parts. (Washington D.C.: Government Printing Office, 1924), II, part 1, pp. 681–782, hereafter cited as *AP*; Austin to Luciano Garcia, October 20, 1832, *AP* (1919), II, part 1, pp. 701–702; Austin to Amos Rawls, June 22, 1824, *AP* (1919), II, part 1, p. 840; Newcomb, *The Indians of Texas*, pp. 343–44; Wallace and Hoebel, *The Comanches*, p. 287; Everett, *The Texas Cherokees*, p. 30; Clarence E. Carter, ed., *The Territorial Papers of the United States: The Territory of Arkansas, 1819–1825*, XIX, pp. 69–70.

50. Treaty between Texas and the Cherokee Indians, February 23, 1836, in *The Indian Papers of Texas and the Southwest, 1825–1916*, ed. Dorman H. Winfrey and James M. Day, I, pp. 14–17, hereafter cited as *IPT*; Everett, *The Texas Cherokees*, pp. 70–71, 86–87; Newcomb, *The Indians of Texas*, p. 343.

51. Foster, *Being Comanche*, pp. 58–69; Kavanagh, *Comanche Political History*, pp. 36–56; Daniel J. Gelo, "On a New Interpretation of Comanche Social Organization," *Current Anthropology* 28 (August-October, 1987): 551–52; Wallace and Hoebel, *The Comanches*, pp. 22–25; Elizabeth Cashdan, "Hunters and Gatherers: Economic Behavior in Bands," in *Economic Anthropology*, ed. Stuart Plattner, pp. 21–22.

52. Though it concentrates on the Lakota Sioux, one of the best explanations of band societies and the role of the chief is in Robert M. Utley, *The Lance and the Shield: The Life and Times of Sitting Bull*, pp. 8–13; Foster, *Being Comanche*, pp. 57–63; Wallace and Hoebel, *The Comanches*, pp. 210–16; Kavanagh, *Comanche Political History*, pp. 36–56.

53. Foster, *Being Comanche*, pp. 55–69; Gelo, "On a New Interpretation of Comanche Social Organization," pp. 551–552; Kavanagh, *Comanche Political History*, pp. 36–56.

54. Newcomb, *The Indians of Texas*, pp. 344–45; William T. Hagan, *Quanah Parker, Comanche Chief*, p. 6.

55. Newcomb, *The Indians of Texas*, p. 345; Francis Paul Prucha, *The Great Father: The United States Government and the American Indians*, pp. 354–55.

56. Noah Smithwick, quoted in Newcomb, *The Indians of Texas*, p. 346; Treaty between Texas and the Tonkawa Indians, November 22, 1837, *IPT*, I, pp. 28–30; Treaty between Texas and the Lipan Indians, January 8, 1838, *IPT*, I, pp. 30–32; Report from R. A. Irion to Sam Houston, March 14, 1838, *IPT*, I, pp. 42–45.

57. Andrew Jackson, First Annual Message, Washington D.C., December 8, 1829, *A Compilation of the Messages and Papers of the Presidents, 1789–1908*, ed. James D. Richardson, II, p. 458.

58. Prucha, *The Great Father*, pp. 187–91, 214–68, 300–9.

59. Grant Foreman, "The Journal of the Proceedings of Our First Treaty with the Wild Indians, 1835," *The Chronicles of Oklahoma* 14 (December, 1936): 394–98; "Treaty with the Comanches, etc., 1835," in Charles J. Kappler, *Indian Treaties, 1778–1883*, p. 435; "Treaty with Kiowa, etc., 1837," in Kappler, *Indian Treaties*, p. 489; Prucha, *The Great Father*, pp. 226–228, 297–98.

60. Theda Perdue, "The Trail of Tears: Removal of the Southern Indians," in *The American Indian Experience, A Profile: 1542 to the Present*, ed., Philip Weeks, pp. 108–9; Prucha, *The Great Father*, pp. 189–90, 195–96.

61. Newcomb, *The Indians of Texas*, pp. 346–48; Everett, *The Texas Cherokees*, pp. 99–100; Smith, *The Caddo Indians*, pp. 141–42.

62. Mooney, *Calendar History of the Kiowa Indians*, pp. 257–60; Maurice Boyd, *Kiowa Voices:*

Myths, Legends and Folktales, II, pp. 49–50, 137–38; Newcomb, *The Indians of Texas,* pp. 348–49; Anderson, "Delaware and Shawnee Indians," pp. 242–43, 246.

63. Newcomb, *The Indians of Texas,* pp. 346, 357–58; F. Todd Smith, *The Caddos, The Wichitas, and the United States, 1846–1901,* pp. 43–45, 51–59; Anderson, "The Delaware and Shawnee Indians," pp. 242–43.

64. Newcomb, *The Indians of Texas,* p. 345.

65. Noyes, *Los Comanches,* pp. 280–84; Newcomb, *The Indians of Texas,* p. 350; Wallace and Hoebel, *The Comanches,* p. 294.

66. Noyes, *Los Comanches,* pp. 288–89.

67. Noyes, *Los Comanches,* pp. 289–96; Newcomb, *The Indians of Texas,* pp. 350–51; Minutes of Council at the Falls of the Brazos, October 7, 1844, *IPT,* II, pp. 103–14.

68. George Catlin, *North American Indians,* pp. 332–33; Wallace and Hoebel, *The Comanches,* pp. 241–42; Mayhall, *The Kiowas,* p. 127. For a general discussion on captives, particularly by such agricultural Indians as the Cherokees, see Reid, *A Law of Blood: The Primitive Law of the Cherokee Nation,* pp. 189–96.

69. Z. Taylor to Adjutant General of the Army, September 13, 1842, Explanatory of Bill Making Appropriation for fulfilling Treaty Stipulations with the Various Indian Tribes, &c., Until July 1, 1844, House Document 99, 27th Cong., 1st Sess., 1842–43, Congressional Serial Set, Vol. 420, p. 4–5, hereafter cited as *CSS;* A. M. M. Upshaw, U.S. Agent for the Chickasaws to T. Hartley Crawford, Commissioner of Indian Affairs, September 4, 1843, Fort Washita, Report of the Commissioner of Indian Affairs, Senate Executive Doc. 2, 28th Cong., 1st Sess., 1843–1844, *CSS,* v. 431, p. 419.

70. Prucha, *The Great Father,* pp. 355–58; Treaty between United States and the Comanche, Ioni, Anadarko, Caddo, Lipan, Longwa, Keechi, Tawakoni, Tonkawa, Wichita and Waco Indians, May 15, 1846, *IPT,* III, pp. 53–61.

71. Treaty between United States and the Comanche, Caddo, Lipan, Quapaw, Tawakonia, and Waco Tribes of Indians, December 10, 1850, *IPT,* III, pp. 130–37; Prucha, *The Great Father,* pp. 358–64; Newcomb, *The Indians of Texas,* pp. 354–55.

72. George Klos, "'Our People Could Not Distinguish One Tribe from Another': The 1859 Expulsion of the Reserve Indians from Texas," *Southwest Historical Quarterly* 97 (April, 1994): 602–4; Smith, *The Caddos, The Wichitas, and the United States,* pp. 39–54; Wallace and Hoebel, *The Comanches,* pp. 301–2.

73. Smith, *The Caddos, the Wichitas, and the United States,* pp. 53–67; Klos, "'Our People Could Not Distinguish One Tribe from Another'," pp. 605–6; Prucha, *The Great Father,* pp. 364.

74. E. J. Gurley to R. S. Neighbors, May 5, 1859, Waco, Texas, Letters Received by the Office of Indian Affairs, Wichita Agency, 1857–78, M234, Western History Collection, Roll 928, 1857–1866, #796, hereafter cited as Wichita Agency Letters; S. Ross to R. S. Neighbors, May 9, 1859, Brazos Agency, Wichita Agency Letters, #790; S. P. Ross to R. S. Neighbors, May 24, 1859, Brazos Agency, Wichita Agency Letters, #787; Capt. J. B. Plummer, Capt. 1st Infantry, to Asst. Adjutant General, May 23, 1859, Headquarters Camp at the Brazos Agency, Wichita Agency Letters, #784; Smith, *The Caddos, the Wichitas, and the United States,* pp. 67–78; Klos, "'Our People Could Not Distinguish One Tribe from Another'," pp. 608–19; Prucha, *The Great Father,* pp. 365–66.

75. Diary of James Reagle, James Reagle Jr. Collection, Western History Collection, University of Oklahoma, Norman, Okla., R–45, 1240, p. 14; C. Ross Hume, "Historic Sites around Anadarko," *The Chronicles of Oklahoma* 16 (December, 1938): 415; Jeanne V. Harrison, "Matthew Leeper, Confederate Agent at the Wichita Agency, Indian Territory," *The Chronicles of Oklahoma* 47 (Autumn, 1969): 242–57; Prucha, *The Great Father*, pp. 421; Newcomb, *The Indians of Texas*, pp. 358–59.

76. Robert Utley, *The Indian Frontier of the American West, 1846–1890*, pp. 95; Wallace and Hoebel, *The Comanches*, pp. 303–306.

77. William T. Hagan, *United States-Comanche Relations: The Reservation Years*, pp. 21–23; Prucha, *The Great Father*, pp. 461; Utley, *The Indian Frontier*, pp. 97; Newcomb, *The Indians of Texas*, pp. 358–59.

78. Utley, *United States-Comanche Relations*, pp. 29–43; Prucha, *The Great Father*, pp. 490, 496; Weeks, *Farewell, My Nation*, pp. 137–38.

79. Hagan, *United States-Comanche Relations*, pp. 44–58, Smith, *The Caddos, the Wichitas, and the United States*, pp. 98–100; Weeks, *Farewell, My Nation*, p. 161.

80. Utley, *The Indian Frontier*, pp. 141–48, 173–74; Hagan, *United States-Comanche Relations*, pp. 75–77; James L. Haley, *The Buffalo War: The History of the Red River Indian Uprising of 1874*, p. 17.

81. David D. Smits, "The Frontier Army and the Destruction of the Buffalo: 1865–1883," *Western Historical Quarterly* 25 (Autumn, 1994): 314–34; Hagan, *United States-Comanche Relations*, pp. 106; Haley, *The Buffalo War*, pp. 24–36; Utley, *The Indian Frontier*, pp. 174–75; Weeks, *Farewell, My Nation*, pp. 163–64.

82. Haley, *The Buffalo War*, pp. 176–83; Hagan, *United States-Comanche Relations*, pp. 108–120; Utley, *The Indian Frontier*, pp. 174–78; Prucha, *The Great Father*, pp. 536; T. Lindsay Baker and Billy R. Harrison, *Adobe Walls: The History and Archeology of the 1874 Trading Post*, pp. 14, 50–74.

83. William T. Hagan, *Quanah Parker, Comanche Chief*, pp. 30–39; Hagan, *United States-Comanche Relations*, pp. 127–34, 148–53; Forrest D. Monahan, Jr., "The Kiowa-Comanche Reservation in the 1890's," *The Chronicles of Oklahoma* 45 (Winter, 1967–68): 451–63.

84. Benjamin R. Kracht, "The Kiowa Ghost Dance, 1894–1916: An Unheralded Revitalization Movement," *Ethnohistory* 39 (Fall, 1992): 456–59; Hagan, *Quanah Parker*, pp. 52–61; Hagan, *United States-Comanche Relations*, pp. 189–94.

85. Clyde Ellis, *To Change Them Forever: Indian Education at Rainy Mountain Boarding School, 1893–1920*, pp. 91–130; Hagan, *United States-Comanche Relations*, pp. 133–35, 194–200. For more information on Indian education, see David W. Adams, *Education for Extinction: American Indians and the Boarding School Experience, 1875–1928*; Sally J. McBeth, *Ethnic Identity and the Boarding School Experience of West-Central Oklahoma American Indians*; and Clyde Ellis, "'A Remedy For Barbarism': Indian School, the Civilizing Program, and the Kiowa-Comanche-Apache Reservation, 1871–1915," *American Indian Culture and Research Journal* 18 (1994): 85–120.

86. Hagan, *United States-Comanche Relations*, p. 166; Prucha, *The Great Father*, pp. 666–71; Smith, *The Caddos, the Wichitas, and the United States*, pp. 142–44; Peter Iverson, *When Indians Became Cowboys: Native Peoples and Cattle Ranching in the American West*, pp. 88–92.

87. Prucha, *The Great Father*, pp. 775–76; Hagan, *United States-Comanche Relations*, pp. 262–294; Smith, *The Caddos, the Wichitas, and the United States*, pp. 143–54.

88. Smith, *The Caddos, the Wichitas, and the United States*, pp. 117–21; Kracht, "The Kiowa Ghost Dance," pp. 462–72; Ellis, *To Change Them Forever*, pp. 41, 54–55, 208 n34; Clyde Ellis, "'Truly Dancing Their Own Way': The Modern Revival and Diffusion of the Gourd Dance," *American Indian Quarterly* 14 (Winter, 1990): 19–33; For an excellent examination of these changes and consistencies to Texas Indian cultures, see Foster's *Being Comanche*.

Chapter 1. Raids and Warfare

1. It is not known what battle is being described here.

2. The incident described here appears to be the infamous Warren Wagon Train Raid of 1871 which led to the arrest-imprisonment of Kiowa chiefs Satanta and Big Tree. Ironically, as the Comanches and Kiowas lay in ambush, they let an earlier wagon train pass unmolested in order to attack the more heavily loaded supply train. The first train held General William T. Sherman on his tour of forts in Texas and Indian Territory. It was Sherman who later had Satanta and Big Tree imprisoned at the Texas State Penitentiary at Huntsville. Utley, *The Indian Frontier*, pp. 143–44.

3. Medicine Mounds, four natural hills ranging from 200 to 250 feet in height, are in Hardeman County, Texas, south of the present-day towns of Chillicothe and Quanah.

4. When the government removed the Chickasaws and Choctaws to Indian Territory in the 1830s, the two Indian nations united. The Chickasaws feared moving too far west near the "wild" Indians and instead made their homes throughout Choctaw Territory, which encompassed most of present-day southern Oklahoma. The Chickasaws even had a seat in the Choctaw National Council. But this arrangement satisfied neither nation, and many arguments developed over land and settlement. Finally, in 1855, the Chickasaws separated from the Choctaws and received their own land extending west to about present-day Chickasha, Oklahoma. Grant Foreman, *The Five Civilized Tribes*, pp. 51, 89.

5. Captain Randolph B. Marcy was one of the early army explorers of the Southern Plains. In the summer of 1849, Marcy explored a route from the Canadian River to Santa Fe, meeting up with bands of the Wichitas, Kiowas, and Comanches. He later made several other expeditions across the plains for the government, searching potential routes for railroads or for the overland migration. In 1859, he wrote and published a guidebook for overland pioneers, titled *The Prairie Traveler*. William H. Goetzmann, *Exploration and Empire*, pp. 271–74.

6. Fort Sill was created January 8, 1869, by General Sheridan during his Winter Campaign of 1868–69 against the Comanches, Kiowas, and other Southern Plains tribes. The location, at Medicine Bluffs in the Wichita Mountains, a sacred site for most Southern Plains Indians, was chosen for its proximity to Southern Plains Indians and as a way to keep them in check. Building the post was assigned to Brevet Major General Benjamin H. Grierson and the Tenth Cavalry Regiment. Camp Wichita officially became Ft. Sill August 1, 1869. The Agency for the Kiowas, Comanches, Apaches, Wichitas, and Affiliated Tribes was established one mile south of the post. Traders and merchants established themselves around the fort and did a brisk business with the Indians, especially in buffalo hides. Gillett Griswold, "Old Fort Sill: The First Seven Years," *Chronicles of Oklahoma* 36 (Spring, 1958): 2–14.

7. The Anadarko Agency was for the Wichita and Affiliated Tribes. The Fort Sill Agency was for the Comanches and Kiowas, and the Fort Reno Agency was for the Southern Cheyennes and Southern Arapahos.

8. Some of Mrs. Plummer's facts are in error. Sam Houston was never head of Indian Affairs, though he did believe in a humane Indian policy. Much of Mrs. Plummer's information appears to be hearsay.

9. Matthew Leeper was born in Charlotte, North Carolina, in 1804. He participated in the California Gold Rush. In the late 1850s, President James Buchanan appointed him as Indian Agent to the Comanches in Texas. He, along with Major Robert S. Neighbors helped the Caddos, Wichitas, and Penataka Comanches escape from Texas to Indian Territory in 1859. In Indian Territory, he was agent for the Wichitas, Caddos, and Penataka Comanches at an agency near Fort Cobb. Once the Civil War began, Leeper sided with the Confederacy and was named as Confederate Agent for these Indian peoples. His agency was destroyed October 23, 1862, during the Tonkawa Massacre. Leeper returned to Texas and died in Sherman in 1894. Harrison, "Matthew Leeper," pp. 242, 249.

10. These peoples were prisoners taken by the government after the Red River War of 1874–75 and incarcerated at Fort Marion, Florida, near St. Augustine. Haley, *The Buffalo War*, pp. 211–14.

11. During the 1840s, Charles and William Bent and their partner, Ceran St. Vrain, were Indian traders operating out of Bent's Fort on the Santa Fe Trail in southern Colorado. To increase trade with the Comanches and Kiowas, they built a few mud structures on the Canadian River in Hutchinson County, Texas. William Bent and St. Vrain later abandoned the Canadian River post and it fell into disrepair, later to become known as Adobe Walls. Baker and Harrison, *Adobe Walls*, pp. 13–14.

12. William "Billy" Dixon of West Virginia was one of the best marksmen among the buffalo hunters holed up at Adobe Walls on that morning of June 27, 1874, when the Indians attacked. Baker and Harrison, *Adobe Walls*, pp. 7–8, 50–77; Haley, *The Buffalo War*, pp. 23, 28.

13. Jonathan Richards was the Agent at the Wichita Agency at Anadarko. Smith, *The Caddos, the Wichitas, and the United States*, pp. 100–2.

14. John Ward was born at Old Boggy Depot, Choctaw Territory, December 28, 1858. He was with the parties that visited the Comanche Indians who were camped at Atoka, Indian Territory, and was present when the agreement was made between the Comanche Indians and the Choctaw Indians for hunting privileges during the fall of 1868. This privilege was in Atoka County for a period of ninety days. John Ward, vol. 67, pp. 3–6, Indian-Pioneer Histories.

15. Councils between the eastern Indians, such as the Creeks, Cherokees, Chickasaws, and Seminoles, and the western or plains Indians were rather common in Indian Territory, especially during the 1840s and 1870s. One of the objectives of these councils was to bring about peace between the two groups of peoples and attempt to convert the plains to a farming area and the "wild" Indians to a lifestyle similar to that of the eastern Indians. Okmulgee is the capital of the Creek Territory. A. M. Gibson, "An Indian Territory United Nations: The Creek Council of 1845," *Chronicles of Oklahoma* 39 (Winter 1961–62): 398–413.

Chapter 2. Southern Plains Cultures

1. Dr. Charles R. Hume, Vol. 30, pp. 222–28, Indian-Pioneer Histories.

2. For more information on the Southern Plains Culture that developed during the twentieth century, see Howard Meredith, *Dancing On Common Ground: Tribal Cultures and Alliances on the Southern Plains*.

3. Squaw corn was a strain of corn with more starch than other varieties and had flat and rounded kernels. Many colors appear in the corn, but white and blue predominate. Squaw corn is also sometimes called flour corn or soft corn. John N. Winburne, *A Dictionary of Agricultural and Allied Terminology*, p. 749.

4. The 1904 Louisiana Purchase Exposition in St. Louis commemorated the centenary of the Louisiana Purchase and celebrated the triumph of American expansionism. The Exposition was also an anthropological exhibition, featuring live exhibits of aboriginal peoples and their cultures from North America and around the world. Quanah Parker, Geronimo, and Chief Joseph attended the Exposition. Robert W. Rydell, *All the World's a Fair: Visions of Empire at American International Expositions, 1876–1916*, pp. 155, 165.

5. A frow, or froe, is a tool used to cut shingles from a larger piece of wood or for cutting staves to make casks and barrels.

6. Shinny was a variation of field hockey played by children by using a club and a ball, a block of wood, or a tin can. This game should not be confused with the more familiar Indian Stick Ball, a variation of lacrosse, which was common among the eastern Indians, such as the Creek, Choctaws, Cherokees, and Chickasaws, but not originally played by the Caddos, Wichitas, and other plains Indians. For more information on stick ball, see Theda Perdue, *Nations Remembered*, pp. 77–80.

7. This game is called the Hand Game and is a popular game of chance still enjoyed by Southern Plains and other Indian peoples to this day.

8. The American Indian Exposition was founded in 1933 by Lewis Ware and Parker McKenzie, both Kiowas, and is still held every summer in Anadarko, Oklahoma. For years, it was the first and only exposition in the United States managed exclusively by Indians. The Exposition, complete with a Princess, is attended by Indian people from all over Oklahoma and the nation, but is strongly represented by the host peoples, such as the Kiowas, Comanches, Apaches, Caddos, Wichitas, Cheyennes, and Arapahos. During the Exposition, great encampments of these peoples surround the grounds. Indian dances and songs, parades, exhibitions, games, and arts and crafts take place. Muriel H. Wright, "The American Indian Exposition in Oklahoma," *Chronicles of Oklahoma* 24 (Summer, 1946): 158–65.

9. The fair described here probably took place in 1879.

10. Old Greer County was a piece of land in southwestern-most part of present-day Oklahoma located between the North Fork of the Red River and the 100th meridian. The State of Texas claimed Greer County, but in March, 1896, the United States Supreme Court ruled that Greer County belonged to the Oklahoma Territory. John W. Morris, Charles R. Goins, and Edwin C. McReynolds, *Historical Atlas of Oklahoma*, p. 54.

Chapter 3. A Spiritual Life

1. St. Patrick's Mission was founded in 1892 as a Catholic mission and boarding school for Indian children. Father Isadore Ricklin founded the mission and school and served as superintendent. The Sisters of St. Francis ran the school. Father Aloyisius Hitta succeeded Father Ricklin as priest and superintendent. Sara Brown Mitchell, "The Early Days of Anadarko," *The Chronicles of Oklahoma* 28 (Winter, 1950–51): 392.

2. The Post Oak Mission near Cache, Oklahoma, was founded as a Mennonite Mission by Reverend Henry Kohfeld in 1894. The mission and its cemetery were near Quanah Parker's home, and it was to the Post Oak Cemetery that Quanah Parker had the remains of his mother, Cynthia Ann Parker, reinterred from Texas in December 1910. When Quanah died on February 21, 1911, he also was buried near his mother at the Post Oak Cemetery. In 1957, because the Fort Sill Military Reservation expanded, the Post Oak Mission and Cemetery were moved to a spot northwest of the town of Indiahoma. The remains of Quanah and his mother were reinterred at the Fort Sill Post Cemetery. Hugh D. Corwin, "Protestant Missionary Work among the Comanches and Kiowas," *The Chronicles of Oklahoma* 46 (Spring, 1968): 55–57.

3. The Green Corn Ceremony was affiliated mainly with the agricultural peoples of the southeastern United States, particularly those of the Mississippian cultural tradition. The Green Corn Ceremony was an important yearly festival and usually took place in the late summer to celebrate the ripening of corn. Though various southeastern Indians celebrated it at different times and in different ways, at its heart it was a ceremony of renewal and purity. The renewal rituals usually included dancing, fasting, purging oneself, offering forgiveness of past offenses to others, extinguishing of fires and then relighting them from a main "sacred" fire and finally feasting. Hudson, *The Southeastern Indians*, pp. 365–66.

4. The Ghost Dance was a revitalization movement that swept through most Indian societies in the American West during the late 1880s and early 1890s. In 1888, Wovoka, a Paiute Indian of Nevada, experienced a vision in which he saw the present world where whites reigned supreme, vanishing, and then being reborn in a pure state with only Indians living in it. The Indian dead, the old ways, and even the great herds of buffalo would return. From then on the Indian people would live happily, free from all the suffering the whites had inflicted upon them. To achieve this vision, the Indians must live harmoniously and honestly, give up all white ways, including alcohol; they must pray and meditate, but especially must dance so that they might be permitted to see a vision of the new earth to come. It was this idea of the return of the dead that gave it the name "Ghost Dance." As Wovoka taught it, the Ghost Dance beliefs were nonviolent. Whites would disappear through spiritual power, not through warfare. Many Indian nations sent people to Nevada to visit Wovoka and learn of these new beliefs and rituals. The Kiowas sent Chief Apiatan who rejected the beliefs as false, but within a couple of years the Kiowas took up the Ghost Dance again. Similarly, Indians all over the West began dancing it and with little interference from government officials. Even the Caddos and Wichitas enthusiastically participated in the dance. Only on the Lakota reservations of South Dakota did the Ghost Dance turn violent. When the Ghost Dance beliefs reached the Lakotas, they added a mili-

tancy to the rituals, such as a belief in shirts that the white man's bullets could not penetrate. As the Lakotas began to dance the Ghost Dance, reservation officials grew fearful of a Lakota uprising and called upon the army to suppress the dance. The Lakota refusal to stop practicing the Ghost Dance resulted in the Battle of Wounded Knee on December 29, 1890, when the 7th Cavalry attacked a Lakota village, killing over one hundred and fifty men, women, and children and losing only twenty-five cavalrymen. Wounded Knee was the last battle of the Indian Wars and brought an end to Ghost Dance practices. Prucha, *The Great Father*, pp. 726–29; Carl Waldman, *Atlas of the North American Indian*, p. 158; Mooney, *Calendar History of the Kiowa Indians*, pp. 221–22, 360.

5. The Reverend John Jasper Methvin (1846–1941) of Jeffersonville, Georgia, served two years in the Confederate Army and became a lawyer, but soon felt called to preach and was licensed in 1870 by the Methodist Episcopal Church, South. In 1885, after an appeal from Bishop Robert K. Hargrove, Methvin cane to Indian Territory as Superintendent of New Hope Seminary, Choctaw Territory and the next year became Superintendent for Seminole Academy. In 1886, Methvin toured the western area of what became Oklahoma, home of the Kiowas, Comanches, Apaches, Caddos, Wichitas, Delawares, Cheyennes, and Arapahos; he was surprised at how little Christian activity had been done among these peoples. In October, 1887, the 42nd Indian Mission Conference met at Vinita, Indian Territory, and assigned Methvin as a missionary to the Western Tribes. Methvin and his family immediately left for the West and arrived at the United States Indian Agency in Anadarko in November, 1887. Methvin decided to concentrate on working with the Apaches, Comanches, and Kiowas as they were the most numerous, and in his opinion, the most war-like. Methvin began preaching, using interpreters to get his points across. Work was slow, and early on few of these Southern Plains Indians showed any great desire for a conversion to Christianity. But Methvin slowly prevailed and his church began to grow large enough to build an actual church house. Eventually, the Kiowa chief To-hau-sin converted and began regularly attending Methvin's church services. This brought even more people into his church. He became so popular among the Kiowas that they elected him to citizenship and gave him an allotment of land. In 1890, with the help of government donated land and a donation of $2,500 from the Missionary Society of the Methodist Episcopal Church, South, the Methvin Institute, a school for Indian children, was begun. It opened with fifteen pupils but soon had over one hundred. The Methvin Institute, operated by the Woman's Board of Missions, operated for about twenty years and had a tremendous impact on the Indian peoples around Anadarko; even the Caddos and Wichitas. Methvin retired in 1908, but remained active in church affairs. He also wrote several books: *Andele, A Story of the Kiowa-Mexican Captive; In the Lime Light—A Story of Anadarko; Fig Leaves and Else and The Lone Cedar and Else*. Methvin died on January 17, 1941. Sidney H. Babcock, "John Jasper Methvin, 1846–1941," *Chronicles of Oklahoma* 19 (June, 1941): 113–18. Also see Bruce David Forbes, "John Jasper Methvin: Methodist 'Missionary to the Western Tribes' (Oklahoma)," *Churchmen and the Western Indians, 1820–1920*, pp. 41–73.

6. The Pine Ridge Reservation of the Lakotas is in South Dakota. A-peahtone [Apiatan]

apparently did visit the Pine Ridge Reservation in South Dakota and then continued his search for Ghost Dance information to Nevada, where he met Wovoka, the Paiute Ghost Dance prophet.

7. This man should not be confused with Chief Sitting Bull of the Lakotas who was present with the Lakotas and Cheyenne against Custer at the Battle of the Little Big Horn in 1876.

8. The Sun Dance was the Plains Indian equivalent of the Southeastern Indian's Green Corn Ceremony. It was a major ceremony for the Kiowas and the Indians of the Northern Plains, such as the Cheyennes, Arapahos, and Lakotas, but not that important to the Comanches. Held annually in the spring or early summer to honor the sun and help bring about the regeneration of the buffalo, it brought the various bands of the nation together. A sacred Sun Dance lodge was built where dances and ceremonies were held. Self-torture was an important aspect of the Sun Dance, except for the Kiowas. For most Northern Plains Indians peoples, the Sun Dance usually entailed a man piercing his breasts with thorns and then tying these thorns with buffalo sinew to a central pole of the lodge. The man would dance until these thorns were torn from his breast. The Kiowas did not allow self-torture during the Sun Dance and even the accidental shedding of blood was taken as a bad omen and serious enough to cancel the dance. Mooney, *Calendar History of the Kiowa Indians*, pp. 242–44; Mayhall, *The Kiowas*, p. 148.

9. Thomas Chester Battey, a Quaker teacher, arrived at the Wichita Agency in October 1871 and taught school among the Caddos for eight months. In 1872, he went to teach among the Kiowas. Rather than building a schoolhouse and requiring Indian children to attend it, he used the novel approach of visiting the Kiowa camps, where he set up a tent and tried to conduct school in the camp itself. He spent two years among the Kiowas, and while not realizing much success with his school, he did make close friendships with such Kiowa chiefs as Kicking Bird and Stumbling Bear. Poor health forced Battey to leave his position in July, 1874. Battey's experiences among the Indians led him to write a book of his adventures that was published in 1875. See Thomas C. Battey, *The Life and Adventures of a Quaker among the Indians*.

10. The actual Kiowa offer probably was only $100. Hagan, *United States–Comanche Relations*, pp. 188–89.

11. The Euchees or Yuchis are a Southeastern Indian people closely associated with the Creek or Muskogee Indians, originally living in southeastern Tennessee, northwestern Georgia, and northeastern Alabama. Hudson, *The Southeastern Indians*, p. 5.

12. Sofkey, or soffkee, is a type of soup made from course grits and drank by the Cherokees, Choctaws, Creeks, Seminoles, and Chickasaws.

13. Black Beaver, a Delaware Indian, was born in 1806 near present-day Belleville, Illinois, and accompanied his people to Indian Territory. In 1834, he served as interpreter for Colonel Richard Dodge during the army's expedition to make peace with the Wichitas, Comanches, and Kiowas. During the Mexican War, Black Beaver served as an army guide and was designated with the rank of "Captain," but his company of Delaware and Shawnee warriors did not see action. Black Beaver seemed to have a wanderlust and spent time wandering in Oregon, California, and among the Crow and Blackfeet Indians of the Northern Plains. His knowledge of the West served him well, and

other army explorers relied heavily upon him. Captain Randolph Marcy hired him to guide him to Santa Fe and California in 1849 as did Lieutenant A. W. Whipple's 1853–54 exploration expedition for a railway from Fort Smith to Los Angeles. As he grew older, he settled down and began farming. Still he was one of the most famous Indians in the West, and his advice and assistance were often sought by government, army, and private individuals. As his reputation soared, he became chief of the Delawares in Indian Territory. Late in life he became a Baptist and even preached. He died on May 8, 1880, with over one hundred and fifty people attending his funeral. He was buried near Anadarko. Carolyn Thomas Foreman, "Black Beaver," *The Chronicles of Oklahoma* 24 (Autumn, 1946): 269–92.

14. Mount Scott is part of the Wichita Mountains and is located near Lawton, Oklahoma.

15. Reverend Elton C. Deyo was born in Wyoming, New York, in 1851. When he was thirty-eight years old, he experienced a religious conversion and attended Colgate Theological Seminary. In 1893, after his graduation, the American Baptist Home Mission Society sent him and his wife, Anna Mullen, to work among the Comanches in southwest Oklahoma Territory. In 1895, Deyo organized the Comanche mission about fifteen miles southwest of Fort Sill and served as a Baptist minister of the gospel to the Comanches and the Indians around Fort Sill and Lawton, Oklahoma, until his death in August, 1926 at Lawton. Jerry B. Jeter, "Pioneer Preacher," *Chronicles of Oklahoma* 23 (Winter, 1945–46): 358–68.

Chapter 4. Education and Health

1. P. B. Hunt was the agent for the Comanches and Kiowas from the spring of 1878 until the summer of 1885. Hagan, *United States-Comanche Relations,* p. 139.

2. Chilocco Indian Industrial School was established as an off-reservation boarding school in Kay County, Indian Territory near the Kansas border and opened in January, 1884. Students came from all the Indian nations in Indian Territory. Prucha, *The Great Father,* pp. 692, 815; Smith, *The Caddos, the Wichitas, and the United States,* pp. 132–33. Also see K. Tsianina Lomawaima, *They Called It Prairie Light: The Story of the Chilocco Indian School.*

3. Reverend George W. Hicks, a Cherokee Indian, and his wife were missionaries in the American Baptist (Northern) Church. They came to Anadarko in 1887 and established a small school and church for the Wichitas and Caddos. Later they began missionary and education efforts among the Kiowas. Corwin, "Protestant Missionary Work Among the Comanches and Kiowas," p. 44.

4. Reverend Silas V. Fait and his wife, Anna, were Presbyterian missionaries who came to Anadarko in 1888. They ministered to the Comanches and Kiowas. In 1892, they built a Presbyterian Church in Anadarko and established the Mary Gregory Memorial School, or Mautame School, four miles east of Anadarko. Anna R. Fait, "An Autobiography," *The Chronicles of Oklahoma* 32 (Summer, 1954): 185–95.

5. Dr. Charles R. Hume came to the area in 1890 as a government doctor and provided health care and medical service for over four thousand Kiowas, Comanches, Apaches, Caddos, Wichitas, and Delawares, spread over fifty-eight hundred square miles. Hagan, *United States-Comanche Relations,* p. 220.

6. By this he means the opening of the Comanche and Kiowa reservation to white settlement in 1901.

7. The Red Store was a small outpost of mercantile stores on the Comanche and Kiowa reservation near Fort Sill where the Indians often came to trade and buy merchandise with the money they earned for leasing their grasslands. Hagan, *United States-Comanche Relations*, p. 243; Gen. R. A. Sneed, "The Reminiscences of an Indian Trader," *Chronicles of Oklahoma* 14 (June, 1936): 140–41.

8. The Riverside Indian School, located on the north side of the Washita River north of Anadarko, is the oldest operating Indian boarding school in the United States. Originally the Wichita School, it was founded by Quaker missionaries Jonathan Richards and A. J. Standing in 1871 as a school for Wichita, Caddo, and Delaware children. In the 1920s, other Indian peoples, such as the Kiowas, began sending their children to Riverside. The school, with its beautiful red brick buildings, is still in operation. Mrs. Tommie P. Hanger, "Notes and Documents: The Riverside Indian School, Centennial, 1971," *The Chronicles of Oklahoma* 48 (Winter, 1970–71): 480–83.

9. Joshua Givens was the son of Kiowa Chief Satank who had been killed en route to the Texas State Penitentiary at Huntsville in 1871. Givens was sent to Carlisle Indian School in Carlisle, Pennsylvania, where he adopted many of the white ways, accepted Christianity, and even became a Presbyterian preacher. When he returned to the Kiowa reservation, he often served as an interpreter for the agency officials and was seen by white officials as being the beginning of a new generation of Indian leaders. When the Jerome Commission arrived at Fort Sill in September, 1892 to begin negotiating the break up of the Kiowa and Comanche reservation, the Commission hired Givens as interpreter. He soon came under suspicion by the Kiowas as not interpreting accurately. Because of this, a Kiowa medicine man cursed him, saying he would become sick and begin to bleed from his lungs. On the date the medicine man predicted, Givens fell sick with tuberculosis and began hemorrhaging. Despite being consoled by the agent, and even sweated in the Indian tradition, Givens soon died and was buried in the Kiowa cemetery. Hagan, *United States-Comanche Relations*, pp. 163, 208, 213; Fait, "An Autobiography," pp. 191–92.

Chapter 5. Life on the Reservation

1. During his administration, President Ulysses S. Grant used a policy of appointing churchmen to run the Indian Agencies rather than government-appointed bureaucrats. Church officials and humanitarians, with the Quakers leading the charge, began clamoring for this policy change once Grant became president, believing that incompetent and corrupt agents caused many of the problems the government had with the Indians. Called the Quaker Policy, or the Peace Policy, neither improved the life of Indian peoples on reservations nor brought peace. Indian raids, churchmen's naiveté, and Army antagonism brought the policy to an end in 1878. Prucha, *The Great Father*, pp. 479–83; Weeks, *Farewell, My Nation*, pp. 148–60, 190–97.

2. These were the Comanche, Kiowas, and Southern Cheyenne prisoners taken at the end of the Red River War of 1874–75 and sent to Fort Marion, Florida. When the Kiowa chiefs returned from prison, before they could go home, they were taken to Riverside Indian School and made to sing gospel hymns to the Wichita, Caddo, and

Delaware children attending the school. Karl Schmitt, "Wichita-Kiowa Relations and the 1874 Outbreak," *Chronicles of Oklahoma* 28 (1950): 154–60.

3. It is not clear whether the payments mentioned here were annuity payments made by the United States government to the Indians, or "grass payments," which were payments made by cattlemen to lease pasture from the Indians on which to graze their cattle.

4. This was a Civilian Conservation Corps camp during the 1930s.

5. This was "grass money," or money the cattlemen paid for the right to graze their cattle on reservation land. The payout was probably done in two manners. In earlier instances, the cattlemen paid the money directly to the Indians, but apparently in the early 1890s, the cattlemen paid the lease money to the government and then the government paid the money to the Indians. Hagan, *United States-Comanche Relations*, pp. 175–82.

6. Major Frank D. Baldwin, a Civil War Medal of Honor winner, assumed charge of the Comanche and Kiowa Agency in November 1894. Often controversial and at odds with the reservation traders and merchants, Baldwin served as agent until he was recalled by the Army to serve in the Spanish-American War of 1898. Hagan, *United States-Comanche Relations*, p. 218.

7. When the Comanche, Kiowa, Caddo, and Wichita lands were opened in 1901, these Indians lost ownership and access to a tremendous amount of land. This loss of these lands hurt their economic prosperity and just about ruined their chances of successful ranching; they now did not possess the land on which to graze large herds of horses and cattle. Hagan, *United States-Comanche Relations*, pp. 271–78.

8. He means Anadarko rather than Ardmore, Oklahoma.

9. W. G. Williams, originally from Kentucky, became a trader among the Caddos in 1859. During the Civil War, he served with the Confederacy's Caddo Frontier Battalion, commanded by Caddo chief, George Washington. Williams married a Caddo woman and began cattle ranching. Williams is now a very common surname among the Caddo people. Sneed, "The Reminiscences of an Indian Trader," p. 145.

10. Lieutenant Colonel James F. Randlett served as agent for the Comanche, Kiowa, and Wichita Agency from 1899 to 1905. Hagan, *United States-Comanche Relations*, pp. 248–49.

11. This story about Cynthia Ann Parker and her son Quanah is accurate except for the last sentence. The Comanches did not force Cynthia to go back to the white Texans; she was recaptured by them in 1861. Hagan, *Quanah Parker*, pp. 6–7.

12. He probably means Kiowa, rather than Crow Indians.

Chapter 6. Old Ways, New Ways

1. Though linguists say that Caddo and Wichita come from the same Caddoan language stock, many Caddo people do not see any connection. Caddo people cannot understand Wichita and Wichita people cannot understand Caddo. Phil Newkumet, interview with the author, Norman, Okla., July 6, 1996.

2. He is probably referring to the Kwahadi Comanches as the warring tribe. However, it is more than likely that it is the Penataka Comanches to whom Pewo is referring that made the first treaties with the United States.

3. In September, 1878, the Comanche-Kiowa agency was moved from Fort Sill to

Anadarko and consolidated with the Wichita Agency. After consolidation, the Kiowa School was established in 1878. Most Kiowas, though, lived still lived near Fort Sill, and so in 1892 the Fort Sill Indian School opened. Hagan, *United States-Comanche Relations*, pp. 199–200.

4. She is referring to the seventy-four Comanche and Kiowa prisoners taken at the end of the Red River War in 1875 who were incarcerated at Fort Marion, Florida. Haley, *The Buffalo War*, pp. 211–13, 220–21.

5. Lake Lawtonka is near Lawton, Oklahoma.

6. Annuity money involved per capita disbursements the government made to individual Indians from moneys promised them in treaties. For example, in the Treaty of Medicine Lodge Creek of 1867, the United States promised to pay the Comanches, Kiowas, and Apaches together a sum of $30,000 for thirty years. Kappler, "Treaty with the Kiowa, Comanche, and Apache, 1867," *Indian Treaties, 1778–1883*, p. 983.

7. It is unclear what Ms. Bedoka means by the Caddos going "back to Texas." The Caddos were removed from Texas to Indian Territory in 1859 and never officially went back to Texas. She might mean that during the Civil War, when the Caddos split into several bands—with some going to Kansas, some going west and some remaining in Indian Territory—that one band did briefly seek refuge in Texas.

8. He probably means Lt. Richard H. Pratt of the United States Tenth Cavalry who led the Indian Scouts during the Red River War of 1874–75. Pratt was put in charge of the Indian prisoners after the war and helped select those who would be sent to Fort Marion, Florida. Pratt eventually became the champion of Indian education and founded the Carlisle Indian School in Carlisle, Pennsylvania. Haley, *The Buffalo War*, pp. 187, 194, 211–12, 220–21.

9. The Treaty of Medicine Lodge Creek between the Comanches, Kiowas, and Apaches and the United States was signed in 1867. The Ghost Dance took place in 1889–90. Mr. Barnes may be confusing the Medicine Lodge Treaty with the Jerome Commission's activities in the 1890s that broke up the reservations and later opened to white settlement in the early twentieth century.

10. James Mooney was an early ethnologist and published several studies on Indian life around the turn of the twentieth century. One of his most famous works was the *Calendar History of the Kiowa Indians*. The Kiowas had kept a yearly calendar, recorded by pictographs on buffalo hides. Mooney published the *Calendar* with the pictographs and explanations.

11. The Kiowas seem to be a people with a truly artistic bent. Beginning in the late 1920s, five young painters, known as the "Kiowa Five," became internationally renown. The "Kiowa Five" included Spencer Asah, James Auchiah, Jack Jokeah, Stephen Mopope, and Monroe Tsatoke. See Maurice Boyd's *Kiowa Voices* for an examination of Kiowa art.

Epilogue

1. Quoted in Francis Paul Prucha, *Indian Policy in the United States, Historical Essays*, p. 239.

2. Quoted in Prucha, *The Great Father*, p. 671.

Bibliography

◆ ◆ ◆ ◆ ◆ ◆ ◆ ◆ ◆ ◆ ◆ ◆ ◆ ◆ ◆

Archival Sources

Béxar Archives. Microfilm, Microtext Department, Sterling Evans Library, Texas A&M University, College Station, Tex.

Diary of James Reagle, James Reagle Jr. Collection, Western History Collection, University of Oklahoma, Norman, Okla., R–45, 1240.

House Document 99, 27th Cong., 1st Session, 1842–43, Congressional Serial Set, Vol. 420.

Indian-Pioneer Histories, Oklahoma Historical Society Archives, Oklahoma City.

Letters Received by the Office of Indian Affairs, Wichita Agency, 1857–78, M234, Western History Collection, Roll 928, 1857–1866.

Newkumet, Phil. Interview with the author, Norman, Okla., July 6 1996.

Papeles de Cuba, Archivo General de Indias, Seville, Spain.

Senate Executive Document 2, 28th Cong., 1st Sess., 1843–1844, Congressional Serial Set, Vol. 431.

Published Sources

Adams, David W. *Education for Extinction: American Indians and the Boarding School Experience, 1875–1928.* Lawrence: University Press of Kansas, 1995.

Albers, Patricia C. "Symbiosis, Merger, and War: Contrasting Forms of Intertribal Relationship Among Historic Plains Indians." In *The Political Economy of North American Indians.* ed. John H. Moore. Norman: University of Oklahoma Press, 1993, pp. 94–132.

Anderson, H. Allen. "The Delaware and Shawnee Indians and the Republic of Texas, 1820–1845. *Southwestern Historical Quarterly* 94 (October, 1990): 231–69.

Axtell, James. "The First Consumer Revolution." *Beyond 1492.* New York and Oxford: Oxford University Press, 1992, pp. 125–51.

Babcock, Sidney, H. "John Jasper Methvin, 1846–1941" *Chronicles of Oklahoma* 19 (June, 1941): 113–18.

Baker, T. Lindsay and Billy R. Harrison. *Adobe Walls: The History and Archeology of the 1874 Trading Post.* College Station: Texas A&M University Press, 1986.

Barker, Eugene C. "The Austin Papers." *Annual Report of the American Historical Association for the Year 1919.* 2 vols., 2 parts. Washington, D.C.: Government Printing Office, 1924.

Barnard, Alan and Anthony Good. *Research Practices in the Study of Kinship.* London: Academic Press, 1984.

Battey, Thomas C. *The Life and Adventures of a Quaker among the Indians.* Williamstown, Mass: Corner House Publishers, 1972. Originally published in 1875.

Baugh, Timothy G. "Ecology and Exchange: The Dynamics of Plains-Pueblo Interactions," *Farmers, Hunters, and Colonists: Interaction between the Southwest and the Southern Plains.* ed. Katherine A. Spielman. Tucson: University of Arizona Press, 1991.

Billard, Jules H., ed. *The World of the American Indian.* Washington, D.C.: The National Geographic Society, 1974.

Bolton, Herbert E. *The Hasinai: Southern Caddoans as Seen by the Earliest Europeans.* Norman: University of Oklahoma Press, 1987.

Bolton, Herbert E., trans. and ed. *Athanase De Mézières and the Louisiana-Texas Frontier, 1768–1780.* 2 vols. Cleveland: The Arthur H. Clark Company, 1914; New York: Kraus Reprint Co., 1970.

Boyd, Maurice. *Kiowa Voices: Myths, Legends, and Folktales.* 2 vols. Fort Worth: Texas Christian University Press, 1983.

Carter, Clarence E., ed. *The Territorial Papers of the United States: The Territory of Arkansas, 1819–1825,* 26 vols, vol. XIX. Washington D.C.: Government Printing Office, 1953.

Cashdan, Elizabeth. "Hunter and Gatherers: Economic Behavior in Bands." *Economic Anthropology.* ed. Stuart Plattner. Stanford, Calif.: Stanford University Press, 1989, pp. 21–48.

Chipman, Donald E. *Spanish Texas: 1519–1821.* Austin: University of Texas Press, 1992.

Corbin, James E. "Spanish-Indian Interaction on the Eastern Frontier of Texas." *Columbian Consequences: Archaeological and Historical Perspectives on the Spanish Borderlands West.* 3 vols, ed. David Hurst Thomas. Washington, D.C. and London: Smithsonian Institution Press, 1989, 269–79.

Corwin, Hugh D. "Protestant Missionary Work among the Comanches and Kiowas." *The Chronicles of Oklahoma* 46 (Spring 1968): 41–57.

Crosby, Alfred W. "Virgin Soil Epidemics as a Factor in the Aboriginal Depopulation in America." *William and Mary Quarterly* 3 ser. 33 (April 1976): 289–99

Din, Gilbert C., and Abraham P. Nasatir. *The Imperial Osages: Spanish-Indian Diplomacy in the Mississippi Valley.* Norman: University of Oklahoma Press, 1983.

Everett, Dianna. *The Texas Cherokees: A People Between Two Fires, 1819–1840.* Norman: University of Oklahoma Press, 1990.

Ewers, John C. "The Influence of Epidemics on the Indian Populations and Cultures of Texas." *Plains Anthropologist* 18 (May, 1973): 104–15.

Ellis, Clyde. *To Change Them Forever: Indian Education at Rainy Mountain Boarding School, 1893–1920.* Norman: University of Oklahoma Press, 1996.

———. "'Truly Dancing Their Own Way': The Modern Revival and Diffusion of the Gourd Dance." *American Indian Quarterly* 14 (Winter, 1990): 19–33

Fait, Anna R. "An Autobiography." *The Chronicles of Oklahoma* 32 (Summer, 1954): 185–95.

Forbes, Bruce David. "John Jasper Methvin: Methodist 'Missionary to the Western Tribes' (Oklahoma)." In *Churchmen and the Western Indians, 1820–1920,* ed. Clyde A. Milner II and Floyd A. O'Neil. Norman: University of Oklahoma Press, pp. 41–73.

Foreman, Carolyn Thomas. "Black Beaver." *The Chronicles of Oklahoma* 24 (Autumn, 1946): 269–92.

Foreman, Grant. "The Journal of the Proceedings of Our First Treaty with the Wild Indians, 1835." *The Chronicles of Oklahoma* 14 (December, 1936): 394–418.

Foreman, Grant. *The Five Civilized Tribes.* Norman: University of Oklahoma Press, 1934.

Foster, Morris W. *Being Comanche: A Social History of an American Indian Community.* Tucson: University of Arizona Press, 1991.

Fox, Daniel E. *Traces of Texas History: Archeological Evidence of the Past 450 Years.* San Antonio, Tex.: Corona Publishing Company, 1983.

Gelo, Daniel J. "On a New Interpretation of Comanche Social Organization," *Current Anthropology* 28 (August–October 1987): 551–52.

Gibson, A. M. "An Indian Territory United Nations: The Creek Council of 1845." *The Chronicles of Oklahoma* 39 (Winter, 1961–62): 398–413.

Goetzmann, William H. *Exploration and Empire: The Explorer and the Scientist in the Winning of the American West.* New York: W. W. Norton & Company Inc, 1966.

Griswold, Gillett. "Old Fort Sill: The First Seven Years." *The Chronicles of Oklahoma* 36 (Spring, 1958): 2–14.

Hagan, William T. *Quanah Parker, Comanche Chief.* Norman: University of Oklahoma Press, 1993.
————. *United States–Comanche Relations: The Reservation Years.* Norman: University of Oklahoma Press, 1976, 1990.

Haley, James L. *The Buffalo War: The History of the Red River Indian Uprising of 1874.* Norman: University of Oklahoma Press, 1976.

Hall, Thomas D. *Social Change in the Southwest, 1350–1880.* Lawrence: The University of Kansas Press, 1989.

Hanger, Mrs. Tommie P. "Notes and Documents: The Riverside Indian School, Centennial, 1971." *The Chronicles of Oklahoma* 48 (Winter, 1970–71): 480–83.

Harris, Marvin. *Cultural Materialism: The Struggle for a Science of Culture.* New York: Vintage, 1979.

Harrison, Jeanne V. "Matthew Leeper, Confederate Agent at the Wichita Agency, Indian Territory." *The Chronicles of Oklahoma* 47 (Autumn, 1969): 242–257.

Hickerson, Nancy. *The Jumanos: Hunters and Traders of the South Plains.* Austin: University of Texas Press, 1994.

Hodge, Frederick W. *Handbook of American Indians North of Mexico,* 2 vols. Washington, D.C.: Government Printing Office, 1907.

Holder, Preston. *The Hoe and the Horse on the Plains: A Study of Cultural Developments Among North American Indians.* Lincoln: University of Nebraska Press, 1970.

Hudson, Charles. "The Hernando de Soto Expedition, 1539–1543." In *The Forgotten Centuries: Indians and Europeans in the American South, 1521–1704.* Athens: University of Georgia Press, 1994, pp. 74–103.

Hudson, Charles. *The Southeastern Indians.* Knoxville: University of Tennessee Press, 1976.

Hume, C. Ross. "Historic Sites around Anadarko." *The Chronicles of Oklahoma* 16 (December, 1938): 410–24.

Iverson, Peter. *When Indians Became Cowboys: Native Peoples and Cattle Ranching in the American West.* Norman: University of Oklahoma Press, 1994.

Jackson, Jack. *Los Mesteños: Spanish Ranching in Texas, 1721–1821.* College Station: Texas A&M University Press, 1986.

Jennings, Francis. *The Founders of America: From the Earliest Migrations to the Present.* New York: W. W. Norton & Company, 1993.

Jeter, Jerry B. "Pioneer Preacher" *The Chronicles of Oklahoma* 23 (Winter, 1945–46): 358–68.

John, Elizabeth A. H. *Storms Brewed in Other Men's Worlds: The Confrontation of Indians, Spanish, and French in the Southwest, 1540–1795.* Lincoln: Neb. University of Nebraska Press, 1975.

Joutel, Henri. "Joutel's Historical Journal of Monsieur de la Salle's Last Voyage to Discover the River Mississippi." *Historical Collections of Louisiana, Embracing Many Rare and Valuable Documents Relating to the Natural, Civil and Political History of that State,* 4 vols, vol. I, ed. B. F. French. New York: Wiley and Putnam, 1846, New York: AMS Press Inc., 1976.

Kappler, Charles J. *Indian Treaties, 1778–1883.* New York: Interland Publishing, Inc., 1972.

Kavanagh, Thomas W. *Comanche Political History: An Ethnohistorical Perspective, 1708–1875.* Lincoln and London: University of Nebraska Press, 1996.

Kelley, J. Charles. "Juan Sabeata and Diffusion in Aboriginal Texas." *American Anthropologists* 57 (October, 1955): 981–95.

Kinnaird, Lawrence, ed. *Annual Report of the American Historical Association for the Year 1945,* 3 vols. *Spain in the Mississippi Valley, 1765–1794: Post War Decade, 1782–1792.* Washington, D.C.: Government Printing Office, 1946.

Klein, Alan M. "Political Economy of the Buffalo Hide Trade: Race and Class on the Plains." *The Political Economy of North American Indians.* ed. John H. Moore. Norman: University of Oklahoma Press, 1993, pp. 133–60.

Klos, George. "'Our People Could Not Distinguish One Tribe from Another': The 1859 Expulsion of the Reserve Indians from Texas," *Southwest Historical Quarterly* 97 (April, 1994): 599–619.

Kniffen, Fred B., Hiram F. Gregory and George A. Stokes, *The Historic Indian Tribes of Louisiana from 1542 to the Present.* Baton Rouge: Louisiana State University Press, 1987.

Kracht, Benjamin R. "The Kiowa Ghost Dance, 1894–1916: An Unheralded Revitalization Movement." *Ethnohistory* 39 (Fall, 1992): 452–77.

Krieger, Alex D. *Culture Complexes and Chronology in Northern Texas.* Austin: University of Texas Publications, 1946.

La Vere, David. "Friendly Persuasions: Gifts and Reciprocity in Comanche-Euroamerican Relations." *The Chronicles of Oklahoma* 71 (Fall, 1993): 322–37.

Lintz, Christopher. "Texas Panhandle–Pueblo Interactions from the Thirteenth Through the Sixteenth Century." In *Farmers, Hunters, and Colonists: Interaction between the Southwest and the Southern Plains,* ed. Katherine A. Spielmann. Tuscon: University of Arizona Press, 1991, pp. 89–106.

Lomawaima, K. Tsianina. *They Called It Prairie Light: The Story of the Chilocco Indian School.* Norman: University of Oklahoma Press, 1994.

Mayhall, Mildred P. *The Kiowas.* Norman: University of Oklahoma Press, 1962.

McBeth, Sally. *Ethnic Identity and the Boarding School Experience of West-Central Oklahoma American Indians.* Lanham, Md.: University Press of America, 1983.

Meinig, D. W. *Imperial Texas: An Interpretive Essay in Cultural Geography.* Austin: The University of Texas, 1969.

Meredith, Howard. *Dancing On Common Ground: Tribal Cultures and Alliances on the Southern Plains.* Lawrence: University Press of Kansas, 1996.

Merrell, James. *The Indians' New World: Catawbas and their Neighbors from European Contact through the Era of Removal.* New York: W. W. Norton & Company, 1989.

Mills, Elizabeth Shown. *Natchitoches: Abstracts of the Catholic Church Registers of the French and Spanish*

Post of St. Jean Baptiste des Natchitoches in Louisiana: 1729–1803. New Orleans, La.: Polyanthos, Inc., 1977.

Mitchell, Sara Brown. "The Early Days of Anadarko." *The Chronicles of Oklahoma* 28 (Winter, 1950–51): 390–98.

Monahan, Forrest D., Jr. "The Kiowa-Comanche Reservation in the 1890's." *The Chronicles of Oklahoma* 45 (Winter, 1967–68): 451–63.

Mooney, James. *Calendar History of the Kiowa Indians.* Washington, D.C.: Smithsonian Institution Press, 1979.

Morris, John W., Charles R. Goins, and Edwin C. McReynolds. *Historical Atlas of Oklahoma.* Norman: University of Oklahoma Press, 1986.

Newcomb, W. W., Jr. *The Indians of Texas.* Austin: The University of Texas Press, 1961.

Newkumet, Vynola Beaver and Howard L. Meredith. *The Hasinai: A Traditional History of the Caddo Confederacy.* College Station: Texas A&M University Press, 1988

Noyes, Stanley. *Los Comanches: The Horse People, 1751–1845.* Albuquerque: The University of New Mexico Press, 1993.

O'Callaghan, Mary A. "An Indian Removal Policy in Spanish Louisiana." In *Greater America: Essays in Honor of Eugene Herbert Bolton.* Freeport, N.Y.: Books for Libraries Press, Inc., 1968; Berkeley: University of California Press, 1945.

Perdue, Theda. *Nations Remembered: An Oral History of the Cherokees, Chickasaws, Choctaws, Creeks, and Seminoles in Oklahoma, 1865–1907.* Norman: University of Oklahoma Press, 1980.

———. "The Trail of Tears: Removal of the Southern Indians." In *The American Indian Experience, A Profile: 1542 to the Present,* ed. Philip Weeks. Arlington Heights, Ill.: Forum Press, 1988, p. 96–117

———. "Women, Men and American Indian Policy: The Cherokee Response to Civilization." In *Negotiators of Change: Historical Perspectives on Native American Women.* New York: Routledge, 1995, pp. 90–114.

Perttula, Timothy K. *The Caddo Nation: Archaeological and Ethnohistoric Perspectives.* Austin: University of Texas Press, 1992.

Peterson, Dennis A. "A History of Excavations and Interpretations of Artifacts from the Spiro Mounds Sites." In *The Southeastern Ceremonial Complex: Artifacts and Analysis, The Cottonlandia Conference,* ed, Patricia Galloway. Lincoln and London: University of Nebraska Press, 1989.

Phillips, Philip and James A. Brown. *Pre-Columbian Shell Engravings from the Craig Mound at Spiro, Oklahoma,* 2 vols. Cambridge, Mass.: Peabody Museum Press, 1978.

Prucha, Francis Paul. *The Great Father: The United States Government and the American Indians,* 2 vols. Lincoln: University of Nebraska Press, 1984.

Ray, Arthur J. "The Fur Trade as an Aspect of Native American History." In *Major Problems in American Indian History,* ed. Albert L. Hurtado and Peter Iverson. Lexington, Mass: D. C. Heath and Company, 1994, pp. 147–56.

Reid, John Phillip. *A Law of Blood: The Primitive Law of the Cherokee Nation.* New York: New York University Press, 1970.

Richardson, James D., ed. *A Compilation of the Messages and Papers of the Presidents, 1789–1908,* 11 vols. Washington D.C.: Bureau of National Literature and Arts, 1909.

Robertson, James A., ed. and trans. "The True Relation of the Hardships Suffered by Governor Hernando de Soto by a Gentleman of Elvas." In *The De Soto Chronicles: The Expedi-*

tion of Hernando De Soto to North America in 1539–1543, ed. Lawrence A. Clayton, Vernon James Knight, Jr., and Edward C. Moore, 2 vols. Tuscaloosa: University of Alabama Press, 1993.

Rogers, J. Daniel. "Patterns of Change on the Western Margin of the Southeast, A.D. 600–900." In Stability, Transformation, and Variation: The Late Woodland Southeast, ed. Michael S. Nassaney and Charles R. Cobb. New York and London: Plenum Press, 1991.

Rollings, Willard H. The Osage: An Ethnohistorical Study of Hegemony on the Prairie-Plains. Columbia: University of Missouri Press, 1992.

Rydell, Robert W. All the World's a Fair: Visions of Empire at American International Expositions, 1876–1916. Chicago: University of Chicago Press, 1984.

Sahlins, Marshall. "Notes on the Original Affluent Society." In Man the Hunter, ed. Richard B. Lee and Irven DeVore. Chicago: Aldine Publishing Company, 1968, pp. 85–89.

Schilz, Thomas Frank and Donald E. Worcester. "The Spread of Firearms among the Indian Tribes on the Northern Frontier of New Spain." American Indian Quarterly II (Winter, 1987): 1–10.

Schlesier, Karl H. "Commentary: A History of Ethnic Groups in the Great Plains, A.D. 150–1550." in Plains Indians, A.D. 500–1500: The Archaeological Past of Historic Groups, ed. Karl H. Schlesier. Norman: University of Oklahoma Press, 1994, pp. 308–81.

Schmitt, Karl. "Wichita-Kiowa Relations and the 1874 Outbreak." The Chronicles of Oklahoma 28 (1950): 154–60.

Secoy, Frank Raymond. Changing Military Patterns of the Great Plains Indians. Seattle: University of Washington Press, 1953; Lincoln: University of Nebraska Press, 1992.

Silverberg, Robert. The Pueblo Revolt. Lincoln and London: The University of Nebraska Press, 1970, 1994.

Smith, F. Todd. The Caddo Indians: Tribes at the Convergence of Empires, 1542–1854. College Station: Texas A&M University Press, 1995.

Smith, F. Todd. The Caddos, the Wichitas, and the United States, 1846–1901. College Station: Texas A&M University Press, 1996.

Smith, Marvin T. Archaeology of Aboriginal Culture Change in the Interior Southeast: Depopulation During the Early Historic Period. Gainesville: University Press of Florida, 1987.

Smits, David D. "The Frontier Army and the Destruction of the Buffalo: 1865–1883." In Western Historical Quarterly 25 (Autumn, 1994): 313–38.

Sneed, Gen. R. A. "The Reminiscences of an Indian Trader." The Chronicles of Oklahoma 14 (June, 1936): 135–55.

Spielmann, Katherine A. "Interaction Among Nonhierarchical Societies." In Farmers, Hunters, and Colonists: Interaction between the Southwest and the Southern Plains, ed. Katherine A. Spielmann. Tuscon: University of Arizona Press, 1991, pp. 1–17.

Swanton, John R. Source Material on the History and Ethnology of the Caddo Indians. Washington, D.C.: Smithsonian Institution, U.S. Bureau of American Ethnology, Bulletin 132, 1942.

Utley, Robert. The Indian Frontier of the American West, 1846–1890. Albuquerque: University of New Mexico Press, 1984.

Utley, Robert M. The Lance and the Shield: The Life and Times of Sitting Bull. New York: Henry Holt and Company, 1993.

Van Creveld, Martin. Technology and War: From 2000 B.C. to the Present. New York: The Free Press, 1989.

Vehik, Susan C. "Cultural Continuity and Discontinuity in the Southern Prairies and Cross Timbers." In *Plains Indians, A.D. 500–1500: The Archaeological Past of Historic Groups*, ed. Karl H. Schlesier. Norman: University of Oklahoma Press, 1994, pp. 239–63.

Waldman, Carl. *Atlas of the North American Indian*. New York: Facts on File, 1985.

Wallace, Ernest and E. Adamson Hoebel. *The Comanches: Lords of the Southern Plains*. Norman: University of Oklahoma Press, 1952.

Weber, David J. *The Spanish Frontier in North America*. New Haven, Conn.: Yale University Press, 1992.

Weddle, Robert S. *The French Thorn: Rival Explorers in the Spanish Sea, 1682–1762*. College Station: Texas A&M University Press, 1991.

Weeks, Philip. *Farewell, My Nation: The American Indian and the United States, 1820–1890*. Arlington Heights, Ill.: Harlan Davidson, Inc., 1990.

Wilcox, David R. "Changing Contexts of Pueblo Adaptions, A.D. 1250–1600." In *Farmers, Hunters, and Colonists: Interaction between the Southwest and the Southern Plains*, ed. Katherine A. Spielmann. Tuscon: University of Arizona Press, 1991, pp. 128–54.

Winburne, John N. *A Dictionary of Agricultural and Allied Terminology*. East Lansing: Michigan State University, 1969.

Winfrey, Dorman H. and James M. Day, eds. *The Indian Papers of Texas and the Southwest, 1825–1916*, 5 vols. Austin: Texas State Historical Association, 1995.

Wintringham, Tom. *The Story of Weapons and Tactics from Troy to Stalingrad*. Freeport, N.Y.: Books for Libraries Press, 1993.

Wolf, Eric R. *Europe and the People Without History*. Berkeley: University of California Press, 1982.

Wright, Muriel H. "The American Indian Exposition in Oklahoma." *The Chronicles of Oklahoma* 24 (Summer, 1946): 158–65.

Index

◆ ◆ ◆ ◆ ◆ ◆ ◆ ◆ ◆ ◆ ◆ ◆ ◆ ◆

References to illustrative material are printed in boldface type.

beading, 89, 90, 92–93, 94, 102, 151, 191
Beal, Knox, 79
Beaty, Henry, 87–88, 94–95, 106, 126–27, 133, 139, 192
bedding, 86, 95, 103, 158
Bedoka, Sadie, 72, 92–94, 189, 223
beef. *See* cattle
Bent, William, 70, 244*n* 11
Big Shield, 23
Big Tree, 43, 52, 138, 243*n* 1
Bird's Fort, Treaty of, 36
bison. *See* buffalo
Biters, 23
Black Beaver, 143–44, 173, 248*n* 13
Black Boys, 23
blacks, 58, 74, 192
blood revenge, 9–10, 22, 26, 31, 34, 35
Boake, R. L., 78–79, 183–84, 198–99
Booher, Jake, 185–86
Brazos River, 4, 8, 9, 15, 38
Brewer, Mr. (sub-agent), 181
Briggs, George, W., 226–27
Britt, Negro, 62
Brooks, Mr., 185
Brown, Morris, 132, 180
Brown, Will, 54
buffalo, 5, 8, 10, 16, 17, 18, 136, 198; hides, 78, 79, 80, 127; hunting of, 9, 24, 38, 43, 63, 71, 77, 78, 79; uses of, 77, 85, 86, 220
Buffalo, Mary, 216
Buffalo Bill Cody, 181–82
Buffalo Hump (Potsanaquahip), 35–36
buffalo hunters, 44, 52, 70, 71
Bullard, Sidney Alonzo, 107
Buntin, John A., 80–82, 156–58, 165–67, 169–70, 192–93
burials, 97–98, 128–29. *See* funerals
Butler, Robert, 201–202
Buxton, Bert, 132

Cache, Okla., 184–85, 200
Caddoan Mounds, 3, 6
Caddo Jake, 194, 219

Caddos, 3, 4, 8, 9, 10, 12, 14, 16, 18, 22, 24, 40, 45, 47, 64, 66, 71–72, 76, 106, 131, 177, 194, 197, 223, 231, 233; Apaches, conflict with, 9; appearance, 89–90, 94, 95, 102, 133, 180, 192, 193; ceremonies and dances, 47, 133–34, 135, 139, 233; councils, 74; disease and treatment, 11, 18, 159, 169, 170, 172, 173, 174; dividing of, 28; during Civil War, 40; farming, 80, 83, 91; funerals, 124, 127; land, 25, 27–28, 39, 213; marriage, 13, 14, 123; Mission San Sabá, attack on, 20–21; Osages, conflict with, 21, 23; ration issue, 189, 192, 193; religion, 6, 120, 139; reservation life, 38, 39–40, 42, 43, 46, 71–72, 82, 85–86, 98, 108, 110, 159, 183, 184, 189, 198, 200; schools, 149, 150, 156, 158, 159, 160–61, 165–66; scouts, 34, 72; Spanish missions, rejection of, 19–20; Texas, exodus from, 40; trade, 13, 15; traditional life, 6–7, 19, 24–25, 78, 84, 87, 88, 89, 91, 92–94, 102–103, 145, 193, 218–19; treaties, 29, 32, 36, 37, 38, 42
Cadodachos, 7, 13, 24
Camp Holmes, Treaty of, 33
Canadian River, 194
cannibalism, 40, 63
captives, 53, 65–70, 137; adopted by Indians, 18, 36, 69; ransomed by Indians, 37, 68, 69; treatment of, 67
Catlin, George, 33, 36
cattle, 84, 85, 152, 166, 184, 201, 209, 210, 211; as ration, 45, 80, 189–90, 192, 193–94
cattlemen, 177, 178, 198, 200, 201, 209, 226–27, 231
Chambers, W. Fox, 208
Chatt, Elsie, 153
Cherokees, 25, 28, 29, 32, 42, 69, 149, 158, 197, 202, 233
Cheyennes, 12, 42, 44–45, 68, 70, 104, 110, 138, 146, 156, 190, 201
Chickasaws, 32, 34, 40, 42, 73, 131, 156, 163, 200, 233, 243*n* 4; raids against, 55–56, 57, 58–59

Wichitas (*continued*) 165; scout, 34; Spanish missions, rejection of, 19–20; Texas, exodus from, 40; trade, 13, 15–16; traditional life, 7–8, 19, 24–25, 77, 103, 192–93; treaties, 32, 36, 37, 38

Wild Cat, 59–60

Williams, W. G., 194, 251*n* 9

women, 67, 99, 104, 105, 173, 216, 220, 223–25; appearance of, 89; capture of, 53; marriage, 18, 26, 46, 123, 223–25; work, 18, 19, 46, 66, 67, 81, 87–88, 95, 96–97, 202

wood. *See* timber

Woodland Period, 5

Wounded Knee, Battle of, 228

Yamparikas, 15, 29

year of the falling stars (1833), 34

Yellow Bear, 226–27

Yellowhead, Kelly, 140–41

Yellowstone River, 23

Yscanis, 8, 24